SHADOW ENEMIES

SHADOW³ ENEMIES

Hitler's Secret Terrorist Plot Against the United States

Alex Abella

&

Scott Gordon

The Lyons Press
Guilford, Connecticut
An imprint of The Globe Pequot Press

The Lyons Press is an imprint of The Globe Pequot Press.

Printed in the United States of America

1 3 5 7 9 10 8 6 4 2

ISBN 1-58574-722-X

Library of Congress Cataloging in Publication Data is available on file.

To our families,
Our wellspring of inspiration,
Our true measure of success.

In war, truth is the first casualty.

—Aeschylus

Contents

Appendices

Acknowledgments

This book began in the hallways of the Criminal Courts Building in Los Angeles, shortly after the O. J. Simpson case. Over stale snack bar coffee we discussed the ways in which certain inflammatory words could affect an entire case just by their utterance. *Ex Parte Quirin*—the Supreme Court decision that lies at the foundation of this book—is one of those cases. Now, several years and several hundred pages later, we have finished the story of the eight Nazis who met an end to their mission in this country.

Along the way we have profited from the help of countless friends and colleagues—not to mention the bottomless patience of our respective spouses, Lisa and Armeen. We are grateful for Greg and Nathalie Gordon, who listened to our innumerable comments about 1942. Of course, we are indebted to our agent, Joseph Regal, and our editors, Brando Skyhorse and Lisa Purcell. Likewise, it would have been hard to round out our story without the assistance of retired FBI Agent Duane L. Traynor, who welcomed saboteur and terrorist George Dasch to the arms of the FBI. We would be remiss if we didn't also express our gratitude to those other retired agents who contributed so greatly to this work, Kenneth Crosby, John J. Walsh, Joseph O'Connor, Thomas Scott, and all the others. Likewise, we are indebted to FBI Public

Affairs Specialist Philip L. Edney, and FBI Public Information Officer Rex Thomb, for pointing us in the right direction.

To Gavin de Becker, Paul Mones, and Mark Fleischer, our trusted counselors, as well as our invaluable supporters at Southwestern University School of Law, Assistant Dean Dori Heyer, Professor Catherine Carpenter, and our incredible research assistant Talia Schulman, we offer our gratitude.

Without the support of friends, a long journey is rarely completed. Judge James Brandlin, Sandra Harris, Jerry McGee, Pete Herley, Lesley Ann Warren and Ron Taft, Ed and Rochelle Begley, Susan Fleischer, Jack Riley of Rand Corporation, Kim Macy + crew, and of course, Jimmy "Gotta Guy" Martz—you certainly have proven your friendship.

Finally, we owe a big debt to our children, Joey, Veronica, and Nicolas, who gave up their dads for months so we could put this story to bed.

To all of you, our heartfelt thanks.

Authors' Note

In the warm days that welcomed June 1942, every aspect of life in the United States was touched in some way by the war in Europe and the Pacific. Popular movies, songs, and books throughout the nation resonated with themes of victory and loss related to World War II. A strong undercurrent of fear that war would again explode on American soil coursed through every town and city.

The nation learned and knew of the events described in this book as the "Nazi Saboteur Case." Throughout this work, the terms *terrorism* and *sabotage* are used. Sixty years, however, have changed the way we look at crimes such as those involved here.

Due to recent tragic events here and abroad, the word *terrorism* has unfortunately become part of the American zeitgeist. In colloquial use, terrorism is associated with splinter or fundamental political groups using terror to advance particular political causes.

In truth, terrorism has been a military tactic since at least the time of the Roman Empire. Many historians recognize the first political/military use of the term during the French Revolution in 1793–1794, associated with the "Reign of Terror." History also records use of the term in the nineteenth century to describe extreme political actions. The modern definition of the word can be best traced to military action in Palestine in 1946–47 during the formation of Israel.

The term *sabotage* derives its origin from the French *sabot*, for shoe. The *sabot* was a metal clamp used to hold railway tracks in place. During labor actions in the early twentieth century, striking French workers earned the nickname "saboteurs" by cutting these clamps or otherwise disabling them to cause damage to the trains. Sabotage has therefore traditionally been associated with destruction or damage done to an enemy's supplies and physical assets.

Recent legislation dealing with terrorism, HR 3162, the USA PATRIOT ACT, provides a new legal definition of "Domestic Terrorism." This includes violence intended to intimidate or coerce a civilian population, to influence the policy of a government by intimidation or coercion, or to affect the conduct of a government by mass destruction, assassination, or kidnapping. The legislation includes specific acts committed against the United States with this intent: destruction of aircraft facilities, arson and bombing of government property, destruction of communication facilities, attacks against mass transportation systems, or train wrecking.

In the legal documents and news articles cited in this book, the terms *sabotage* and *saboteurs* are most commonly used. Judging the conduct of the men in this story from a modern perspective, however, this is a story of terrorism.

—*Alex Abella & Scott Gordon*

SHADOW
ENEMIES

In the News Today

WASHINGTON, D.C., June 19, 1942—Today Army Chief of Staff George C. Marshall said, "The losses by submarines off our Atlantic seaboard and in the Caribbean now threaten our entire war effort." General Marshall is alarmed by the spread of Operation Drumbeat—Germany's sudden and systematic attack of Allied shipping off the coast of the United States. Operation Drumbeat was responsible for the sinking of nearly 400 ships in American waters—including the Eastern Seaboard, the Gulf of Mexico, and the Caribbean in 1942. Operation Drumbeat or Operation Paukenschlag was a coordinated German response by its U-boats to the Japanese attack on Pearl Harbor, personally ordered by Hitler.[1]

CHAPTER 1

Four Lucky
Porcupines

It was around midnight on June 13, 1942, when Farrar Teeple, a pretty 22-year-old brunette, decided to take a stroll with her younger sister Carol on the boardwalk near the family home in Amagansett, on the South Fork of Long Island, New York.[2]

The fog was thick that evening, so thick that Farrar could barely distinguish what appeared to be the movements of four men down on the beach. Farrar thought they wore uniforms, possibly khaki colored; some of them seemed to be wearing caps with visors. One of them waved at her. The four didn't act overtly suspiciously, but something struck her as odd. The encounter unsettled her, putting her on immediate alert.[3]

Since the surprise attack on Pearl Harbor only six months earlier, the war against the Axis powers—the Germans, Japanese, Italians, and their sundry allies—had made all Americans wary of another, perhaps even larger, attack. That month of June, the New York FBI offices had reported hundreds of calls from citizens convinced they had witnessed enemy landings; some even saw secret spy messages in the way neighbors hung the laundry on their clotheslines.

America and its Allies were facing a critical juncture in the war. At that very moment, the Japanese navy was still clashing with American ships after the crucial battle of Midway, which would decide dominance over the South Pacific. In Europe, the seemingly invincible Nazi war machine had penetrated the Soviet Union, settling in around Stalingrad, where a desperate Joseph Stalin had ordered a last stand. In Libya, Nazi Field Marshall Erwin Rommel drove his *Afrika Korps* closer to Alexandria and the Suez Canal.[4] On the home front, German U-boats seemed to have free rein over the Atlantic coastline, sinking ships and creating havoc at will.

For the first time in the twentieth century Americans had to face the fact that the ocean was no longer a moat but a highway—we could be vulnerable to foreign attack on our very own soil.

Still, Farrar was not certain of what she saw, so instead of calling the Coast Guard station a half mile away, she returned home and told her father, Ralph, of her suspicions. Like any protective parent, Mr. Teeple stuck his head out the window, took a look at the enveloping fog, sniffed the air, decided his daughter was overreacting, and urged her to go to bed. To assuage her fears, he promised they would call the Coast Guard in the morning—after all, who could see anything in that pea soup out there?

What Farrar had actually seen were four men disgorged from *Kreigsmarine* U-boat number 202, type VIIC, built by the Krupp Works at Kierl, Germany, in 1941, with a crew of forty-five, commanded by *Kapitänleutnant* Hans-Heinz Lindner. The four men waded out of the shadows for a planned mission of terror unprecedented in United States history—one not to be duplicated until almost sixty years later.[5]

A few hundred yards away from Farrar's house, moving as quickly as they could under the cover of the foggy darkness, the four Nazi agents were about to bury four boxes containing TNT, blasting caps, timing devices, and assorted instruments of destruction. George John Dasch, a gaunt man with wide hazel eyes and a shock of white hair, headed the team. His faction was the first of two groups that would land in the next few days, the vanguard—if successful—of a series of operatives intent on wreaking terror and death in the heart of America.[6]

Their German superior had told them before seeing them off from a Nazi-controlled port in France, "You will cause more damage to the American war effort than a whole division of soldiers."[7] But first, the terrorists had to get inside America.

It had taken the group seventeen days to reach Long Island, the debarkation site Dasch chose because he had once lived near Amagansett, in a furnished apartment in Southampton.[8] He knew there they would find access to transportation and that his men, German-Americans who still spoke with accents, would easily blend into the polyglot crowd in their final destination, the great metropolis of New York City.[9]

Two sailors from the submarine had accompanied them, helping to paddle through surf so strong at times it had threatened to overturn their rubber dinghy. The sailors could also supply extra muscle if needed, for most of the men whom the Nazi High Command had sent on this expedition did not bear weapons and were not professional soldiers, even if they dressed as German marines. They had been chosen on the basis of their fluency in the English language and previous residence in the United States. They had received their education on terrorist tactics during three weeks of intensive training at a school located on a farm near Brandenburg, Germany, once owned by a Jewish family. There, the men had been taught how to prepare bombs, disable water canals, and cripple magnesium and cryolite factories. Most important of all, they had been drilled to spread panic among defenseless civilians by bombing Macy's, Gimbel's, and Penn Station—the great hubs of people and movement in New York.[10]

The four Nazi invaders had not been taught discipline and coordination, however. They ambled aimlessly on the shoreline, discarding their uniforms at will. They had worn them to insure protection under the Geneva Convention's rules for prisoners of war, in case they were captured at landing.

Their leader, Dasch, had rejected Nazi insignia, instead opting for the American clothes he had kept from his long residence in the

States. The only emblem he shared with his comrades was one of four tin porcupines he had ordered made and distributed to each of them. The porcupines, meant as good luck charms, were the emblems of the U-boat that had brought them over. Dasch thought the figurines would also be a good way for the terrorists to recognize members of the group, and send messages to each other through third parties when necessary, with the prefatory phrase, "Greetings from Dick."[11]

Dasch carried with him $85,000 in cash, the equivalent of about $750,000 in today's money, given to him by his German trainers as the extent of help they would receive upon landing. The men had been told that once they landed, there was no turning back. They would only return to Germany after victory—or death.[12]

Dasch goaded his men to finish burying the heavy boxes away from the water line. So far, luck had been with them. Dasch was in the shallows, helping the U-boat sailors tip over their dinghy to empty out the water it had taken, when he glanced over his shoulder. A light was moving slowly down the beach, just a short distance away. Dasch turned to his men but they had moved away to higher ground and didn't notice the beam cutting through the thick fog. What should he do?

The light that shone on Dasch came from a lantern held by red-haired John Cullen, all of nineteen years old. A Seaman Second Class in the Coast Guard, Cullen was about a half mile away from the Amagansett station where he had begun his three-and-a-half-mile shore patrol.[13] Dasch was unaware that the area of Long Island he had landed in had been classified as an important military region by the War Department and was patrolled regularly, day and night. Young, inexperienced men, who called themselves "sand pounders," however, usually carried out the patrols. Due to the scarcity of armaments at that early stage of the war, these shore patrols had not been issued weapons. Sometimes they patrolled with dogs, but most often a flashlight was their only protection. In case of danger or unusual circumstances, the patrols were required to report immediately back to their stations.[14]

National Archives/United States Army Signal Corps

John Cullen, the young Coast Guard seaman who discovered the Long Island team landing while he was on an unarmed beach patrol.

Dasch splashed through the water, thinking of the young guardsman, *boy, you don't know what danger you're walking into.* Just before landing, the captain of the U-boat had ordered Dasch to overpower any intruder who might surprise them and send him back to the submarine to be disposed of. If the terrorists couldn't handle him, the sailors who had accompanied the agents had submachine guns with them to finish the job. Their dinghy by their side, the two husky men stood in the shallow water, waiting for their cue.[15]

"Are you guys fishermen?" asked Cullen. "Are you having trouble? Did you get lost?" His flashlight cut through the swirling wreaths of fog.

"We're a couple of fishermen from Southampton and we ran ashore here," said Dasch.

"What were you fishing for?"

"Clams."

Cullen thought it was highly unlikely anyone would be out clamming at this time of night. Besides, there was something odd about the thin man before him: his slight accent, his jittery mannerisms, the way he brought his finger to his nose to emphasize a point. Cullen glanced over at the two men in the shallow water, and then at a fourth man some distance away who seemed to be in his underwear. Cullen shone the light again on Dasch.[16]

"What are you fellows going to do about it?" asked Cullen.

"We'll stay here until sunrise and then we will be all right."

Cullen told Dasch that the sun would not be up for another four hours and that he had better accompany him to the Coast Guard station just down the beach.

Dasch hesitated a moment, then said, "All right," and began to walk away with Cullen. But after a few feet he stopped and turned.

"I am not coming with you."

"Why not?" asked Cullen.

"I don't have any papers or permit to fish," replied Dasch.

"More reason to come along," said Cullen, who somehow found the courage to grab Dasch by the arm and pull him away. Dasch broke free.

"Now, wait a minute. You don't know what this is all about."

"No, I don't."

"How old are you, son?"

"Nineteen."

"You have a father and a mother, don't you, boy?"

"Yes, I do."

"Well, if you ever want to see them again, please do exactly what I tell you. I wouldn't want to have to kill you."

Just then another member of the group came out of the fog, dragging a large canvas bag in which the terrorists' soggy Nazi uniforms had been stashed. Cullen, not knowing what it contained, asked him, "Hey—you got clams in that sack?"[17]

The man, Ernst Peter Burger, surprised at seeing the coast-guardsman, didn't reply but asked Dasch in German, "Is there anything wrong, George? Do you need any help?"

Dasch wheeled about, slapping his hand over Burger's mouth.

"You damn fool, why don't you go back to the other guys?" he told him in English.

Cullen stood his ground, uncertain of what to do. If these men were Nazi spies, as he was beginning to suspect, he had to get help before they overpowered him. Dasch looked at him, also uncertain of his next step. He could call over the two sailors but that would mean death for the young man. But Dasch also couldn't go to the Coast Guard station as Cullen had requested.

Dasch extracted a leather tobacco pouch, from which he removed several bills. He counted quickly, about one hundred dollars.

"Forget about this and I will give you some money and you can have a good time."

Cullen refused the money, but Dasch would not hear of it. He peeled off more bills, bringing the total to $280, and pressed them into Cullen's hands, his voice steely with conviction this time.

"Please, you have undoubtedly given your oath to do your duty. I am telling you by taking this money, which I am offering you, you are doing nothing else but your duty so please take it."[18]

Cullen, realizing he had no other way out, accepted the bribe. He was about to run off to safety when Dasch stopped him.

"Just a minute. I want you to shine your light in my face."

Dasch took off his hat as the young guardsman illuminated the strange invader. In the spotlight, Dasch stood alone, as though on a stage, his wide, cryptic eyes glaring at whatever future awaited him.

"Take a good look at me. Look in my eyes." He repeated, "Look in my eyes. My name is George John Davis. You will hear from me in Washington."[19]

Dasch paused to make sure that his words sank in. Cullen did not know it but he had done more than just discover the first-ever Nazi invasion of the United States, he had also become Dasch's possible ticket to freedom. For Dasch, who always wanted to keep his options open, was contemplating the end of the mission—and the role he might have to play in its demise. Now, concerned about the reaction of the others in his group, Dasch motioned at Cullen to go. He asked, jovially, "What will you do with your money?"

"Some of it I will give to my parents, some of it I will put in the bank, and I will have a good time," babbled Cullen, realizing his life was in peril.

"Boy, do just that, but please go now and you will hear from me in Washington."

"Thank you, sir," said Cullen, who turned off his flashlight, backed off into the fog until he could no longer see the man—or be seen by him—and then took off running as fast as he could to the Coast Guard station.

Dasch ordered the sailors back to the U-boat, wading out into the water to push their boat beyond the surf.[20] By the time Dasch rejoined his men, Burger had told the group of the encounter with Cullen. One of them, Richard Quirin, a true believer in the Nazi cause, grumbled that they were supposed to kill anyone they encountered. Dasch replied, in German, "Boys, this is the time to be quiet and hold your nerves. Each of you get a box and follow me."

Collection of Duane Traynor

The United States Coast Guard Station at Amagansett.

Dasch could see that they had landed practically within earshot of a small, one-story wooden house, which was visible through the thinning fog across the road, so he took the three men inland, heading northeast along the curvy beach. They went over two sand dunes and into a gulch where he stopped and told them to begin digging. Quirin was still muttering about not killing Cullen.

"Look," said Dasch, "I know what I'm doing and everything is going to be all right. Now shut up and get to work."

Concerned that Cullen would soon return with armed men, Dasch urged them to dig as fast as they could. They opened a hole about two yards wide and one yard deep and stacked the four two-foot-by-three-foot boxes inside. Then he ordered them covered up. Unbeknownst to Dasch, one of the Nazis, Peter Burger, had dropped a pack of cigarettes in the sand some distance away;

and another, Heinrich Heinck, had been nipping from a bottle of schnapps, which he later also surreptitiously discarded in the dunes.

Once the hole was covered, Dasch ordered the men to plant sea grass around it, so when the sun came out it would look dry. As they were about to leave, he noticed some of their wet German army uniforms scattered behind them. He had his men retrace their steps, gather up the clothes, and then bury them as well. In their haste to depart, however, Dasch failed to notice that one of their small shovels had been left by the hole, sticking up as though a marker to indicate where their dangerous cache lay hidden.

The team stumbled over the sand dunes in the darkness. None of them had thought of bringing a map, a compass, or a flashlight, so they drifted around in circles. Finally, Dasch led them away from the sound of the surf, reasoning that way they were sure to be heading inland. Then they heard the sound of a shot. All the men dropped to the ground as a red flare arched in the sky above them, shining through the fog.

"My God, they're after us!" said one of the Germans.[21]

For a moment Dasch too feared for their safety, then he remembered that the sailors in the dinghy had been given a flare in case they couldn't make their way back to the sub. The boat had a light line that was tied to the sub but if it was cut or lost, the flare was to be used to signal it. Dasch explained this to the group, but in their desperation, the men refused to believe him.

"You're crazy. They're looking for us and it's all your fault, George," insisted Quirin. "You should have killed that guy on the beach, or we should have done it! I ought to kill you right now. If I had a gun I would!"

Just then a green flare exploded out in the open sea, where the U-boat was located.

"There, you fools. That's the submarine's answer. Now let's get going."[22]

The sailors had made it to the U-boat, which was trying to hurry away, but it was trapped in a sandbar. Its electric engines did not have enough power to pull it out so the captain had ordered its mighty diesels turned on. The roar of the engines could be heard for miles, an unmistakable grinding sound echoing throughout the beach—even down to Cullen, who had come out of the Coast Guard station house with a group of four armed men, heading back to the place where he had spotted the Nazis. The thick mantle of fog made it impossible for them to establish the exact location of the sub, or find the Nazis' disembarkation site, so the coastguardsmen had to sit on the beach for more than two hours, waiting for the first light of dawn before resuming their search.[23]

A few hundred yards away, hidden by the enveloping fog, Dasch and his men sat by another dune, also waiting for the light. When they were finally able to see a little better, they walked toward the main highway that crossed Amagansett to Montauk Point. Not knowing where the town was located, the saboteurs headed to the right. They came to a house that had its lights on, with a number of cars parked around it. A car engine revved and voices floated menacingly in the air. The men hit the ground again.

Dasch realized they had walked into a campground, with trailers and pup tents scattered throughout. Afraid of falling into a trap, yet intent on making their getaway, the four men zigzagged around the site, continuing down the road until they came to railroad tracks.

There they stood at a junction. To their right, a solitary line of track vanished into the fog, while to their left, three and four tracks coalesced into a many-fingered grid. Reasoning that the city must lay in this direction, Dasch and his men headed left, following the tracks for about two or three miles.

Throughout their walk, the men complained of the cold, of being lost. Heinrich Heinck, a melancholy type who always expected the worst in life, wondered aloud what their punishment would be when the Americans caught them. Dasch quieted them all with bluster and resolve, spurring them on through the mist, telling them he knew exactly where they were heading even though he felt just as lost as the rest. Finally, shortly before five in the morning, they reached a little railroad station with a weathered sign reading, "Amagansett."

The team dusted themselves off as best they could. Their clothes, woolen suits and cheap cotton shirts, saved from their stays in the United States years before, were wrinkled and smelled of diesel fuel from the long journey in the U-boat. Now they were also stained from walking through dirt, wet sea grass, and sand.[24] But there was no one in the station to watch them and disapprove—or tell.

According to the posted timetable, the first train to New York would come at 5:25 A.M. The men sank onto the bench outside the station and waited as the sun came up. They could see a flock of sandpipers scampering along the edge of the water, pecking at the sand, then bolting into the air; the birds flew in formation over the ocean, flashing the bright white underside of their wings before disappearing from sight.

Soon the morning commuter crowd gathered, the ticket booth opened, and Dasch bought four passages to New York. No one said anything, no one even looked twice at the men as the train hissed and rumbled into the station. The sight of city fishermen, who had caught nothing but sand and wet clothes on their outing, was common enough at that time of day. Dasch played up that angle, commenting to the ticket agent that the fishing was lousy, as he paid the four men's $20.40 fare to New York.[25] The men boarded, leaving for New York City. Down on the beach, about a dozen military men scoured the grounds, searching for the tracks of the vanished Nazis.[26]

In the News Today

NEW YORK, N.Y., July 1, 1942—R. F. Fruendt of 11 East 75th Street, Manhattan, today pleaded guilty to spying for the Nazis by conspiring to provide critical defense industry information to the Germans.

NEWPORT, R.I., July 1, 1942— Nicholas Hansen, a twenty-seven-year-old man from Newport, Rhode Island, has been arrested by the FBI after threatening to blow up the Newport torpedo station for Hitler.[27]

CHAPTER 2

"This Is What We Germans Are Supposed to Do"

In early December 1941, just a few days after Pearl Harbor, German Fuehrer Adolf Hitler personally authorized the terrorist mission against the United States. Although the United States had been off limits while it remained neutral, after Hitler declared war on America on December 11, anything in the country was fair game. The terrorists were to be trained at a special German army school for spies and saboteurs that had already been sending agents, with great success, into Belgium, Russia, Czechoslovakia, and other countries.[28] Since the mid-1930s the respective heads of German Intelligence, *Reichfuehrer* Heinrich Himmler for the Gestapo, and Admiral Wilhelm Canaris for the *Abwehr*, or Army High Command Intelligence Section, had been in competition for control of overseas operations.[29] The Abwehr's responsibilities ranged from making reconnaissance flights over Poland and England prior to the Polish campaign to preventing the sabotage and nuisance activity carried out by Allied commandos, as well as Nazi sabotage groups behind the enemy lines.[30]

Historians have described Admiral Canaris as the hidden hand of the *Wehrmacht*, or German army, Resistance. Urbane, astute, and a lover of Spanish culture and the Latin way of life, Canaris had become head of the Abwehr in 1935. Under his supervision, the Abwehr played according to the rules of war. As he told his underlings when he took over, "The intelligence service is the domain of gentlemen."[31] Within three years he was involved in coup attempts against Hitler. Canaris, who was ultimately executed in 1944, is credited with saving hundreds of Jews from concentration camps.[32] He was also openly critical of the SS during its bloody pacification campaign in Poland and he even tried to arrange a secret end to the war after he personally contacted the head of the Office of Strategic Services, William "Wild Bill" Donovan, offering a peace plan that was ultimately rejected by President Roosevelt.[33] Yet Canaris was such a persuasive speaker and could spout Nazi ideology so fluently that no one suspected his betrayal until 1943, when an outraged Hitler blamed him for the defection of key German spies to the Allies.

Canaris, who was already in close contact with the Nazi resistance in 1941, had managed to wrest control of the sabotage school away from Himmler, putting it under the Abwehr's direct supervision. One can only speculate how far he really intended for the school's American side to succeed.[34]

Walter Kappe, formerly number-two man of the German-American *Bund*, a pro-Nazi organization dedicated to the creation of a fascist fifth column in the United States, was placed in charge of the school's American component.[35] Kappe, working in conjunction with the Nazi organization that tracked Germans overseas, the Ausland Institute, located and recruited Germans who had lived for years in the United States. With the arrival of Dasch and his cohorts for their training, Kappe assembled a twelve-man team of German-Americans. They were but one of several groups of operatives from many nations around the world, including Ireland, India, Ukraine, Syria, Egypt, and other countries.[36]

Reinhold Barth

Walter Kappe

Walter Kappe, center, who recruited the eight men to return to Germany and served as their superior officer during their training in the Nazi sabotage school.

Kappe was a short, obese man with a fondness for drink and ornate language. He had used his long stay in the United States to advance in the strangely insular Nazi world, earning himself the rank of lieutenant in the Abwehr. Kappe had toured all of Germany hunting for likely terrorist candidates, sometimes plucking them from factories, as he did with Heinrich Heinck and Richard Quirin, two German-Americans who were working at a Volkswagen plant when Kappe came to speak. Heinck, who had met Kappe in New York City when Kappe published the Bund newspaper, the *Deutscher Weokruf und Beobachter*, eagerly volunteered for the job. Quirin followed suit.[37]

The school itself was in a large farm located at Quentz Lake, near Brandenburg, more famous for Bach concerti than for terrorist training camps. Formerly owned by a Jewish shoe manufacturer, the facility was situated in an old lakeside estate, surrounded by a large park and garden. Heavily guarded, the grounds were encircled by a high fence to keep away the curious.[38]

The first members of the Long Island group to arrive at the camp were Quirin and Heinck on the afternoon of April 1, 1942. The men took a train to Brandenburg, where, following specific instructions, they boarded a streetcar and rode it to the end of the line. From there they took a bus that dropped them off in front of the dirt road that led to the farm's entrance. They walked about fifteen minutes to the farm's iron gate, then up a grade for half of another block before arriving at the main farmhouse.[39] The Quentz Lake manor, a two-story, twelve-room stone building with a cellar, was set on a spread of several acres. A caretaker and his family occupied about half of the house while the school's personnel and recruits were located in the other half. South of the main house was a small stone building where some workers lived, growing greens, vegetables, and flowers in a nearby hothouse. East of the hothouse, the Abwehr had erected a two-story building; the first floor was a garage, the second housed a classroom and a laboratory. There was also a gymnasium, a barn with cows and pigs, a pistol range, and a rifle range about a thousand feet in diameter where explosives and incendiary devices were tested.[40]

Quirin and Heinck were met by Kappe, who showed them to the sparsely furnished room they would share. Later that day Heinck and Quirin met the other men who had been recruited for the American terrorism and sabotage group. After a brief introduction in the vast living room, the terrorists were given a broad outline of their duties and responsibilities once they graduated.

Kappe told them that the German soldiers on the Russian front were doing their duty and that now it was up to them, his handpicked group, to do theirs by stopping production of armaments and supplies in the United States. This was as important as any battle the Germans would ever wage. In fact, he told his charges that their efforts could well decide the outcome of the war. Their training would include courses in the construction and use of explosives, primers, fuses, and timers; they would also learn which weak spots to strike in American factories, bridges, railroads, and canals.[41]

German technicians, engineers, and experts in all kinds of industry had studied the American war machine and decided on their plan of attack. The group would concentrate on destroying the American aluminum and magnesium industry, as well as plants processing cryolite, then an indispensable component of aluminum manufacturing. Special mention was made of the Alcoa plant in Tennessee and the cryolite plant in Philadelphia. Destruction, or even just effective sabotage, of these places would set back the manufacturing of aluminum and the Reich would be able to better prepare for future American attacks.

Other terrorist targets included:

1. the Chesapeake and Ohio railroad lines;
2. the new Pennsylvania depot at Newark, New Jersey;
3. the Hell Gate Bridge connecting Long Island with the Bronx;
4. the New York City water supply and electrical system;
5. hydroelectric plants at Niagara Falls, New York;
6. inland waterways and sluices between Cincinnati and St. Louis;

7. Aluminum Company of America plants at Alcoa, Tennessee; Massena, New York; and East St. Louis, Illinois;

8. the cryolite plant of the Philadelphia Salt Company in Philadelphia, Pennsylvania; and

9. Horseshoe Curve of the Pennsylvania Railroad at Altoona, Pennsylvania.

Then, as sort of a ghastly afterthought, Kappe advised the men to plant bombs in major American railroad stations—New York's Pennsylvania and Grand Central stations, Washington, D.C.'s and Chicago's Union stations—as well as in prominent Jewish-owned department stores such as Macy's, Gimbel's, and Abraham & Straus.

The purpose of the civilian bombings was not only to sow terror among the population, but also to link the bombings to Germans so that the United States government would overreact, persecuting German-Americans indiscriminately. This would then cause, in theory, all Americans of German origin to close ranks and support the Reich by default. This theory had very recent historical precedent: "Kappe, who dreamed up the scheme, pointed to the way the [American] people reacted against the many good citizens of Japanese extraction who were herded into detention camps away from vital war centers. Kappe was, of course, convinced [this] idea was the most valuable part of the mission."[42]

Oddly enough, when one of the men asked Kappe if they were also expected to use bio-terrorist weapons such as anthrax or poison gas on the civilian population, Kappe said they need not go that far. The Germans did not anticipate Americans using that kind of weaponry so there was no need for the Nazis to be the first to do so. There had been enough fatalities from the use of mustard gas during World War I and, apparently, even the Nazis followed some rules of armed engagement.

Kappe's announcement that George Dasch would be the leader of the first group came as no surprise—Dasch had helped formulate the plan of attack by working in close consultation with Kappe and other members of the Abwehr. In fact, Dasch also had a hand in the selection of the candidates for the group, judging their fitness for the mission after a study of their knowledge of the United States and the American way of life.[43]

Dasch, like the other members of his expedition, had been born to a lower-middle-class family in Germany and had never risen far above it throughout his whole peripatetic existence. He was born on February 7, 1903, in Speyer on the Rhine, a medieval town in the verdant Rhine valley of Germany noted for its majestic Romanesque cathedral. One of thirteen children, his father was a carpenter; his mother, in spite of the innumerable duties her large household entailed, was a politician—a city councilwoman on the Social Democratic ticket. Dasch fashioned himself a political progressive and credited his mother for his basic socialist political ideals.[44]

Brought up Roman Catholic, at thirteen Dasch entered a seminary to study for the priesthood. After a year, at the height of World War I, he was drafted to carry out clerical work in Speyer on the Rhine. A few months later he volunteered to do the same for the German army, which assigned him to a battalion in northern France. When he was discharged by the army at the end of the war in 1918, the city administration of Speyer on the Rhine hired him as a French interpreter.

He rejoined the seminary at seventeen, but life on the battlefield and in society had soured him on a priestly calling. He left for Holland and then Hamburg, trying unsuccessfully to get work as a seaman, living by his wits through the terrible depression years of Weimar Germany. Finally, he stowed away on an American ship and illegally entered the United States through the port of Philadelphia on October 4, 1922.[45]

His first few steps in this country were very similar to those of millions of other immigrants who arrive here, lonely and bereft, relying on the kindness of their own people who had migrated earlier for a handout and a step up. As Dasch recounted in his autobiography, when he landed he first went around to a German bakery, where the baker took pity on him.

" 'So you came here without any papers or visa or anything!' Shaking his head, he continued, 'Look, boy, don't let the boss know. He'll exploit the daylights out of you. Go upstairs and get to work and I'll take care of him for you.' "[46]

He lived in the bakery for a week, and when he got his first week's pay—five dollars—friends told him on which highway he should try to hitch a ride out of town. Dasch then moved to New York, working in a number of restaurants and hotels, but never staying in any one place for more than a few months.

The following year Dasch was advised to settle his legal status in the country, a much more lax procedure than it is today. To obtain the necessary paperwork he sailed back to Germany, visiting his mother in Speyer, then returned to New York in late 1923. The following four years after his return found Dasch continuing to drift between waiter jobs in several New York restaurants, with one season spent at a hotel in Miami Beach.[47]

In 1927 Dasch enlisted as a private in the United States Army Air Corps. Charles Lindbergh had just flown his *Spirit of St. Louis* in a daring solo flight from New York to Europe in May of that year, and Dasch, like so many others, was fascinated with the dashing new field of aviation. He was assigned to the Fifth Composite Group of Newton Field, in Honolulu, and served with the Seventy-second Bombardment Squadron, but after a year, he purchased his exit from the army, receiving an honorable discharge.

Dasch again drifted to waiter work in San Francisco, Sacramento, Los Angeles, and back in New York for two more years until he met a slender, pretty girl named Rose Marie Guille, a hairdresser from Walston, a coal-mining town in Pennsylvania. They were married in the spring in a small ceremony, Rose Marie being the sole survivor of her family. Dasch called her Snooks; she would remain with him her whole life, serving as his only anchor. On their honeymoon they visited Lake George in Canada; then in November of that year, they sailed to Europe to visit his mother in Speyer on the Rhine. When they returned in March of 1931, they settled in New York City at 119 West Eighty-eighth Street, in a walk-up

George John Dasch with his wife, Rose Marie "Snooks" Guille.

just a few blocks away from the gothic spires of the Museum of Natural History.[48]

The following year, itching to try another line of work, Dasch moved to Chicago, where he became a salesman for the Mission of Our Lady of Mercy, offering sanctuary supplies in southern Illinois. Later his responsibilities widened to include Missouri, and for a while he resided there in Overland. But in 1933 he returned to New York and again went back to work as a waiter.[49]

Already a certain pattern of conduct was emerging in Dasch's life: a restless, constant striving, yet with an unwillingness to devote the time necessary to achieve anything other than a superficial advancement, along with a predisposition to blame anybody but himself for his own shortcomings. He left the air corps, he wrote, because he felt he would not be able to advance fast enough to reach his goal of becoming an aviator.[50] Then, in 1935, he blamed political extremists for his defeat as a union representative.

While working in White Plains, New York, he had helped to start a culinary workers union, becoming at first a member of the executive board of the Bartenders and Waiters International Union at Mount Vernon and later being voted into its executive board. He attended the labor college of the Amalgamated Clothing Workers of America Union to study parliamentary procedure and union organization and ran for the office of business agent for Local 168. He lost, he said, because the local "was, to my sincere belief, in the hands of a bunch of chiselers and Communists. I made this an issue and fought them at every turn. . . . Due to the fact that the other side of the gang knew that nothing would stop my being elected, they had to use trickery to stop me."[51]

In 1939, a visit by Dasch's mother proved to be a crucial turning point in his life. She spoke glowingly of Germany under Hitler, how unemployment had been virtually eradicated, and the country was prospering. As long as people didn't get involved in politics, she said, life was wonderful under the Nazis. Although Dasch, by his own account, argued with his mother over her politics—or lack thereof—he was forced to admit to himself that he was going nowhere in America.

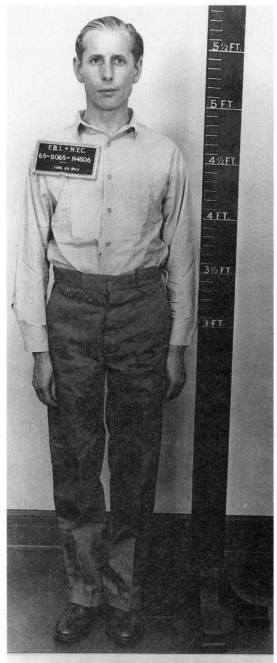

George John Dasch

Collection of Duane Traynor

Disillusioned, he never followed through on a United States citizenship application, and began to make plans to return to Germany.[52]

On hearing that Germany was paying for the return trip to the *vaterland* for émigrés, he contacted the New York German consulate. He was given the cold shoulder there for his lack of professional degrees and his use of common German—his many years in America had made him forget the complex High German or *Hoch Deutch*. But using his native facility for prevarication, he concocted a story about owning an import-export company that steered contracts to Bund members and German nationals. He was immediately placed on a waiting list for embarkment.[53]

The route to Germany was long and difficult. One had to travel for several months, first by bus to San Francisco, from there by ship to Japan, then board another ship to Korea, and then to the Soviet Union, traveling by train through Siberia and across the great Eurasian landmass all the way to Moscow and finally down to Berlin. All of this was done under the auspices of the Ausland Institute, the branch of the Nazi government in charge of supervising and controlling the lives of Germans abroad—and keeping them under close watch once they returned to Germany. Despite the ordeal, tens of thousands of Germans made the trip back from the United States, drunk on the heady potion of Nazi war victories in Europe.

A few weeks after Dasch had put in his application, he received the news that his trip had been approved—he had less than twenty-four hours to pack up his belongings and ready himself for the journey. He claimed to have misgivings, but even so, he left behind his beloved Snooks in the hospital, recuperating from an operation, and took the bus out to San Francisco. He made arrangements for his wife to later board a Spanish cargo ship to join him in Germany. Those plans came to naught when a British warship intercepted her vessel. Rose would spend the rest of the war at an internment camp in Bermuda.[54]

On March 22, 1941, Dasch took a bus from New York for the West Coast and on March 27, he boarded the Japanese steamer *Tattuta Maru* headed for Yokohama, Japan.[55]

Dasch alleged that other repatriating Germans on the ship to Japan suspected him of being an American spy because he would not automatically say "Heil Hitler" by way of greeting and would refuse to engage in other ostentatious displays of Nazism. He claimed even to have had a physical confrontation with some Hitler thugs but that ultimately he came to an uneasy truce with them for the remainder of his trip.[56]

No doubt Dasch's skepticism was reported to the Ausland Institute. Upon arriving back in Germany, every German was met by a member of the AI and questioned about whether he intended to stay in Germany permanently or was returning only for a visit. If the person was a member of the AI in a foreign country, he was required first to report to party headquarters to give his whereabouts in Germany. Then, if his stay was permanent, his file was transferred to the party branch nearest to where he intended to settle. In addition, all Germans were required to report to a Gestapo agent, a finance agent, and an agent from the Labor Front in order to obtain all possible information from the returning Germans regarding their foreign country of residence. They were also questioned regarding their political ideology, their finances, occupation, relatives in Germany, and whether the returnees were members of the Nazi Party and the AI, and if not, why not—in other words, they had to prove they were good Germans deserving of another shot in Hitler's Aryan paradise.[57]

All the same, within weeks of finally getting to Berlin, Dasch was assigned a plum government job—listening to American radio broadcasts and making summaries of them for the Foreign Office. The man who secured him that job was Walter Kappe, who would later offer Dasch the most perilous decision of his life: joining the Abwehr's top-secret sabotage school.

The dozen men Kappe and his Abwehr superiors had chosen were a motley group, linked only by their long stay in America and their seeming loyalty to the Reich. Besides Dasch, Kappe had assembled the following crew:

Ernst Peter Burger

Collection of Duane Traynor

1. **Ernst Peter Burger**: An early follower of National Socialism, Burger had participated in Hitler's failed Munich Beer Hall *Putsch* of 1923; he had then migrated to the United States and had eventually become an American citizen and a member of the Michigan National Guard. Now in his early thirties, Burger had returned to Germany around 1933, affiliating himself with the head of the Storm Troopers, the SA or *Sturmatbeilung* leader Ernst Roehm.[58]

When Roehm lost an internal power struggle with SS chief Heinrich Himmler, and thousands of his followers were slaughtered, Burger almost lost his own life. An outcast, he had been tortured and held for almost two years in a concentration camp by the Gestapo for criticizing the German occupation of Poland. When offered a place in the terrorist mission, Burger eagerly took it.[59] A highly educated journalist, he was the group's second in command.

2. **Richard Quirin**: Born in Berlin, Quirin was a mechanic who had lived in the United States from the 1920s to 1939. While living in the States, he had been a member of the German-American Bund and openly supported the Hitler regime. Upon his return to Germany he had gone to work at a Volkswagen plant before being recruited for the espionage mission.[60] Dasch and Kappe thought of him as a cool, cruel man who would not hesitate to kill anyone to accomplish the mission's objectives.

3. **Heinrich Heinck**: A machinist who had emigrated to the United States from Hamburg, Germany, in the 1920s, Heinck had been an early recruit of the German-American Bund; he had belonged to the group's bodyguard section, the OD or *Ordnungs Dients*. Heinck had migrated back to Germany shortly before the war, his fare paid by the German consulate.[61] According to records obtained by FBI agents during a search of the trash of the New York German Consulate, Heinck was in the direct pay of the Nazis during his stay in America.[62] Dasch considered Heinck a bully and a coward who might run if confronted by superior force.

4. **Edward John Kerling**: A ruddy-faced, blue-eyed native of the Rhineland, 33-year-old Kerling had migrated to the United

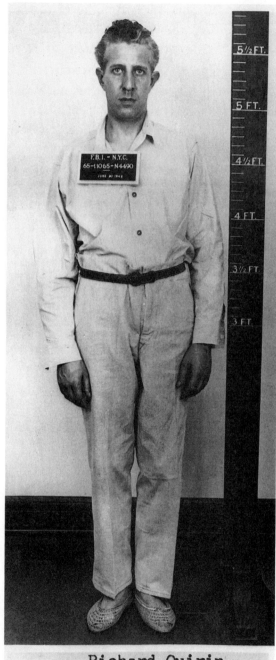

Richard Quirin

Collection of Duane Traynor

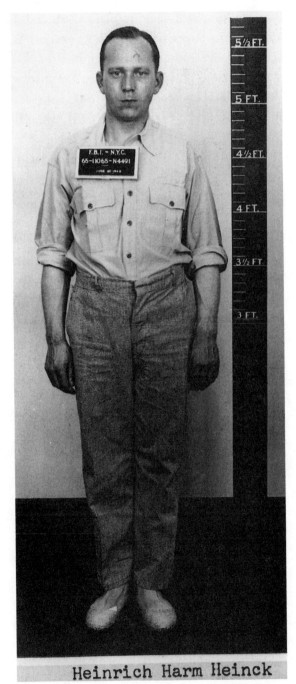

Heinrich Harm Heinck

Collection of Duane Traynor

States in 1928, working at a packing plant in Brooklyn, New York, smoking hams. After his marriage in 1931 to Marie Sichart, also a German immigrant, he worked as a chauffeur for a Jewish bridge builder, Ely Culbertson, on Long Island, while his wife worked as the family's domestic. The two of them would continue working for a number of other wealthy families until 1939, when his outspoken support for Hitler ultimately cost Kerling his job.

Before migrating to the United States, Kerling had been among the first 80,000 men to join the Nazi Party in Germany, a mark of honor in the Third Reich for which he had received a special lapel insignia. According to FBI informants, Kerling was a highly placed member of the Bund who traveled to Germany every two years under the auspices of the Freud Society.

In 1940, to get around a travel embargo to Germany, Kerling, along with a number of Nazi Germans and another future terrorist, Hermann Neubauer, purchased a yacht. The *Lekala* sailed from New York City down the eastern seaboard, followed by United

© Bettmann/CORBIS

Edward John Kerling, left, aboard the *Lekala* in 1940.

Edward Kerling

Collection of Duane Traynor

States Coast Guard vessels. The sloop was stopped in North Carolina and the crew questioned by the FBI. They were released and ultimately sailed to south Florida, where, after more confrontations with the authorities, the yacht was intercepted as it attempted to sail to Germany. Eventually the yacht was sold in Florida, where Kerling spent several months in and around Jacksonville working as a waiter.

It was there that he met his future mistress, 31-year-old Hedwig "Hedy" Engemann, a German immigrant who worked without much distinction as a waitress, domestic, and store clerk in Miami Beach. Upon learning of the affair, Kerling's wife, Marie, whom friends described as below Kerling's social level, returned to New York to live with friends. Chastened, Kerling followed, but shortly thereafter bought passage on a boat to Lisbon and from there made his way to Germany while his wife stayed behind.

Like Dasch, Kerling had also worked at the Foreign Office, monitoring news broadcasts. When Kappe had come to recruit him, Kerling was working for the Propaganda Ministry, staging pro-Nazi theater plays.[63]

5. **Hermann Otto Neubauer**: A seaman and cook born in Hamburg, Germany, Neubauer lived in the United States for nearly ten years before returning to Germany. Dasch described him as a tough fellow and a devoted member of the German-American Bund. Tall, dapper, and dark haired, he had married an American, Alma Wolf, from Chicago. According to FBI files, Neubauer, under the code name "Hofweg," had been transporting secret letters during his travels to and from Germany.

A friend of Kerling, Neubauer had been one of the investors in the ill-fated *Lekala*. When the yacht was sold and the group disbanded, Neubauer, a.k.a. Hofweg, left the United States on a German passport via a clipper ship to Lisbon, but not before "his wife made some boastful remarks to the effect that Neubauer was carrying important papers." The German Consulate in New York paid part of the cost of their trip.

Hermann Otto Neubauer

Collection of Duane Traynor

Upon his return to Germany with his wife, Neubauer was drafted into the German army and sent to the Russian front, where he was seriously wounded by shrapnel just three days after the declaration of war between Russia and Germany. While convalescing at an army medical center in Austria, Kappe wrote to Neubauer, asking if he would be willing to accept a secret assignment to the United States. Neubauer agreed and was ordered to report to the house on Quentz Lake.[64]

6. **Herbert Haupt**: The youngest and perhaps the most American looking and sounding of the group, Haupt was a dreamy-eyed, 22-year-old high school dropout from Chicago. He had migrated to the United States when he was six and was an American citizen. Fond of loud, flashy clothes and "jive talk," Dasch referred to him contemptuously as "a drugstore cowboy."[65] Yet even FBI files refer

HERBERT HANS HAUPT

National Archives/Federal Bureau of Investigation

to him as "a romantic type," a seeming ne'er-do-well who had been involved in some interesting scrapes.[66]

An apprentice optician, Haupt had been active in the United States Army Reserve Officers Training Corps; he was, however, also a faithful member of the German-American Bund. Friends recall seeing him "goose stepping down Western Avenue in front of the Queen of Angels Guild Hall in his brown-shirt uniform."[67]

Haupt had left Chicago in June 1941 after his girlfriend, Gerta Melind, an exotically beautiful 23-year-old widow, told him she was pregnant. Whether he was unwilling to accept his responsibilities, or just looking for a last fling before settling down to enforced parenthood—abortion then being highly illegal and hard to procure—Haupt quit his job at Simpson Optical Company, a defense material manufacturer. Accompanied by his best friend, Wolfgang Wergin, Haupt drove to Mexico in his Chevrolet after attending a colorful Mexican fiesta in Chicago's North Side. Both men carried the princely sum of $80 for their trip. Haupt was twenty-one; Wergin was eighteen. According to interviews with military authorities who supervised his work at Simpson, Haupt intended to travel all the way to Central America to look for work in Nicaragua.

In Mexico, Haupt and Wergin sold their car for living expenses—then were denied passage back into the United States by Mexican border officials until they paid taxes on the sale of the car.[68] Broke and unable to return to the United States, they drifted back to Mexico City, where German Embassy officials put them in touch with a German sausage factory owner who housed them for a while. Mexican authorities, who suspected the boys' host of being a Nazi spy, detained Haupt and Wergin for questioning. Haupt and Wergin were released on July 15, 1941, after the Mexican police determined their immigration papers were in order. In Mexico City Haupt met one Paul Schmidt, also known as Swensen-Swede, who would later also join Dasch's group.[69] According to reports from an FBI informant in Mexico, Haupt was visiting a German-Mexican family when the Mexican police burst in. Schmidt, who did not have papers to be in Mexico, escaped by diving out the bathroom window.[70]

There is no clear evidence of what drove Haupt to take his next fateful step, whether he was already a Nazi agent or, as muddled-headed youths often do, he took the path of least resistance. One thing is clear—the German consulate paid for his return trip to Germany via Japan. On July 27, 1941, he sailed from Manzanillo to Yokohama aboard the SS *Jinoya Maru*, along with several other Germans.[71]

Haupt would later tell his family that upon arriving in Japan, he was practically starving and had to go work on a farm to earn his keep.[72] He told Dasch, however, that he had stayed at the Tahiti Hotel in Tokyo and had received a daily allowance from the German Embassy. Nazi officials put him on a steamer that sailed to Europe out of Kobe. The trip lasted eighty-three days, during which time Haupt was put to work, utilizing his optics experience by tending to every pair of binoculars aboard the ship. His freighter evaded the British blockade around Nazi-occupied France. Dasch reported having read newspaper accounts of Haupt spotting a British warship while serving as lookout on the German steamer. This act earned Haupt an Iron Cross, second-class, from a grateful Reich, plus another special medal for running the blockade.[73]

7. **Werner Thiel:** A toolmaker who lived in New York and the Midwest for fourteen years before his return to Germany, Thiel was also a member of the German-American Bund and the Friends of New Germany. Dasch said Thiel, short and slight of build, was moody and prone to drink. A porter for three years at the Home for the Aged and Infirm on New York City's Central Park West, Thiel had returned to Germany on the same trip as Dasch.[74] Dasch said that as soon as their ship had left American waters, Thiel, along with several other migrants, changed into Nazi clothing and obnoxiously prodded the passengers into singing Nazi songs.[75] Thiel thought Dasch was an FBI agent and was duly surprised when he met him again at the Quentz Lake training camp. He was a close friend of Kerling.

8. **Jerry Swensen:** The oddest man in an already odd bunch, his real name was Joseph Paul Schmidt. A perfect Aryan-looking

Werner Thiel

blond, blue-eyed, tall, and muscular man with Nordic features, who spoke English with a high-pitched voice, Schmidt was called "the Swede," even though he hailed from the Rhine valley. About thirty years old, he had lived in the United States and Canada for more than fifteen years. In the United States he had been a farmer; in Canada, he had operated a trucking business hauling fish during the season. Off-season he was a fur hunter and trapper. When war broke out between Germany and Great Britain, the Canadian government had seized Schmidt's fur farm and attempted to arrest him as an enemy alien. Schmidt, however, had fled to Mexico. He was extremely strong and often performed tricks, such as bending heavy pieces of metal with his bare hands. Dasch thought he had anti-Nazi sympathies, at one point overhearing him say that if the Germans couldn't get along with the rest of the world, they would be destroyed.[76]

9. **Ernst Zuber**: A mentally ill veteran of the Russian front, Zuber's involvement with the saboteurs was brief. A quiet man, about thirty-eight years old, small and slight, with thinning blond hair, he was known at the school as Wanne. He was a native of the Sudetenland and had met Kappe in Cincinnati, where he had been an active member of the Bund. Kappe was very fond of him and pulled him out of the Russian front to take part in the mission, according to Dasch. But when Zuber was told the details of the enterprise, he refused to participate.

Zuber told Dasch he couldn't repay the kindness that America showed him by terrorizing it and causing needless deaths. Dasch thought he was suffering from some kind of mental disturbance, battle fatigue as he called it, but Kappe, feeling betrayed, turned him over to the Gestapo, who took him away.[77]

10. **Bill Dempsey a.k.a. Billy Braubender**: A former prize-fighter and trainer, Dempsey matched Dasch's wiliness in maneuvering the Nazi system. About forty-five years old, he was the oldest in the group; he would only remain at the school for about a week before departing, saying "I'll see you boys over there," since he would come in on another landing.[78]

Dempsey was a gambler and womanizer who was only in the mission for the money—and a chance to return to America. A former middleweight contender, Dempsey had fought throughout the United States under the name Billy Smith. He had spent World War I in New York but had returned to Germany by the time Hitler seized power in 1933. When they first met, Dasch was surprised at how well Dempsey spoke English despite having lived in Germany for so long. Married and hurting for money, he talked Dasch into giving him a leather jacket Dasch had brought over from America. Like most boxers of the era, he was missing some teeth and had others crowned with gold that shined when he talked. Dasch called him "a shrewd old fox."[79]

11. **Scotty**: A former tie salesman in the Midwest, Scotty was working as a bookkeeper in Hamburg when Kappe recruited him. Single, about five feet, five inches tall, with dark hair combed back, he claimed to be very popular with women. Nevertheless, he struck a very sour note with the men in the group, who could not stand him. He was dropped from the mission after three days.

Supervising the group were Kappe, two instructors, Drs. Gunther Koenig and Walter Schultz, as well as Reinhold Barth, a mild-mannered bookkeeper who was married to one of Dasch's cousins. A devoted Nazi who had lived in the United States for nine years, Barth had been instrumental in putting Dasch in contact with Kappe and had advised Dasch on what to do in order to be included in the mission. Barth, a former draftsman with the Long Island railroad, would instruct the men on how to sabotage railroads and railroad equipment.[80]

Kappe first had everyone adopt an alias and make up a false personal history. The men were then separated into two groups. In Group One, with Dasch—who became known as George John Davis—were Richard Quirin, now called Richard Quintas; in his false identity he was of Portuguese extraction because of his hook nose and swarthy complexion. Heinrich Heinck became Henry

Kayner, of Wilkes-Barre, Pennsylvania (a town name he would never quite learn how to spell).[81] Burger's name remained the same. In the second group, Hermann Neubauer became Henry Nicholas, while Kerling became Edward Kelly. Werner Thiel was reborn as John Thomas, a recent Polish immigrant, to disguise his thick accent. Haupt, a United States citizen like Burger, retained his true name and origin, while Dasch and Kerling were said to have been born in San Francisco before 1906—which meant their records had been lost in that city's earthquake and fire.[82]

All the men except for Haupt received forged Social Security cards and Selective Service Registration cards with their false names.[83]

The course of instruction lasted about three weeks. The terrorists were forbidden to take notes and had to memorize all the information, including a host of formulas for explosives and incendiaries. Much like in German primary schools, classes were given six days a week—from nine o'clock in the morning to five-thirty in the afternoon Monday through Friday, and from nine to noon on Saturdays. On Sundays, Kappe allowed the men to go down to a nearby village to drink some beer and relax. Even in their off time they were training, to the point of singing American tunes such as "Oh Susanna!" during walks in the woods.[84]

The men were divided into two study groups. The first was headed by Dasch and composed of all those who would land with him—Heinck, Quirin, and Burger, along with Swensen. The second was headed by Kerling, who early on, because of his pro-Nazi zeal, was designated the subhead of the entire expedition. Four German officers who were not part of the expedition took classes with the German-Americans as well. Two were naval officers and two were non-commissioned officers, all dressed as medical doctors. Dasch never knew where exactly they were supposed to be going, even though he surmised they were also supposed to come to the United States at some point in the future.[85]

Their days, filled with activity, were models of Teutonic punctiliousness. Dasch, Kerling, and Kappe had single rooms in the main house, while the rest of the terrorists shared rooms. They would all rise at seven in the morning, exercise until precisely seven-thirty, then make their beds, and at eight o'clock have breakfast. From nine to noon they would attend school, supervised by the gloomy Dr. Schultz, who would go over the mechanical principles and physics behind their lessons on explosives. The men would then have lunch back at the manor house. At one o'clock there was compulsory reading of American magazines and publications to keep abreast of the latest news and trends. This lasted until two o'clock, at which time they returned to the laboratory, to put into practice the lessons learned in the morning. Then from four to five-thirty they had sports and physical training—including soccer, boxing, wrestling, and, as a titillating addition, tossing hand grenades and shooting rifles and pistols.[86]

First, the groups learned how to make and use incendiaries. They were given suitcases that would burst into flames, to be used in airplanes, trains, and department stores. They were also given ignition formulas, such as potassium permanganate, flour, and sulphur, which in the right proportions would be sufficient to ignite the incendiaries.

The saboteurs were also taught how to construct and use unusual timing devices. One of the most inventive was a glass beaker or test tube filled with dry peas, and sealed loosely with a cork bearing a contact. Water would be added to the tube so that when the dry peas absorbed the liquid hours later, they would push the cork upwards and make contact, triggering the explosion.

Another ingenious timing device was made out of an ordinary wooden matchbox, reinforced on one side with a strip of wood. A razor blade split in half was placed at one end of the strip. A piece of rubber or rubber hose soaked in benzene or gasoline was placed over the razor blade. The soaking would cause the rubber to expand, bending the razor blade outward. A wire extending a fraction of an inch was placed through the end of the rubber hose. A second wire was attached to the blade. When the gasoline or benzene evaporated and the rubber hose dried, it contracted, releasing the pressure on the razor blade, which made contact with the wire, closing the circuit and setting off the charge.[87]

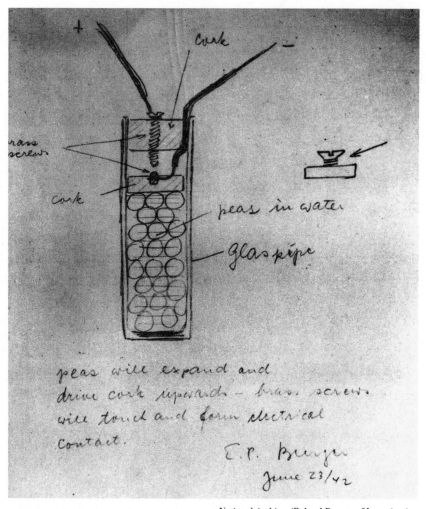

National Archives/Federal Bureau of Investigation

Drawing by Peter Burger of bomb trigger made from a glass tube, dried peas, water, screws, and small pieces of cork.

The men were also taught how to make a chemical timing device by using sulphuric acid, powdered sugar, and potassium chlorate. The sulphuric acid was placed in a bottle and the bottle sealed with a paper cap. The sugar and potassium chlorate were then placed under the cap, and the bottle held upside down over it. Once the acid ate through the paper cap, it would splash on the dry mixture, creating an instant hot fire.

During their afternoon practices the men, in pairs, blew up railroad tracks laid around the grounds of the farm, discovering through trial and error the exact amount of explosives required in a given situation. During one exercise, they were told a certain building was a power plant and that Kappe, Schultz, and Barth were guards around the installation. Their job was to sneak in and plant the explosives, without being caught. Everyone passed the test.

The last formal course of instruction was on secret writing. They were taught several formulas to make invisible ink using common everyday preparations sold over the counter. One employed Ex-Lax or any laxative that turned blue in water—the ink would be used on cloth or paper and would be developed by straining water through cigarette ashes.[88] They were also taught that secret writing could be produced by the simplest of materials; for instance, placing a dry sheet of paper over a wet sheet and writing on the dry sheet with the end of a toothpick wrapped in cotton. This would leave a legible imprint on the wet paper; after the paper dried, it could be used to write an innocuous looking letter on the opposite side, thus disguising its true content.[89]

After two weeks of instruction the men were given a week's break, during which time all of them returned to see their families—most for the last time. Dasch visited his mother at Speyer on the Rhine but he told her nothing about his mission to America. Instead, he repeated his cover story, which he had used earlier as the reason for his dismissal from the Foreign Ministry: He had been sent to work at the German Embassy in Chile. His mother was worried about Dasch's wife, but Dasch assured her he would make every effort to get her freed as soon as he left the country.[90]

When they returned from their vacation, the men received their final week of instruction. Kappe and the instructors took them to Berlin, where at a railroad yard Barth showed them how to sabotage locomotives, pointing out the bearings into which they should throw sand or abrasives.[91] He also showed them chunks of TNT coated with plastic to resemble ordinary lumps of coal. Schultz told them this explosive could be thrown into a railroad locomotive or any other kind of coal-burning furnace or steam boiler. The explosive would crack and ruin the boiler.

The terrorists were then taken on a tour of the I. G. Farben aluminum and magnesium plants in Dessau, Bitterfeld, and Aachen. Engineers there showed Kappe and Dasch the complete plans of American aluminum plants built in the Tennessee Valley before the war under contract by Farben for Alcoa. The technicians who explained the plans were the very same ones who had supervised their construction. They told them sabotaging the plants was a simple matter—it would just require cutting off the power supply for eight to ten hours. This would cause the electrolytic baths in which the metal was refined to solidify. To be removed the metal would have to be dynamited out, thereby destroying the baths. Rebuilding the baths would take eight to ten months.

The engineers advised Dasch to have his men blow up the steel towers carrying high-tension wires into the plant. If they took the towers out of commission in mountainous terrain, which repair crews would have trouble accessing, the men could accomplish their job without much risk. This was one of their first assignments, to be undertaken within three or four weeks after arriving in America.[92]

During his inspection of one of the I. G. Farben plants, Dasch noticed large numbers of slave laborers—Jews and other undesirables who had been spared death in the concentration camps. Company officials referred to them as "foreign labor." They explained to Dasch that the company paid them the same as regular workers but that nearly 60 percent of their wages went to the government. The little they were allowed to keep was given to them in scrip redeemable only at the company commissary. Men and women were kept in separate camps; marital privileges for husbands and wives were granted only on the basis of what the Nazis judged to be good behavior. To Dasch the workers looked famished, filthy, and overworked. "I couldn't understand how people could be so inhuman," he later recalled.[93] Dasch said that he wanted to speak up and protest but he didn't dare. He remembered earlier that year when he had heard an Abwehr officer laughing as he boasted of how he had shot an old Jewish woman when she wouldn't leave the corpse of her daughter in Russia. Dasch had complained to Kappe about the officer's wanton cruelty.

"What kind of Dutchman are you?" Kappe had snapped. "This is what we Germans are supposed to do, kill all the Jews. And don't you get so chicken hearted."[94]

After their tour of the plants, the men were taken to inspect sluices in canals around Berlin. Kappe and Barth pointed out the different kinds of locks and the best way to plant dynamite to disable them. They were told it was almost impossible to destroy a whole lock but that by damaging the hinges, they could prevent the lock from opening. The instructors mentioned the locks in the canals around Ohio and also the Panama Canal, but advised the men to stay away from Panama because it was heavily guarded.

At the end of their tour they were given money for their expenses. Kappe had promised it would be a sizable amount and it was—$160,000, the equivalent of more than $1.7 million today, all in fifty-dollar bills. As leader of the expedition, Dasch was entrusted with the funds, but to avoid suspicion, Dasch asked Kappe to give half of the money to Kerling, who was second in command. This appeased Kerling, who during their training had complained to Kappe about Dasch's lack of attention to the classes, his tardiness, and his cavalier attitude toward the Nazi party line.[95]

Finally Schultz and Koenig showed the men the sealed wooden boxes they were to transport to America. Schultz explained that inside each wooden box was a sealed tin container to make the box waterproof. The boxes held, among other things, several square blocks of ordinary TNT, pieces of TNT painted black to resemble coal, fuses, detonating caps, time clocks, incendiary pencils and fountain pens, and state-of-the-art spy equipment. The boxes were to be buried in the sands or woods where they landed. Later, the men were to buy a farm or some other business to establish a front and, when it was safe, return to their landing site and retrieve the boxes.

While awaiting their departure in Berlin, Kappe took the terrorists to a public school to receive their German navy uniforms, to be worn when landing in case they should be sighted and arrested. The uniform consisted of a pair of khaki pants, a plain slipover khaki jacket, a cap with a swastika, heavy shoes, gray socks, and a woolen belt. They were also to bring their own civilian clothes to change into if they managed to land without being noticed. All the men were guaranteed a salary to be paid to their wives or family in case of death. They were also ordered to sign a secrecy agreement, which specified that the price for disclosing any information about their mission was death. All were promised comfortable jobs after the war, when they would certainly return to a victorious Germany. Dasch was assured he'd be posted as a consul in a foreign country, possibly the United States, after the war. Kappe was convinced the conflict would be over in two years, possibly sooner. But Dasch told him, "You don't know what's coming to you fellows."[96]

After about a week in Berlin, Kappe ordered his terrorists to report the next day for departure. The eight men, along with Swensen and Kappe, left for France by train. They arrived in Paris the morning after and stayed for three days at the Hotel de Deux Mondes on the Rue de l'Opéra, on the Left Bank. The men were at liberty to explore the city's cultural wonders, which they did, as well as its brothels and bars. At one point Heinck got so drunk at the Deux Mondes that he confessed to a Parisian prostitute that he was a German spy on a mission to America. Fortunately for Heinck, the woman did not speak German and the other people who overheard him were probably German spies themselves, as the hotel was a notorious rendezvous point for Gestapo officers and Nazi undercover agents.[97]

While in Paris, Dasch's group lost Swensen, who complained of a flare-up of a case of gonorrhea he had previously contracted, and

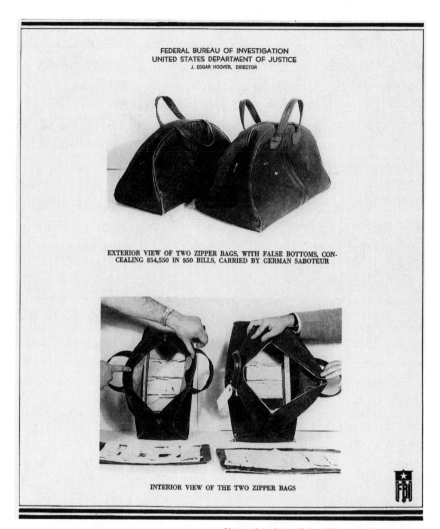

FEDERAL BUREAU OF INVESTIGATION
UNITED STATES DEPARTMENT OF JUSTICE
J. EDGAR HOOVER, DIRECTOR

EXTERIOR VIEW OF TWO ZIPPER BAGS, WITH FALSE BOTTOMS, CONCEALING $54,550 IN $50 BILLS, CARRIED BY GERMAN SABOTEUR

INTERIOR VIEW OF THE TWO ZIPPER BAGS

National Archives/Federal Bureau of Investigation

The false-bottomed bags the Nazis carried to conceal more than $54,000.

returned to Berlin. Dasch, however, didn't believe Swensen was really ill and surmised he was angry over the fact that Quirin, and not he, had been made second in command in Dasch's group. Kappe told the men that should the mission be successful, he and Swensen would be coming over to America later that year.

Finally, on May 26, the men were taken to Lorient, a port in Brittany housing the German submarine fleet. Kerling's group was given its final orders and left that day for Florida in a submarine.[98]

Two days later, Dasch and his men departed for New York aboard U-boat 202, with *Kapitänleutnant* Hans-Heinz Lindner at the helm. It would take them seventeen days to complete the journey to Amagansett, Long Island, where an unsuspecting country awaited.

In the News Today

DETROIT, MICH., July 2, 1942—Restaurant owner Max Stephan was convicted of treason in a Michigan court today. As his wife seated beside him sobbed, the court handed down the sentence to a stunned Stephan. A restaurant owner, Stephan was convicted of aiding Hans Peter Krug, an escaped Nazi prisoner of war. Stephan faces death by hanging.[99]

BELIZE, BRITISH HONDURAS, July 4, 1942—British authorities have broken a Nazi spy ring in this tropical port. Twenty men were arrested today as enemy aliens who conspired in an espionage plot that extended to the Panama Canal. The men were accused of supplying U-boats for operations in the Caribbean and off the American Coast with the assistance of a local gangster known as the "King of Belize."[100]

CHAPTER 3

The Friendly Sea

The America into which Dasch and his crew disappeared after their landing had long been prepared by secret Nazis and assorted demagogues of every stripe. In the United States, support for Nazi Germany was always intertwined with fervid anti-Semitism, often disguised as anti-Communism. The roots of that poisonous tree were fertilized by anti-Semitic tracts such as *The International Jew* and the spurious *The Protocols of the Secret Elders of Zion*, both of which held the Jews accountable for most of the world's miseries.[101]

Widely publicized statements from such prominent figures as auto magnate Henry Ford, Catholic radio preacher Father Charles E. Coughlin, and aviator Charles Lindbergh, had justified the rise to power of the National Socialists in Germany and their concomitant attacks on Jews. Up until the attack on Pearl Harbor, these national heroes warned that a world war against the Axis powers would only serve the interest of the Jews, whom they saw as a cabal intent on world domination. As Charles Lindbergh said: "The greatest danger to this country lies in the large Jewish ownership and influence in our motion pictures, our press, our radio and our government."[102]

A number of groups espousing fierce anti-Semitic propaganda, denouncing the so-called "Wall Street bankers" whom they blamed for the Great Depression, had created a climate favorable to Germany and its supporters. The America First Committee, as well as the

Mothers Movement, the Committee of One Million, the Christian Front, the National Workers League, and the Christian Mobilizer, all actively engaged in isolationist politics aimed at keeping the United States out of war, and lent an air of legitimacy to the activities of Nazis here and abroad—at times even harboring spies. In all, close to two hundred different groups were fascist or had ties to fascist groups in the 1930s.[103] None of these pro-Nazi forces were as potentially dangerous or disturbing as the American paramilitary associations, such as William Dudley Pelley's Silver Shirt Legion who aped the National Socialist ethos, down to the jackboots and fascist salutes.*

These groups recruited openly for years, gathering crowds at New York's Madison Square Garden, raising funds at Park Avenue society soirees, and setting up youth camps throughout the country. According to American government officials, their membership surpassed the hundred thousand mark, with hundreds of thousands of others as sympathizers.[104] In fact, all but one of the terrorists who landed in the United States during those early June days of 1942 had belonged to the most feared, rabidly pro-Nazi organization of all, the German-American Bund.

Today there's hardly a vestige left of the German-American *Bund*, or League, which for a period was described as one of the greatest threats to freedom in the United States.[105]

During its heyday in the 1930s, the Bund claimed thousands of members, with a network of supporters extending throughout the entire Midwest, the East, and great portions of the Southwest and California. One of its covert goals was the establishment of a separate homeland for German-Americans, somewhere in the West or Midwest, in its own version of Hitler's *Lebensraum*, with its own laws, press, and political representatives.[106]

The Bund originally was an offshoot of the Teutonia Club, one of many German cultural associations in the Midwest, where the

---

*For further information regarding Pelley and the Silver Shirt Legion, see Appendix 1.

bulk of the nation's German immigrants resided. The Teutonia Club bore the distinction of having been set up by Franz Gizzibl, a German immigrant to Detroit who had participated, along with Peter Burger, in Hitler's abortive Beer Hall Putsch in Munich in 1923. In 1925 the Chicago unit of the Teutonia Club patterned itself after Hitler's Brown Shirts and adopted the swastika as its emblem. Five years later the organization became the Friends of the Hitler Movement, under the leadership of Heinz Spanknoebel, a young German photo-engraver who had come to the United States claiming to be a clergyman. According to sworn testimony before congressional investigators, Spanknoebel had been handpicked by the Nazi government to head the organization.[107]

The Friends of the Hitler Movement and other similar groups were supported and subsidized by the Ausland Institute or *Deustche Ausland Institute*, the recruitment and propaganda outfit for Germans abroad, which had been set up by the National Socialists. In its yearbook in 1936, the Institute stated that it supported more than 20,000 German organizations in the United States.[108] Eventually it came under the control of the Abwehr, the German Army's Intelligence section.

In the United States, the Ausland Institute spun off from the Friends of the Hitler Movement a new group called Friends of the New Germany (*Freunde des Neuen Deutschlands*) after Hitler became Chancellor on January 30, 1933. Later that year, when a federal grand jury indicted Spanknoebel on charges of being an unregistered German agent, he disappeared and was never heard from again. According to law enforcement sources, he was kidnapped by German secret service men, who forced him at gunpoint to board a steamer and kept him prisoner until the boat reached Germany.[109]

The new leader, or *Bundesfuhrer*, of the Friends of the New Germany, handpicked by the German authorities themselves, was a short, thick-browed man with a heavy German accent and little patience named Fritz Julius Kuhn. At the time, he stated that his organization's mandate was to explain the new Reich to the American public.[110]

Kuhn was a man with a colorful past, framed in shades of military black and brown. Born in Munich on May 15, 1896, to a middle-class family, he served as a lieutenant in the Bavarian army during World War I in France, Italy, Serbia, and Romania, earning an Iron Cross. A chemist by profession, he migrated to Mexico in 1923, where he married a fellow student from the University of Munich, Elsa, with whom he had two children. A few years later he entered the United States and moved to Detroit, becoming a naturalized American citizen in 1934.

When questioned by a congressional committee on why he had migrated to Mexico from Germany, Kuhn replied:

> Because the revolution [in Germany] was going on; inflation was there. Every second man was out of work. I lost my job. I had a very good job with one of the greatest chemical concerns. We were thrown out by the French Army of Occupation. A colored regiment came in. A woman was not safe anymore there. . . . I had to go somewhere.[111]

Yet there were reports at the time that Kuhn had actually left Germany because he was guilty of petty theft at his employer's warehouse. His boss, a Jew named Reinhold Spitz, who was a friend of Kuhn's family, fired him but declined to press charges. Instead, he set up a collection to raise funds to buy Kuhn's ticket to Mexico.[112]

Because Kuhn worked at Henry Ford's Rouge River automotive plant in Detroit, and took an unpaid leave of absence to head the Bund, there has always been speculation that Ford himself was financing the Bund. Regardless of whether there was actual money exchanged, the record is clear that Ford was an avowed anti-Semite who approved of the Bund's aims and adoration of Adolf Hitler. The feeling was certainly mutual, for Hitler saw Ford as an inspiration for his anti-Semitism and had a picture of the industrialist in his office. On July 30, 1938, in Detroit, representatives of the Hitler regime awarded Ford the Grand Cross of the German Eagle, the *Verdienstkreuz Deutscher Adler*, on the occasion of the industrialist's seventy-fifth birthday. The medal was a golden cross surrounded by four small swastikas, finished in white enamel and strung on a red ribbon. The German consul in Cleveland then read from a congratulatory message sent by Hitler. This honor was also bestowed on Charles Lindbergh in Berlin later that year.[113]

When Kuhn took over the Friends of the New Germany, the organization boasted about 5,000 members. Three years later, the group changed its name to The German-American League and announced a new aim: to direct the American way of life in the same direction as Nazi Germany's, fighting Jews and Communists. Just one year later the League was incorporated in Buffalo, New York, under the name The German-American Bund.[114] Some estimates placed the number of Bundists at one point at up to 350,000 members, but in actuality it had closer to 40,000.[115]

Backed by Nazi money and under the direction of the Ausland Institute, the Bund flourished. It divided the United States into three *gaue* or districts, each with its own *fuehrer* or *gauletier*: The Eastern District or *Gau Ost*, with forty locals; the *Gau Mittelwest* or Midwest District with nineteen locals; and the Western District, the *Gau West*, with ten locals. The greatest concentration of members was in the East Coast, with up to 25 percent living in the Greater New York area.[116]

Applicants to the Bund had to take the following pledge:

> I herewith declare my entry into the League of the Friends of the New Germany. The purpose and aim of the League are known to me and I obligate myself to support them without reservation.
>
> I acknowledge the leadership principles according to which the League is being directed.
>
> I do not belong to any secret organizations of any kind (Freemasons, etc.). I am of Aryan descent, free of Jewish or colored racial traces.[117]

The Bund's appeal in the depths of the Great Depression was considerable, especially to Americans of German descent. Although the Bund's message resonated with many other ethnic groups, particularly Irish Catholics, its core was comprised of recent immigrants:

When the Depression struck, many of these newly arrived Germans found themselves in dire straits. Unemployed or engaged in menial tasks like dishwashing, these disappointed people found solace in the Bund. They could leave their cramped cold-water flats, head for a local [beer hall] and sit around drinking beer. The conversation often turned to the Jews and to the misery of living in Roosevelt's America. Tens of thousands of such people attended Bund meetings and rallies. Better-educated leaders, like Fritz Kuhn, found them easy to manipulate.[118]

Each Bund district was divided into cells, with each cell subdivided into uniformed Storm Troopers (*Ordnungs Dienst*); male and female Hitler Youth Corps (*Jungenschaft* and *Madchenschaft*); a Women's Auxiliary *(Frauenschaft)*; and a German-American Business League (*Deustcher Konsum Verband*).

Funds for the Bund were derived from sales of literature, collections, donations, and subsidies from Germany. The dues were 75 cents per month, and the initiation fee $3, the equivalent of about $9.50 and $37, respectively, in today's dollars. Their publications included:

Blood and Race
The Riddle of the Jew's Success
Bolshevik Atrocities in Spain
The Truth About the Jews in Germany
The International Jew by Henry Ford
Communism with the Mask Off by Joseph Goebbels.

There were twenty-four Bund Camps throughout the United States, the spiritual antecedents of today's Aryan Nation compounds. Nineteen youth camps were attached to them, and it was these that attracted the most attention during the camps' inception—not all of it favorable:[119] "Many found it offensive to see in newsreels five- and six-year-olds, dressed in brown or blue shorts or skirts, white blouses and Hitler scarves, marching in unison and heiling Hitler as they did so. . . . The children ate, slept, talked, and dreamed Nazism just as the *Jugend*, the Hitler Youth, did."[120]

During the late 1930s, visitors to one such compound—Camp Siegfried, near New York City in Yaphank, Long Island—reported being met by storm troopers in gray uniforms at the entrance, where everyone was stopped and questioned. At the 44-acre camp, German slogans were placed throughout: *Deutschtum Erwache*—Germans Awake—and *Ein Volk, Ein Reich, Ein Fuhrer*—One People, One Country, One Leader. German was the only language spoken. Swastikas were painted or built onto the masonry facades of the year-round homes. Great emphasis was placed on marching, military training, and indoctrinating the principles of the National Socialist movement.[121]

Yet, the Bund went beyond mere social, pro-Hitler gatherings. German consulates around the country cooperated with the Bund, which in turn served as the eyes and ears of the Nazi party in the United States. Fritz Kuhn boasted at one point that he had succeeded in getting many consuls removed from their posts because of his reports to Berlin.[122]

The Bund also provided cover to Nazi agents in the United States, who dispersed propaganda and made their influence felt in every social class of the country. Dasch and his saboteurs were to make contact with several Bund members whose names had been written in secret ink on a silk handkerchief that he had prepared.

It's no coincidence, then, that the trainer and recruiter of Dasch's mission, Lieutenant Walter Kappe, had been one of the founders of the German-American Bund. According to an FBI memo, he had been the editor of the *Deutsche Zeitung*, the official newspaper of the Teutonia Society.[123]

This paper later became the *Deutscher Weokruf und Beobachter*, the official propaganda sheet of the Bund, with offices in New York City. Kappe was one of its founders in 1935. He also edited the German-American Bund's Yearbook for 1937. That year, however, Kuhn ousted Kappe from his post—allegedly for spending too much of the party's money on entertainment—and Kappe returned to Germany.[124]

In 1935, Rudolf Hess, then secretary of the National Socialist Party in Germany, issued a directive that emigrant German citizens not become entangled in the political affairs of their host countries; as a result, the Bund restricted membership to German-Americans, like Kuhn. But soon the organization turned a blind eye to this requirement, continuing to pad its rolls with German nationals, even as the Bund's involvement in American politics became more pronounced.[125]

In addition to continually encouraging anti-Semitism and a strict neutralist policy for the United States—which made the Bund a bedmate of the isolationist America First movement—in 1936 the Bund endorsed Republican candidate Alf Landon for president against Franklin Roosevelt. Kuhn made his endorsement after a trip to Germany, where he had turned over a $3,000 check to Adolf Hitler as the group's contribution to a new Germany. On his return, Kuhn hinted that Hitler himself had encouraged him to support Landon, telling him, "Go back and carry on your struggle."[126] When this was reported in the news media, the German Embassy disavowed any such endorsement and publicly began a hands-off policy toward the Bund. The Bund, however, continued to grow in strength and numbers.[127]

The Bund's apogee occurred at an infamous meeting in Madison Square Garden, on February 20, 1939, when more than 22,000 people came to hear Kuhn and other speakers on what Kuhn called "a pro-American celebration of George Washington's birthday." Seventeen hundred police officers were on hand to prevent any violent outbreaks. A huge figure of George Washington flanked by giant swastikas towered high above the platform, as twelve hundred Storm Troopers walked into the hall to the muffled sound of drums and *Sieg Heils*. Speakers derided President Franklin Delano Roosevelt as a Jew bloodsucker "Rosenfeld."[128] Kuhn declared:

> We now know that it was the Jews who were responsible for America's entering the World War through pressure brought upon President Wilson. . . . We, the German-American Bund, organized as American citizens with American ideals and determined to protect ourselves, our

German-American Bund color guard, holding American flags and a banner inscribed with the Nazi swastika, stand before an immense portrait of George Washington at the 1939 rally at New York's Madison Square Garden.

homes, our wives and children against the slimy conspirators who would change this glorious republic into the inferno of a Bolshevik paradise.[129]

During the speech, a Jewish demonstrator named Isadore Greenbaum tried to come up on the stage. Storm Troopers beat him unconscious then removed him from the hall, as Kuhn watched and smiled. Afterward, Storm Troopers roamed the streets around the Garden, beating up anyone who looked Jewish.[130]

For a while it seemed as though there was little the American government could do to stop the growing strength of the German-American Bund. In the mid-1930s, alarmed by the growing popularity of Nazi-supportive organizations in the United States, the House of Representatives, under Representative John W. McCormack, had set up a committee to investigate the Bund, the Friends of New Germany, and other extremist groups—the forerunner of the House Un-American Activities Committee of the 1950s. A parade of witnesses testified to the links between the Friends and Germany but, aside from the resignation of the group's then-president, Heinz Spanknoebel, nothing much came of it.[131]

Then, in 1938, Representative Martin Dies of Texas asked for another Congressional investigation into the "un-American activities of Nazis, Fascists, Communists, and White Russians," and the committee was reassembled. In May 1938 the House approved the establishment of the Dies Committee.

The Dies Committee explored the makeup of the Bund and in its interim report, stated that it and other similar groups were "potent organizations for espionage and sabotage if war breaks out." Although the Committee was severely critical of the Bund, calling it "a money-making racket based on the credulity of the American people," it was unable to stop the Bund's activities, since they were, in essence, legal—repugnant as they might be to democratic principles.[132] It fell to Kuhn himself to destroy the organization.

On May 2, police officers investigating charges of embezzlement raided Kuhn's offices and seized papers acting under a warrant issued by District Attorney Thomas Dewey. A popular politician who would become three-term Republican governor of New York (1943–55) and unsuccessful Republican candidate for president in 1944 and 1948, Dewey called Kuhn "a common thief." On May 25, 1939, Kuhn was indicted on charges of embezzling almost $15,000 of Bund funds. He was arrested near Allentown, Pennsylvania, along with other leaders of the organization. Kuhn denied the allegations and pleaded not guilty.[133]

While on bail, Kuhn continued with his Jew-baiting comments, saying at the start of war between Germany and Britain, "We shall see how far the Jewish warmongers go; how far our youth will be driven into war." He also ridiculed the Dies Committee's decision to seek his indictment for perjury and for being an unregistered agent of a foreign government.[134]

Kuhn's boasting and arrogance did not serve him well during the trial. Jurors did not believe his assertion that there had been no misappropriation of funds, as he had always been at perfect liberty, according to the Bund's charter, to spend the organization's money as he saw fit for the good of the group. On December 6, Kuhn was convicted of defrauding the Bund and was sentenced to prison to serve a sentence of two and a half to five years.[135]

Kuhn's second in command, Gerhard Wilhelm Kunze, was named head of the Bund, but from that point on the organization lost its vital force, for Kunze was not only a German sympathizer; he was also an actual German spy.

Born in Camden, New Jersey, in 1906, the son of German immigrants from Saxony, Kunze was a restless lower-middle-class wanderer. Like George Dasch, he had held a variety of jobs all over the United States, as well as Mexico and Trinidad: salesman, truck driver, butler, chauffeur, steward on ocean liners. He joined the Friends of the New Germany in 1933 and in August 1937, was appointed National Public Relations Officer by Kuhn himself.[136]

That year Kunze traveled to the Fifth Reich Congress of Foreign Germans in Stuttgart, Germany, where, dressed in the uniform of the Bund—a gray and black imitation of a Storm Trooper's—he gave a speech praising the aims of the Third Reich, blasting Jews and their pernicious influence in the United States. During the next two years Kunze used his post to whip up even more public sentiment against Jews and Communists, both through speeches and through his control of the Bund's official newspaper, the *Deutscher Weckruf Beobachter.* In its September 29, 1938, issue he wrote a greeting to Bundists which concluded with the words, "Make propaganda your cause! . . . Don't let anyone rob you of your German language and the pride in your German racialism!"

The more time went by, however, the clearer it became that what remained of the Bund was only a shill for the Nazi regime, backed and supported by Berlin. In fact, on July 8, 1940, during an appearance before a Senate judiciary committee, Kunze protested against proposed legislation that would have required registration of foreign-controlled organizations, saying it would destroy the Bund. In subsequent speeches he declared that the Germans were being persecuted for their beliefs and their race, and in a special feature article in the *Deutscher Weckruf Beobachter* he wrote, "German Americans! Wake up and fight the Democratic Reign of Terror!"[137]

Ironically, although the FBI kept close tabs on Kunze throughout his ascendancy to leadership in the Bund, a local statute triggered the ultimate downfall of Kunze and the Bund.

In spite of a marked reduction in Bund membership following the Kuhn embezzlement trial, Kunze had not curtailed his inflammatory rhetoric against Jews; he had actually redoubled his efforts. This resulted in Kunze and several other leaders of the Bund being charged in 1940 with violating a New Jersey statute forbidding incitement to racial hatred. He was convicted of the charge in January 1941 and sentenced to serve twelve to fourteen months in state prison. Freed pending an appeal of the conviction—which was overturned by the New Jersey Supreme Court late in 1941 on grounds the statute was unconstitutional—Kunze disappeared.[138]

Accompanied by other leaders of the Bund, Kunze made an extensive trip throughout the Midwest and along the West Coast, obtaining detailed military information on possible weaknesses in national defense. In Chicago he contacted a known White Russian spy, Count Anastase Vonsiatsky, who gave Kunze money to leave the United States so that the Bund leader could take his military secrets to Germany. Afterward Kunze fled to Mexico. In his absence, a federal judge in Hartford, Connecticut, charged him with attempted violation of the Espionage Act of 1917.[139]

Kunze had intended to travel to Germany out of Mexico. But after Pearl Harbor and the declaration of war between the United States and Germany, the German consul in Mexico advised Kunze to lie low so as not to displease the local authorities. Undeterred by the warning, Kunze moved to Boca del Rio, a fishing village south of Veracruz on the Gulf of Mexico. There, he used the money Vonsiatsky had given him to buy a boat in which he intended to travel to the Azores in the mid-Atlantic and from there reach Germany. Mexican police grew suspicious of his activities, however, and he was detained for questioning. While he was being held, the authorities discovered that the man they knew as Alfonso Graf Cabiedes, ostensibly the son of a Mexican mother and a German father, was none other than Wilhelm Kunze.

Kunze was flown to Mexico City by personal order of Mexican President Manuel Avila Camacho and then transported to Brownsville, Texas, where FBI agents picked him up. (Coincidentally, Kunze was captured just a few days after news broke of the landing of the Nazi terrorists.)[140] Having been returned to Hartford, Connecticut, on August 21, 1942, Kunze pleaded guilty to attempted violation of the Espionage Act of 1917 and was sentenced to fifteen years in a federal prison.

Following a nationwide crackdown by the FBI on all Bund members suspected of illegal activities—as many as 10,000 people were picked up by the FBI for investigation during the first six months of 1942—the Bund was eliminated as an overt political force.[141] But for years the Bund remained a potential fifth column, with federal authorities fearing that its thousands of former members were waiting only for an occasion to once again render their services to Nazi Germany.

In the News Today

WASHINGTON, D.C., July 9, 1942—F.B.I. spokesmen today announced the arrest of seventy-two members of the German-American Bund. The Nazi sympathizers were taken into police custody after twenty-nine of the Bund leaders were arrested in sweeps across the country.[142]

CHAPTER 4

Franz Daniel Pastorius

On the morning of June 13, when their train from Amagansett reached Jamaica Station in Queens, New York, all four Nazi saboteurs—George Dasch, Peter Burger, Richard Quirin, and Heinrich Heinck—debarked without any trouble. To their relief, no one on the train had commented on their wet, sandy clothes. Nor had the Coast Guard alerted local law enforcement agencies to keep a lookout for Dasch, of whom coastguardsman Cullen had already given a description.[143]

On the train Dasch had bought copies of the morning newspaper and handed them out to his cohorts. The headlines blared news about an American victory in the Coral Sea over the Japanese navy; the steady advance of Rommel's *Afrika Korps* in Libya; and President Roosevelt's call on Americans to donate old rubber from houses and garages to contribute to the war effort.[144] But all of that seemed distant to Dasch, who was ecstatic at seeing the sights of New York again, the American stores, the English-language signs, the abundance of consumer goods—coffee, cars, clothes, and food—all of which were in tight supply back in Germany. After outfitting themselves with new suits, the men separated. Burger and Dasch stayed together while Quirin and Heinck went their own way. The men agreed to meet again at three o'clock that afternoon at an automat, the Horn and Hardart Cafeteria on Thirty-fourth Street and Eighth Avenue in Manhattan.[145]

Dasch and Burger went to several men's haberdasheries to buy new clothes, purchasing a cheap suit in one store, a shirt in another, and shoes and hats in still another. They changed in the men's room of a restaurant then unceremoniously dumped their old clothes into garbage cans. Still, Dasch felt a touch of regret at discarding his old suit—it was the one he had worn when he had left New York the year before on his way back to Germany.[146]

Once in Manhattan, Dasch and Burger rented two nearby rooms at the Governor Clinton hotel, in midtown, Thirty-first Street and Seventh Avenue, a 31-floor skyscraper built in the Italian Renaissance style. That afternoon they met with Quirin and Heinck at the Automat, all of them congratulating each other on a safe passage as they enjoyed the seemingly limitless quantities of American food. Dasch had two kinds of salad, his dietary weakness in the summertime, which he washed down with a bottle of milk and followed with a piece of coconut pie.[147]

Since they all stayed on the west side of Manhattan, Dasch and his men might not have been aware that at the precise moment they were enjoying America's culinary delights, more than half a million people were taking part in a "New York at War" parade down Fifth Avenue. Starting in Washington Square and concluding at Seventy-third Street, members of management, labor, air raid wardens, and all sundry branches of the armed forces demonstrated America's might, rumbling uptown in serried ranks of people, tanks, guns, and military vehicles.[148]

After the terrorists finished their late lunch, Dasch suggested Quirin and Heinck check into the Chesterfield Hotel. They were to meet next at one o'clock in the afternoon on Sunday at a restaurant called the Swiss Chalet on West Fifty-second Street. If for some reason they could not keep that appointment, they were all to meet at Grant's Tomb on Riverside Drive and 120th Street on Sunday at six o'clock.[149]

Quirin was eager to start his mission, but Dasch urged them all to settle in first. They should go around, do as they pleased, and reacquaint themselves with the pleasures of America. Meanwhile Dasch, as the group leader, would make contact with the local collaborators, former members of the Bund and others who harbored deep Nazi sympathies. [150]

In reality, Dasch wanted to make sure he had Burger's allegiance. In Germany the two men had briefly discussed their mutual dislike of the government, but neither had been very explicit. Now, in the relative safety of New York, Dasch meant to gauge Burger's true feelings.

Although Dasch had been one of the architects of the terrorist operation, he intended to betray it. Caught in the lunacy of wartime after his return to Germany, Dasch had seized on the terrorist mission as a means of escape back to the United States. This was the reason for his neglect of the lessons at the training camp that Kerling had complained about; it was also the reason why he had let Cullen live, telling Cullen he would hear from him in Washington. Whether from allegiance to America, or from simple revulsion at bloodthirsty Nazi tactics, Dasch had no intention of carrying out the carnage that had been planned. He was going to go to the FBI and turn them all in.[151]

If his plan worked out, Dasch was convinced the Americans—and even the Germans—would hail him as a hero when Hitler was defeated. Dasch believed that the majority of Germans detested the Nazi party and just went along with its program out of fear and convenience. He also saw that Germany alone did not have much of a chance in a war against the mighty Americans. Now that he was back in the United States, Dasch could supply the American government with all sorts of confidential information on the operations of the Abwehr. With the money that he had brought, he might even open a short-wave radio station to broadcast propaganda back to Germany. Then, when the Allies triumphed, Dasch would return to occupy the paramount place of importance in the postwar German government that he had earned by his cunning, enterprise, and patriotism.

That night, after a nap, he and Burger went to Rockefeller Center, where Dasch pointed out to Burger a mural illustrating the history of humankind from slavery to the present day. He hoped Burger would confide in him and talk about his experiences with the Gestapo and his dislike of the Nazis, but Burger kept his thoughts to himself.[152]

On the way back to the Governor Clinton, Dasch stopped at a couple of restaurants where he had worked before leaving New York. At the time he had told his friends he was going to Russia to help fight the Nazis. Coincidentally, Soviet Foreign Minister V. M. Molotov had arrived to visit the United States a few days before, and some of Dasch's old colleagues ribbed him that he had come riding back with Molotov.[153]

That night Dasch tossed and turned in bed, debating the dangers of his possible defection. All the members of the expedition had been authorized to kill anyone who betrayed the mission. If he confessed his true feelings, and Burger turned out to be an unrepentant Nazi, Dasch would be signing his death warrant.

On Saturday morning, he and Burger had breakfast in his room. After the dishes were cleared, Dasch opened a window and looked down on the street eleven floors below as Burger watched apprehensively. Dasch then turned to Burger and told him the two of them were going to have a talk; if they didn't agree with each other, only one of them would leave the room alive, for the other would go flying out the window. The time had come for Burger to tell him all about himself and the Nazis and the concentration camp.[154]

Dasch's confrontation blasted open whatever reluctance Burger still carried. The two men spoke for hours. Burger detailed his life story, how the Gestapo had abused him. He also told Dasch that he had long suspected him of being an American agent, especially after noticing his lack of interest in the terrorist training they had received. "George," Burger concluded, "because I cannot go through with this mission, I want you to help me and tell me what to do."

Dasch explained he was not an American agent but that he wanted to report the mission to the FBI all the same.

"What's your reaction to that?" he asked.

Burger stared back at Dasch for a long moment then he put his arms around him. "I'm with you one hundred percent!" he said.

Because their trainers had informed them that German secret agents had infiltrated every FBI field office except for FBI headquarters, Dasch told Burger he had decided to go to Washington and speak to J. Edgar Hoover himself. With his knowledge of wartime Germany, he figured he would be put to work in some kind of anti-Nazi propaganda operation. Burger said he too had detailed inside knowledge of the Nazi wartime apparatus.

Dasch, already contemplating a hero's laurels in postwar Germany, told him, "Kid, you are a godsend. God brought us together. We are going to make a team. What you know I will try in my way to bring over back to them. Something the whole people don't know. And if we cannot help them open their eyes and help to create a revolt, then nothing will help them."[155]

The two men spoke so long that they lost track of time, missing their lunch rendezvous with Quirin and Heinck, so they hurried to keep the appointment at Grant's Tomb. There, the other two terrorists sat waiting on benches. They followed Dasch and Burger up the hill to Broadway, near Columbia University, where the men stopped to confer. Quirin and Heinck had been ready to leave New York if Dasch and Burger had not shown up that evening. Dasch assuaged their fears and urged them to get an apartment, since they had just spent the night at a cheap hotel—a recommendation from a stranger on the subway. They agreed to meet a day later at the Automat once more and the two pairs separated.[156]

That night Dasch and Burger had dinner and drinks at a bar-restaurant known as the Queen Mary on Fifty-eighth Street and Madison Avenue. On their way out, they stopped at a hotel on Madison and Fifty-third where Dasch placed a phone call to the New York FBI office from the lobby while Burger waited outside the building.[157]

Calling himself Franz Daniel Pastorius, Dasch told the agent who answered that he would be coming to Washington to offer J. Edgar Hoover some very important information on Thursday or

Friday. He said he had recently arrived from Germany and could only relay his facts to the Director in person. Dasch refused to give any more details and hung up. He walked outside and related the call to Burger, who congratulated him, saying the ground had been prepared. Neither man suspected that the agent, thinking the caller was crazy, made only a brief note of the information and filed it, never bringing it to the attention of his supervisor, much less Hoover himself.[158]

New York, N.Y.
June 14, 1942
RE: F. D. POSTORIUS [sic]

MEMORANDUM FOR THE FILE:

Please be advised that at 7:51 P.M. on this date, FRANK DANIEL POSTORIUS [sic], called this office by telephone, and advised the writer that he had made the call for the purpose of having a record of it, in this office. POSTORIUS advised that he had arrived in New York City two days ago from Germany. He would not reveal his present address in the city, and remained uncommunicative concerning any information that he might be able to furnish this office. He stated that he was going to Washington, D.C. on Thursday or Friday of this week, and would talk to Mr. HOOVER or his secretary. He refused to come to this office and report his information and asid [sic] that he had come to see a certain person in Washington, first, but he wanted this office to make a record of his call and to notify our Washington office that he was coming there.

This memo is being prepared only for the purpose of recording the call made by POSTORIUS.

Respectfully submitted,

D. F. McWhorter
Special Agent

After the call, Dasch and Burger then went to yet another watering hole, the 18 Club on Fifty-second Street, where Burger hooked up with a call girl. Dasch left him there and returned to their hotel.

The following day, Monday, Dasch and Burger had lunch, then Dasch went to visit one of his old friends at Mayer's, a restaurant on Forty-eighth Street. A pinochle game started and Dasch sat down to play nonstop for the next thirty-eight hours—using the money the

Nazis had given him. At the end he came out $250 ahead, returned to his room, and slept for about five hours.[159]

Burger came to see him, warning him that Quirin and Heinck were suspicious of him, but Dasch told Burger to explain to them that he was out making contacts in New Jersey and that they would all regroup when he returned. That night he and Burger ate at Dinty Moore's, an Irish restaurant on Forty-sixth Street and Broadway, then Dasch returned to his hotel to rest while Burger, Quirin, and Heinck went to an expensive whorehouse.

The next day Dasch bought a leather briefcase, packed the group's cache of money, $83,000, and took the train down to Washington, after leaving a letter for Burger in his room.

"Gentlemen, let me tell this. It is a long story. Let me tell it in my own way from the beginning to the end," insisted the rail-thin man with the haunting eyes and shock of white hair. "I have been planning this for a long time. I want to help America fight the Nazis."[160]

The morning of Friday, June 19, 1942, at FBI headquarters in Washington, D.C., Special Agent Duane L. Traynor had a problem on his hands—an almost hysterical Dutchman (as German-Americans were called back then), who claimed he had been sent by Adolf Hitler to bring America to her knees.

Three agents had picked up the man at his hotel after he had rung up FBI headquarters, demanding to speak to Director J. Edgar Hoover. As far as Traynor was able to gather, the man had come down from New York, where he had called the local field office, advising them he would be traveling to Washington to speak to Mr. Hoover.

Once in the capital, the man had first called the office of the provost marshal general of the United States army, where he had been transferred to the desk of a Colonel Kramer, who was not in at the time of the call. The man then called FBI headquarters, which had put the phone call through to Traynor. Colonel Kramer had called the man back before the FBI agents arrived but, when informed that the agents were on their way, Kramer had deferred the case to the Bureau.[161]

Traynor was in charge of espionage matters, a job that back in 1942 required only a handful of agents. He worked directly under D. Milton "Mickey" Ladd, assistant director in charge of the FBI's security division, who reported directly to Hoover. Born in South Dakota, and trained as a lawyer—Hoover wanted his FBI agents to be either attorneys or accountants—Traynor was thirty-two years old, married, with a little girl and another child on the way. A five-year veteran of

Collection of Duane Traynor

Special Agent Duane Traynor, the man who brought in George Dasch.

the Bureau, he had joined just after Congress had finally given agents permission to carry weapons and make arrests, instead of depending on the United States Marshals to provide the muscle.[162]

By nature polite and methodical, Traynor did his best to restrain his skepticism as the Dutchman rambled on. Every day hundreds of people called FBI offices around the country with tales of purported espionage and sabotage. Sometimes they showed up at FBI offices, sometimes agents brought them in for questioning, and sometimes they even told the truth.

Traynor recalled the Duquesne case, which had started with just one such agitated caller. William Sebold, a naturalized United States citizen, had reported to an American consulate in Germany that he had lost his passport—and that the Gestapo was pressuring him to become a spy when he returned to the United States. The case was passed on to the Bureau, which at first refused to believe the German-born engineer, even assigning an agent to live with him for a month once he returned to the States just to see if the story was true.[163]

Sebold proved, however, not to be a counterespionage pigeon but a bona fide spymaster. Within months he and FBI agents had set up a short-wave transmitter on Long Island, sending spurious information back to Germany. As other German agents reported back to Sebold, the circle widened and more evidence of espionage and prospective sabotage was gathered. When the ring was finally broken and all the suspects arrested, thirty-three people were ultimately convicted, dealing a mortal blow to Nazi espionage activities in the United States.[164]

That was before Pearl Harbor. With war now raging across the world, it was very possible that the Germans just might try what the Dutchman in Traynor's office was babbling about.

The man said the code name of his operation was Franz Daniel Pastorius, after the first German immigrant to the United States, a Mennonite who, seeking religious freedom, founded Germantown, Pennsylvania, the first permanent settlement of German immigrants in the 1600s. He claimed other saboteurs had been sent with him and that many more would follow until the whole country was riddled with deadly fifth columnists.

The more Traynor listened, the more he felt inclined to dismiss the man as another lunatic, another would-be hero longing to bask in the reflected glory of the homeland war effort. He might even be an inspired con man, utilizing his knowledge of wartime Germany for a quid pro quo moneymaking scheme. Yet the man seemed to have a very extensive knowledge of life under the Nazis, constantly interjecting details that only someone who was recently in Germany would know.[165]

Traynor observed him for a while and realized that in spite of his ravings, he was highly intelligent.[166] His speech might be a bit broken but he used a number of unusual words; talkative and animated, he also had the habit of interjecting "Christ's sake!" and "For Christ!" in his conversation. Traynor noticed that when he wanted to press a point, the man would place his finger to the bridge of his nose and nod vigorously.[167]

Then the Dutchman confirmed Traynor's worst fears: He said he had enough materiel to blow up the Empire State Building, Penn Station, Grand Central Station, Macy's, Gimbel's, the Hell Gate Bridge connecting Long Island to New York, and assorted aluminum plants. He added that the explosives had been buried in sand dunes in Amagansett, New York.[168]

A chill coursed through Traynor when he heard the man speak so blatantly about the explosives. Knowledge of the landing in Long Island was classified. The information had been kept out of the papers and off the radio, and only a handful of agents were aware of it. Traynor scrutinized the man again and recalled the description a coastguardsman had given of the man he had encountered—gaunt, with large eyes, and a shock of white hair.[169]

Traynor asked the man whether he would mind if a stenographer wrote down their conversation.

"Not at all," said the man. "I want this to be official."

Traynor excused himself, ostensibly to have the stenographer sent up, then stepped outside his office. He called the acting agent in charge and asked him to send agents to search the man's room at the Mayflower, a luxury hotel located on Connecticut Avenue just four blocks from the White House—and, coincidentally, at the time, the location of J. Edgar Hoover's favorite spot for dinner, whether at the bar or in the Rib Room.[170]

Traynor reread the tickler, or brief interoffice report that had been filed on the secret Nazi landing, and then he returned to his office. The Dutchman was busy telling a joke to the agents in the room and to the stenographer, who had arrived. Traynor chuckled, and turned to his visitor:

"Now that we have the stenographer here, would you mind telling us what is your real name and where were you born?"

"My name is George John Dasch and I was born in Speyer on the Rhine, Germany," said the man. "My trainers in Germany gave me the name George Davis."

Traynor kept his excitement to himself. He would have to if he wanted more information. Now it was only a matter of letting the man talk his way into the welcoming arms of Uncle Sam.

"That's good, George. Tell us again what happened to you."[171]

At first, Dasch claimed that he had been originally recruited to drop a parachute over England, and that he had only agreed to do so because he wanted to leave Germany and fight the Nazis. But gradually as he warmed up to his subject, Dasch gave broader hints as to the manner of his arrival.[172]

After about an hour, Traynor was called to the phone by one of the agents he sent to search Dasch's room at the Mayflower Hotel. The hotel manager had been very cooperative and let the agents into the room without a warrant. There they had found Dasch's belongings, as he claimed. The agents had also intercepted a letter on hotel stationery that Dasch had left with the manager, apparently intended for his fellow saboteur in New York, one Peter Burger.[173]

My dear Pete:
　　I bet you begin wondering why I didn't write to you sooner.
　　In my last letter to you from here, I stated that I had found the right way and right persons to tell our story. Since that time things began to happen. I've been working like hell from daybreak until

dawn. What I have this far accomplished is too much to describe here. I can only tell you, that everything is working out alright. Have faith and patience. You will hear or see me in the near future. Please stick to your role and keep the other boys contented and please don't loose their sights. Also don't tell them, that I've been here, tell them that you have heard from me from Pittsburgh.

I also beg you to destroy this letter after having read it, for it would be awful if Henry and Dick would ever read this letter.

So please Pete take good care of yourself, have fullest confidence that I shall try to straighten everything out to the best of every one concerned. Until you hear from me again, accept my best regards & wishes.

Your friend,

George J. Dasch[174]

Then the shocker: They had found a leather case stashed under the bed, containing close to $83,000. Traynor thanked the men for a job well done and returned to his office.[175]

The interview dragged through the day. Dasch eventually admitted he had landed by submarine but said he wanted to get to that point at its proper time. Traynor, always a believer in giving a man enough rope, let him ramble on. At one point Dasch became hungry and asked for something to eat. Traynor ordered him a sliced chicken sandwich and a glass of milk, which Dasch ate as he continued to dictate. That afternoon, Traynor supplied him with two packs of cigarettes. Then, at seven, a dinner of clam chowder, ham and salad bowl, and milk.[176] Finally, at around midnight, Traynor talked Dasch into leaving the FBI offices and returning to the Mayflower. Dasch pulled out of the closet a canvas satchel with leather piping he claimed had been given to him in France when he had sailed off.

Traynor asked Dasch just how were they supposed to have survived in this country, whether they had been given any money in addition to their deadly supplies.

Dasch looked at Traynor, then at the agents skulking in the room. He realized he was all out of secrets. Grinning sheepishly, he searched under his bed and brought out a leather bag. He opened it, revealing the $83,000 in fifty-dollar bills.

"Now, you weren't going to hold out on us, were you, George?" asked Traynor.

"Not at all, fellows. Look, I have even put in the note in here to tell everyone what this money is. See?" Dasch extracted from the sheaves of bills a piece of paper on which he had scribbled:

$82,350
—money from German government for their purpose—
to be used to fight their Nazis
George J. Dasch
alias George J. Davis
alias Franz Pastorius.

"I have always wanted to use this money to fight Hitler. I am the enemy of the National Socialism. They just never knew who they were dealing with."

"I'll say," muttered Traynor.[177]

As required by the stringent regulations of the FBI, Traynor issued a steady stream of memoranda on his findings to his superior, Assistant Director Ladd, who in turn passed on the information to FBI Director J. Edgar Hoover.

An astute player of politics, especially in wartime, Hoover was keenly aware he personally had as much at risk in the success or failure of the Pastorius Operation as did the nation at large.

Then forty-seven years old, Hoover had been with the Bureau almost since its inception in 1919 as the General Intelligence Division, with the express mission of rounding up and deporting alien radicals following a series of anarchist bombings against prominent figures, such as oil magnate John D. Rockefeller, financier J. P. Morgan, and the United States attorney general, A. Mitchell Palmer.[178]

He had guided the Bureau through a series of scandals in the 1920s, making it the preeminent law enforcement agency in the country, if not the world, during its drawn-out and successful battle in the 1930s against gangsters such as Al Capone, "Pretty Boy" Floyd, John Dillinger, Bonnie and Clyde, and "Machine Gun" Kelly.[179]

With the success of the Sebold case in 1942, the FBI was enjoying an even greater wave of popularity. FBI agents, or G-men, were

the closest things to demigods in the law enforcement pantheon—
an omniscient force that could foil all attacks against the nation.

Hoover wanted to use this public adulation of the FBI to halt
the encroachment on his turf by his archrival, William S. Donovan. A
tall, personable, Yale-educated lawyer, "Wild Bill" Donovan was the
head of the OSS, the Office of Strategic Services, which would become the Central Intelligence Agency at the end of the war. Belong-
ing to President Roosevelt's inner circle, and sharing the same
background of patrician privilege as the president, Donovan had already succeeded in eroding Hoover's authority.[180]

Just days after Pearl Harbor, Donovan had asked President Roosevelt to let the antecedent to the OSS, the Office of the Coordina-
tor of Information, or COI, coordinate all intelligence agencies in
the government. Hoover virulently objected, and he marshaled all
his considerable political and intelligence resources against Donovan, who responded in kind. To solve the dispute, in January 1942,
FDR mimicked the Catholic Pope's Treaty of Tordesillas—in 1494,
after the discovery of America, he divided the world into Spanish
and Portuguese spheres of influence. Given that the FBI had been
collecting intelligence on fascist activities in Latin America since
1940 through its Special Intelligence Service (SIS), the Bureau would
retain responsibility for the Western Hemisphere, while Donovan
and his COI, soon renamed the Office of Strategic Services, would
be in charge of the rest of the globe.[181] Although he graciously accepted the President's fiat, Hoover never forgave Donovan, and
after the war he settled the score by persuading President Truman
to abolish the OSS and fire Donovan.[182]

At this point in 1942, any news that the FBI was anything less
than invincible in its intelligence capabilities would simply be additional fodder for Donovan. Hoover thus had not only to ensure that
the Nazis failed for the sake of the country, but also for that of his
own political career. He could not let Donovan, or anyone, for that
matter, know that the failure of the plot sprang not from the extraordinary sagacity of the FBI but from a lucky turn of events. Hoover
feared that anything other than superhuman perfection would tar-

nish the image of the Bureau, apparently forgetting that all investigations require a lucky break to proceed.

Hoover's instructions to Ladd were simple: not a word of the landing was to be whispered to the press. When an enterprising reporter somehow got wind of the investigation and called the New York field office wanting confirmation of reports of a Nazi submarine landing saboteurs in Long Island, the reporter was politely but firmly turned away, admonished that no such event had taken place.

It all fell upon Traynor then, and the information he could secure from the ever voluble, mercurial Dasch. The stakes were high, for the rest of the terrorist team was still at large in New York. And even though Dasch said one of them, Peter Burger, was willing to cooperate with the FBI, the other two were diehard Nazis. Not only that, any one of them was at liberty to begin operations any time he saw fit. Terrorist attacks had not ensued simply because Dasch had persuaded the group into first settling in before launching their operations. Nonetheless, they had been in the country almost a week already, and if they suspected that Dasch had gone over to the Americans, they might very well begin their campaign.

Dasch named the true believers as Richard Quirin and Heinrich Heinck, although he said they would be calling themselves Richard Quintas—purportedly Portuguese—and Henry Kayner—supposedly from Czechoslovakia—to make themselves more inconspicuous. Burger, because of his background, was much more likely to cooperate with the FBI. In fact, Dasch said Burger was equally desirous of foiling the entire operation. He would be found in his hotel room, waiting for Dasch.

The question facing Traynor was, were these men still where Dasch reported them to be? Or had they slipped away, having made contact with underground supporters, perhaps activating sleeper cells of terrorists? If so, could they be stopped in time before they launched any of their operations?

The only man who knew the answer to these questions was Dasch. He, however, refused to give straight answers, insisting instead on telling the whole story his way, as though setting an official record for some ulterior motive.

At one point during the first day of interrogation, Dasch gave Traynor a silk handkerchief. It contained, he said, the names and addresses of contact people for the group, Nazi sympathizers, or perhaps even agents, who would be able to help them if necessary. Unfortunately the names had been written in invisible ink and Dasch had forgotten the formula to make it legible again.[183]

Traynor sent the handkerchief to the FBI lab and proceeded to grill Dasch, even as he made plans for surveillance of the remaining terrorists. It was then, at the end of the first day of questioning, when Traynor felt like he had the situation under some form of control, that Dasch dropped yet another bombshell:

There had been another landing.

Four other men were supposedly at large in the country, all intent on carrying out their deadly mission. An anxious Traynor suddenly saw the urgency of his job increase a thousandfold—there weren't just two rogue agents but possibly six, perhaps even more, with funds and weapons, free to roam and destroy at will around the country. When questioned about their whereabouts, Dasch said all he knew was the location of the landing: Florida.[184]

Traynor then asked Dasch if the two groups were supposed to communicate with each other. Dasch replied they had all planned to meet in Cincinnati, Ohio, on the Fourth of July to coordinate their activities and begin their campaign. That was the latest date he had been able to secure from their trainers. He added that both groups were to prepare the way for more Nazi agents, who were scheduled to be arriving every six weeks or so. Other than that, Dasch had no way of contacting them, except for the silk handkerchief—and unfortunately, he still couldn't remember the formula to make the invisible ink legible.[185]

The following day, June 20, a team headed by the special agent in charge of the New York Office, T. J. Donegan, began surveilling Peter Burger, hoping he might lead them to the other terrorists.

It was a warm sunny Saturday afternoon in Manhattan. Throngs of shoppers headed for Macy's, Gimbel's, and Abraham & Straus— the latter advertising a fabulous new product, leg makeup that simulated silk stockings. New gasoline rationing rules had somewhat lessened the chaotic prewar traffic jams around Herald Square, dotted here and there by the brown and white uniforms of soldiers and sailors on leave.

Four agents had been posted in and around Burger's room at the Governor Clinton Hotel. At 2:40 P.M. they spotted Burger leaving his room, number 1421, and heading out of the building.[186]

The G-men surreptitiously followed as Burger walked north on Seventh Avenue to Thirty-third Street past Gimbel's. For a moment they may have wondered if Burger was out to catch the matinee showing of James Cagney's *Yankee Doodle Dandy* at the air-conditioned Hollywood Theater on Broadway and Thirty-first, but instead Burger continued east past Broadway to Fifth Avenue and Thirty-third Street.

Burger stopped and stood in the doorway of the tony men's store, Rogers Peet, where he seemed to be examining the cut of a fine suit displayed in the window. After ten minutes the agents noticed two other men joining him in the doorway. After a brief conversation, the group entered and walked through the haberdashery, buying several clothing items and conversing the entire time. The agents did not know it, but they had just located all three Nazis who had landed with Dasch—the men accompanying Burger were Quirin and Heinck.[187]

After half an hour the terrorists left the store with bags in hand and crossed the street to the Old Oxford Restaurant where they ate a late lunch. Assistant FBI Director E. J. Connelley joined Donegan and three other agents in the surveillance, waiting for the right moment to detain the suspects.

Connelley was one of the top men in the FBI. Previously in charge of the New Orleans office, in 1936 he had helped Hoover personally capture Alvin "Kreepy" Karpis, the Bureau's Public Enemy Number One. Connelley was in New York on a personal mission from Hoover, to make sure nothing went wrong.[188]

The FBI agents weren't aware that during the lunch Burger had to calm the nerves of his two rattled cohorts; they kept asking where was Dasch and why weren't they proceeding with their mission. Quirin and Heinck's suspicions had been aroused by a letter Dasch had left Burger when he had taken off for Washington. The two had found the letter stashed in a bureau drawer in Burger's room while Burger was shaving.

> Dear Pete:
>
>   Sorry for not have [sic] been able to see you before I left. I came to the realization to go to Washington and finish that which we have started so far.
>
>   I'm leaving you, believing that you take good care of yourself and also of the other boys. You may rest assured, that I shall try to straighten everything out to the very best possibility. My bag and clothes I'll put in your room. Your hotel bill is paid by me, including this day. If anything extraordinary should happen, I'll get in touch with you directly.
>
>   Until later,
>   I'm your sincere friend,
>   George.[189]

Burger, afraid that after reading it they might toss him out the window before he could come up with an explanation, hurried out of the bathroom and walked out of the hotel with them. That had been two days ago. Since then Burger had managed to give them a plausible explanation for the missive. Still, Quirin and Heinck were on edge. They were contemplating leaving for Chicago if Dasch didn't return soon.

At about 4:10 P.M., the three men left the Old Oxford, trailed by the FBI agents to the corner of Fortieth Street and Fifth Avenue, two blocks from the Public Library. There Burger shook hands with Heinck and Quirin, then walked back to the Governor Clinton Hotel.

Quirin and Heinck crossed the street and caught an uptown bus on Fifth Avenue, back to a room in an apartment on Seventy-ninth Street and Amsterdam Avenue that they had rented. The agents scrambled to their cars and followed the bus as it wended its way up-town and across Central Park.

Quirin and Heinck left the bus at Seventy-second Street and Broadway, then walked to Amsterdam Avenue and headed north. At the corner of Seventy-fourth Street the two men separated, as Heinck entered a delicatessen while Quirin continued walking north. Afraid the two might slip away in spite of their surveillance, or that other conspirators might show up unexpectedly to help the Nazis, Assistant Director Connelley gave the order for the arrest.

At the corner of Seventy-sixth Street and Amsterdam Avenue, at approximately 4:30 P.M., Donegan and Special Agent H. G. Foster approached Quirin in the presence of Connelley and Special Agent B. F. Wiand.

"Richard Quirin?" asked Donegan. Quirin glanced at the four agents who crowded around him.

"Yes?" came his reply.

"We're with the FBI. Please come with us." Quirin moved as if to bolt but Donegan grabbed hold of his sleeve, telling him not to try anything foolish, and then tucked him inside one of the nondescript Bureau sedans that had followed him all the way from midtown.

Connelley then hustled down the street to the deli, where Heinck was about to pay for his purchase. The assistant director waved at five other agents to accompany him and they all entered the narrow-aisled establishment. Heinck's face turned ashen when he saw the phalanx of G-men. Trembling, he dropped his purchase to the floor.

"Mr. Heinck?" asked Connelley.

"I know. You're the FBI."

"Please come with us. We have a few questions to ask you."

Heinck too was placed inside a Bureau car and transported to the FBI field office downtown.

Little over an hour later Burger finally arrived at Room 1421 at the Governor Clinton Hotel. The two agents who had been sta-tioned there and the other two who had trailed Burger back from his meeting now waited in the lobby until Assistant Director Connelley arrived. When he did, they all rode the ornate elevator up to the fourteenth floor.

At approximately 5:45 P.M. they knocked at Burger's door.

"Come on in," said Burger.

In trooped the frightened hotel manager and the nattily dressed FBI agents, their hands on their guns. Burger looked up, smiling sardonically.

"How may I help you fellows?"

"Are you Peter Burger?"

"Yes, I am."

"I'm Assistant Director E. J. Connelley from the FBI. You're under arrest."

Burger shook his head, and smiled through a wreath of cigarette smoke.

"I have been expecting you."

Burger rose from his bed, quickly packed his belongings, and left with the agents for his own long days of questioning. Among the personal effects at the time of his apprehension were counterfeit Social Security and Selective Service Registration cards, a Detroit, Michigan, Safety Inspection Certificate for a .32 Colt automatic pistol (but no gun, since it had been confiscated in Germany in 1933), and a leather pocketbook inside of which appeared the following inscription: "Bucyrus Erie Company Safety Contest, 1930, 'Always Be Careful.' "[190]

When Traynor received news of the arrests, he was jubilant but still worried. Four down, four more to go. Everything now hinged on the cat-and-mouse game he was playing with Dasch, who would only answer Traynor's questions in ways that would absolve him from guilt and responsibility.

Sometime into the second day of Traynor's marathon questioning of Dasch, one of the men from the FBI laboratory called with the news that they had finally figured out the formula to make legi-

EXAMINATION OF TNT BLOCK, TECHNICAL LABORATORY, FBI

National Archives/Federal Bureau of Investigation

ble the invisible ink on the handkerchief. It was an outstanding performance from one of the stellar components of J. Edgar Hoover's intelligence service.

The FBI laboratory had been set up in the wake of a hearing on the controversial Sacco and Vanzetti murder case. Hoover had been impressed by the use of scientific evidence in the hearing and agreed that the Bureau should be the central clearinghouse for law enforcement in the country in matters dealing with criminological work. In 1932 the first FBI laboratory was opened in a converted lounge in Washington, chosen apparently because it had a sink. At first it had exactly one employee, a handful of equipment, and a Packard sedan the agents called Old Beulah, used for traveling to crime scenes. Within three years the Bureau had established its National Police Academy, which would eventually become the

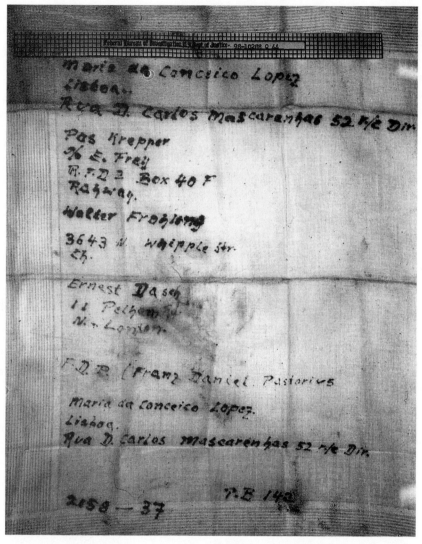

National Archives/Federal Bureau of Investigation

Dasch's "invisible ink" handkerchief. The FBI figured out the formula to expose its secret message—names of Nazi contacts and the password, "Franz Daniel Pastorius."

FBI National Academy in Quantico, Virginia, and its laboratory was offering services to local police across the country.[191]

The handkerchief had presented a particular challenge, because Dasch, whether by forgetfulness or guile, did not provide the formula for revealing its contents. If the technicians took too many chances and experimented with too many formulas, the entire message might be wiped out. The information on the handkerchief was of critical importance; it was the only way that the agents could track the whereabouts of the second team that Dasch had disclosed. Dasch's by now notoriously unreliable memory failed him when it came to addresses and names of contacts. Fortunately, one of Dasch's offhand comments provided the clue: exposing the secret ink to ammonia fumes made it visible.

The handkerchief's information proved intriguing. The name and address of a woman in Lisbon, Portugal, Maria da Conceico Lopez, had been written twice—the second time with the letters FDP over it. When Traynor showed the handkerchief to Dasch, he explained he had written it twice to dupe the Nazi handlers into thinking that he was putting in more information than was necessary. FDP was simply shorthand for Franz Daniel Pastorius, the code name for the terrorist mission. The location in Lisbon was a mail depot for the group members to communicate with their handlers back in Germany. Portugal had been selected since it was a neutral country, and there were no direct postal communications with Germany after the breakout of the war.[192]

There were two other addresses on the handkerchief and they provided the essential clues. One was the name and partial address of a Pas Krepper, and the other of a Walter Froehling. Dasch said Krepper was a minister, Pastor Krepper, and that he lived in Rahway, New Jersey. The second man was somehow related to a man he identified as Eddie Kerling, the leader of the second terrorist group.[193]

It was another lucky break. Traynor realized that without this information, the Bureau might never have been able to trace the second group. The members of the first group were already in custody, but all they knew about the second was their purported landing in Florida, and their eventual rendezvous in Cincinnati on the Fourth of July to coordinate their terror campaign. Given the unreliability of communications, and the knowledge that the groups could initiate their plans independently, for all Traynor knew the second, and even a third, team may have slipped into the country. Traynor passed on the information to his superior, Ladd, asking him to put a tail on the two people mentioned in the handkerchief. Traynor then returned to the odd, long story of Dasch and his terrorist cohorts.

By this time, having captured all the members of the first team, Hoover proudly informed Attorney General Francis Biddle, who passed on the news to a relieved Roosevelt. The FBI director and the president were an odd match, yet in many ways they complemented and appreciated each other. In fact, back in 1933 when he had first taken office, Roosevelt had kept Hoover on the job, in spite of the opposition of several top congressmen—among them Senator Kenneth Douglas McKellar, head of the subcommittee presiding over Justice Department appropriations. Many high-ranking political figures not only feared the concentration of power in one man's hands that the FBI directorship entailed; they were also annoyed by Hoover's appetite and knack for publicity and media relations.[194]

But Roosevelt, who also knew how to handle the media in his own inimitable style, always appreciated the press-savvy professional. His son Elliot wrote that his father thought Hoover's "competence was unquestionable, so Father made it a practice never to interfere, this in spite of the fact that he knew there were many rumors of Hoover's homosexuality. These were not grounds for removing him, as Father saw it, so long as his abilities were not impaired."[195]

Politics is the art of getting the maximum amount of credit with the least amount of exposure; therefore, Hoover adroitly fudged on exactly how the terrorists had been apprehended. He had earlier communicated to Attorney General Biddle that the men had landed on Long Island but that he was confident they would soon be apprehended. As Biddle wrote in his memoirs, "All of Edgar Hoover's imaginative and restless energy was stirred into prompt and effective action. He was determined to catch them all before any sabotage took place. He had steadily insisted that his war could be fought without sabotage. But he was, of course, worried."[196]

Shortly after the discovery of the cache of weapons in Amagansett, the Bureau had set up a post in that beachside town, interviewing anyone who might have seen the Nazis and combing the sands for more evidence. As was the FBI's custom, agents had also checked immigration records for a George Davis, and they had even traced the laundry marks of the few American-made garments that had been found on the beach, discarded by the invaders. But all of that had led to a dead end.

Now, with Dasch turning himself in, the Bureau was again in the lead and in control. But Hoover still insisted on keeping the appearance of invincibility, especially since his gamble that his men would break the case had paid off. In retrospect, it's doubtful even Hoover could have kept his job if the Nazis had struck and the public had then found out it had deliberately been kept in the dark—and that no preventive measures had been taken lest they tip off the terrorists.

Hoover informed the president by wire that his men had apprehended "all the members of the group which landed in Long Island," and that the FBI expected to catch the second group in short order as well. Of course, that all depended on the accuracy of his agents and the information they were able to gather.

The other members of Dasch's team were now talking with different agents in New York. Their accounts coincided in the general aspects of the case, corroborating Dasch's story. The detailed information on the history of the operation continued to come from Dasch, however, because in essence, he had been there since the beginning.

Nonetheless, no matter how much Dasch attempted to minimize his involvement, it was becoming clear that the operation the Nazis had planned was a major undertaking. It was without precedent in American history—but had succeeded in other countries, such as Czechoslovakia and Holland, where a small but determined number of terrorists had crippled those nations' industrial capacities.[197] The Nazis had boasted that the efforts of Dasch's group would do more damage to the United States than a whole division of soldiers. Traynor had to make sure he stopped the operation. The only way to accomplish this was to get the rest of Dasch's story.

By the time Dasch would finish telling his odyssey, and practically his entire life story, five days and four nights would go by. Traynor would employ six different stenographers, who took down 254 single-spaced pages of the terrorist's narrative. Traynor did not see his family during that period, sleeping instead for a few hours each night on a cot in his office, spending the rest of his time reviewing the pages of Dasch's confession after they were transcribed, assembling the details into a coherent narrative.[198]

Traynor still had questions. How had the mission begun? Whose idea was it? And just how thorough did the Nazis intend the terrorist mission to be? Were they ready to keep sending group after group until America really was on her knees? Could the country be rid of saboteurs and terrorists like Dasch and his ilk without losing her values? Or would the United States have to become as ruthless as the enemy to triumph?

Those were the questions that Traynor urgently needed answered. America's security depended on it.

In the News Today

WASHINGTON, D.C., July 17, 1942—
F.B.I. Director J. Edgar Hoover announced today that in the twelve months preceding June 30, 1942, the F.B.I. obtained 1,471 convictions for espionage, sabotage, and Selective Service Act violations. The F.B.I. reported to the attorney general that train wrecking, attacks against defense plants, damage to interned enemy ships, and other acts of sabotage accounted for 218 convictions.[199]

CHAPTER 5

Welcome In America

E ven as Traynor continued his marathon questioning of Dasch, dozens of FBI agents coordinated by Assistant Director Ladd shadowed the Nazi contacts named in the secret handkerchief. Ladd had no photographs of the men in the second group, nor did he have any precise idea of where they would be heading or how soon they would start operations—or even where they would strike first. His only hope was that somehow the Nazis would do something to give themselves away. It was a tense period, for as Ladd explained in a memo to Hoover, FBI agents were getting little cooperation from other German-Americans in New York and Chicago, where the contacts lived.[200] Not only that—the second group was having much more luck than the first.

Although Kerling and his men had departed Lorient two days before Dasch's team, they arrived several days afterward due to the greater distance involved. Unlike Dasch's team, they slipped into the country unobserved, in spite of a Coast Guard boat patrolling the Florida shore the night they arrived. They landed June 17, 1942—the same night that Dasch initially contacted the FBI office in New York, only to be rebuffed as a madman.[201]

The moon was still glowing around four-thirty that morning when the U-584, under the command of *Kapitänleutnant* Joachim Deecke, maneuvered his vessel to within fifty yards of a desolate spot on the beach outside Ponte Vedra, Florida. Kerling's team—Herbert Haupt, Werner Thiel, and Hermann Neubauer—slipped into a rubber dinghy and rowed ashore. They carried four wooden boxes of equipment and explosives bound with steel straps and tied with rope. One of the boxes bore on the outside a double red X mark and another a single X mark, while the other two had none—exactly like the boxes buried in Long Island.[202] The terrorists, dressed in German navy uniforms, were escorted by a machine gun-toting sailor.

When they made landfall, Kerling scouted around a little to make sure there were no houses or other inhabited structures nearby. Seeing none, he gave the go-ahead to the sailor, who re-

National Archives/Federal Bureau of Investigation

Boxes of explosives and equipment discovered by the FBI at the Ponte Vedra landing site.

turned to the submarine, which then sailed away. The saboteurs immediately stripped and changed into civilian clothes, then opened a hole in the sand to bury the boxes. Kerling made a mental note of the location, observing that the site was behind some sand dunes, close to a clump of palm trees. Nearby, a barbed-wire fence ran east to west, while a portion of an old foundation lay just a few hundred yards away. When the men walked inland out of the sand they found themselves on Highway 140, about four miles south of the town of Ponte Vedra Beach, eleven miles south of Jacksonville.[203]

It was dawn by then and the men walked to Ponte Vedra Beach, where they had breakfast and waited until about 11:00 A.M., when they took a bus to Jacksonville, the state capital. In Jacksonville, Kerling and Neubauer, using the names Kelly and Nicholas, booked a room at the posh Seminole Hotel, a favorite of local politicians, while Haupt and Thiel registered elsewhere. That afternoon, Kerling and his group did the very same thing that Dasch and his men had done once safely in America—they went shopping. Haupt in particular made good use of the $5,000 each man was allowed, purchasing fancy clothes, Oxford shoes, a Bulova red gold wristwatch, a leather wallet, and a number of other luxury items, all on the Reich's account.[204] Murder and mayhem may have been on their agenda, but deprivation was not.

Later that afternoon the four men met at a park and arranged to split up. Haupt and Thiel would leave the following morning for Cincinnati. From there Haupt was to go on to Chicago, where he would make contact with Bund members and Nazi supporters, while Thiel waited in Cincinnati. Kerling was scheduled to meet him on Saturday afternoon at the restaurant of the Gibson Hotel, yet another luxury establishment, once famous for its resident jazz band. The following day Kerling and Neubauer left for Cincinnati, where Neubauer made a brief stop, announcing he was going to Chicago, where he would be staying at the Blackstone Hotel, or at any event, "to a hotel employing Negroes inasmuch as they were not so observant as white persons."[205]

On June 20 Neubauer left for Chicago from Cincinnati while
Kerling purchased sleeper car railway tickets for himself and Thiel
for New York. If all went well, both terrorist groups—Kerling's and
Dasch's—would meet back at the Gibson Hotel on the Fourth of
July to begin operations.[206]

Kerling and Thiel arrived in New York on Sunday, June 21,
1942, and checked into the Commodore Hotel, a 30-story charmless
hotel for businessmen and conventioneers next door to Grand Central Station. Surprisingly, no one in Kerling's group contemplated
the possibility of Dasch's betrayal. They went about their business
as though their stay in Germany had been as harmless as a weekend
jaunt to Havana.[207]

More than anything else, sex provoked Kerling's arrest—or, to
be more charitable, his romantic liaisons did. His marriage to Marie
had always been rocky. Even before he met Hedwig Engemann during his fateful boat trip to Florida, he had close relationships with
several women. One was a Miriam Adams of Cambridge, Massachusetts, to whom he wrote, confiding his pride at being a member of
the National Socialist party.

On June 4, 1940, he sent her a letter with a return address in
New York City, condoning the Nazi invasion of Europe: "We know
we have to fight in Europe, not for the fun of it but to live—not to
have some sort of government or some ideals, it is just for room. You
may not understand this here, and it look like American [sic] wants
once more to save the English democracy, which at present is more
brutal than dictatorship in Russia."

Later that month Adams received another letter from Kerling,
this one postmarked Lisbon, Portugal, stating he had left the country and was trying to get a ranking position in the German army. In
December of 1940, Kerling sent her another letter, bearing a return
address in Wiesbaden, in which he confided, "I am in Berlin again.
Have been for 3 months with the army in France. After the war I
may visit the States again . . . but I won't stay long: there is work in
Europe to be done. I have a very interesting job here at present but
I burn to get back in the Army again."[208]

When he did return to the United States, Kerling did not attempt to contact Miss Adams—by then she was married and known as Mrs. Eldridge Preston, of Malden, Massachusetts. Instead, on the night of his arrival, Kerling, accompanied by Thiel, took the subway and went to visit an old friend, Helmut Leiner, who lived at 21–58 Thirty-ninth Street in Astoria, Queens—which just happened to be one of the addresses written in secret ink on Dasch's handkerchief and one of the two locations that the FBI was casing. Leiner, a close friend of Kerling, had lived in the States for thirteen years. A member of the Nazi party since he was nineteen, Leiner was a Bund member and had met Kerling at a Bund meeting.

Thiel was the first to approach Leiner's house in the largely lower-middle-class neighborhood of Astoria. Kerling and Thiel were surprised to find a number of people on Leiner's porch, conversing. Out of caution Kerling asked Thiel to ask Leiner to step outside so Kerling could speak to him. Leiner was a close friend of Kerling's wife, Marie, which was the main reason why Kerling had contacted him.

Leiner, who thought Kerling had gone to Mexico, was surprised to see him. He explained that the people in his house were visiting

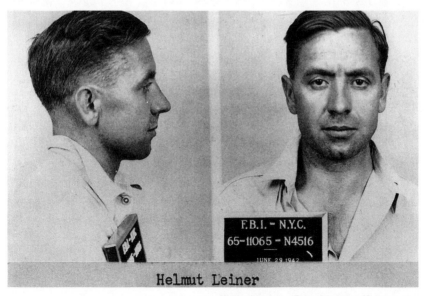

Helmut Leiner

National Archives/Federal Bureau of Investigation

relatives. He then offered to put Kerling in touch with Marie, who was working as "a cook in a fashionable New York apartment."[209] Kerling then excitedly told him about his training and landing. Leiner agreed to help him by exchanging some of the fifty-dollar bills he'd been given by the Abwehr. They agreed to meet again with Marie at a restaurant next to the Shelton Hotel, on Lexington Avenue and Forty-eighth Street in Manhattan.

FBI agents continued tracking Kerling and Thiel after they left Leiner and returned to their hotel room in Manhattan. During the next two days Kerling also contacted his mistress, Hedy, who lived at Eighty-sixth Street and Second Avenue in Manhattan. Kerling told her he'd returned to the States as a secret agent, and showed her the almost $60,000 he had brought with him. Since she was working in a store, he asked her to help him exchange the large bills as well. He then promised her they would build a life together; he asked her to rent them an apartment in New York, where they would live for a few weeks, and to accompany him during his travels in the United States on his terrorist mission afterward. She agreed to all he asked.[210]

For his part, Thiel contacted a friend from Bund days, Anthony Cramer, a 41-year-old mechanic who lived in the Upper East Side neighborhood of Manhattan known as Yorkville, home to thousands of German-Americans. Leiner contacted Cramer for Thiel, giving him the cryptic message: "Franz from Detroit" wanted to meet him at the Grand Central terminal information desk. Cramer kept the rendezvous, and over drinks at a nearby bar, Thiel told Cramer of their secret landing by submarine and of their mission, then asked Cramer to hold for him $3,670 of the $5,000 each of the terrorists had been given for expenses. A conscientious Cramer promptly laid away $3,500 of Thiel's money in a safe-deposit box.[211]

The FBI agents tracked the pair's movements for the next two days, to see whether they were in contact with any other parties. Leiner, in the meantime, contacted Mrs. Kerling, who was thrilled to hear her wayward husband was back in town. During their long separation from each other, Marie had come to the conclusion that her feelings for Kerling were more sisterly than marital; she had met with Kerling's mistress, Hedy, and agreed to grant him a divorce.

On Tuesday, June 23, Kerling and Leiner went out to New Jersey to try to contact Pastor Krepper, one of the contacts whose name was written in the secret message on the handkerchief. They were unable to locate him and concluded the FBI had detained him. Nevertheless, not suspecting they themselves were being followed, they pressed on with their plans. Kerling had wanted to leave the boxes of explosives with the preacher, but now he began to think of buying a farm out in Pennsylvania where he could stash the materiel. But first Kerling wanted to finally close the loop on his complicated love life. He was to meet with both Marie and Hedy that night at the restaurant of the Shelton Hotel, near Times Square, to work out a final arrangement.

Leiner called Marie and asked her to meet him at Hedy's store in Yorkville. In the meantime, Kerling met with Thiel and Cramer at a bar before walking five blocks east to Lexington and Forty-ninth. There he paced for close to fifteen minutes outside the restaurant, waiting for the women to arrive. He would never talk with them. FBI agents arrested Thiel a few blocks away; then, at 10:00 P.M., they scooped up Kerling as well while he waited outside the Shelton, immediately transporting him to the New York field office for questioning. Marie, Hedy, and Leiner showed up an hour later but after waiting in vain past midnight, they finally went home. They would all be taken into custody during the next two days.[212]

News of Kerling and Thiel's arrest reached Traynor on the fourth day of his marathon interview with Dasch. By then Traynor had bonded with his unlikely Nazi, who even called the agent by his nickname, "Pie," after the Pittsburgh Pirates third baseman Harold Joseph "Pie" Traynor. But Agent Traynor was becoming concerned about the Dutchman's mental health—Dasch seemed to be cracking under the pressure.

During a dinner conversation, Dasch told Traynor he was depressed for fear that the main mission he had embarked on when he came over to the States—namely, to fight Hitler and Nazism—

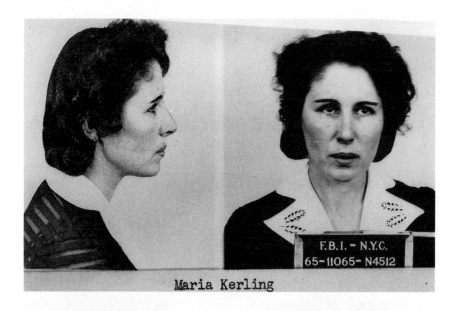

Maria Kerling

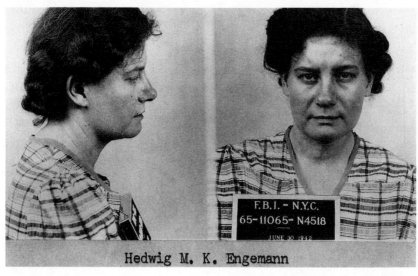

Hedwig M. K. Engemann

National Archives/Federal Bureau of Investigation

would fail. In a memo to Ladd, Traynor described Dasch as an egomaniac who pictured himself as two characters. One was George John Davis, the stool pigeon and informer—a traitor to the German government. The other was good George, George Dasch, the patriot fighting for the Germans who were opposed to Hitler.[213]

Dasch said he wanted to take part in the reconstruction of Germany after the war. He told Traynor he had planned to use the money the Abwehr had given him to start a short-wave radio station that would broadcast back to Germany and open the eyes of its people as to what Hitler was doing. But Dasch added that if he didn't succeed in his propaganda efforts, he would rather be taken out as a spy and shot. He said he would even take his own life if this were not done, and would take the life of others with him.[214]

Alarmed, Ladd and Traynor came up with a plan that made use of Dasch's avowed patriotism, as well as his concern over the fate of his family in Germany if news surfaced that he had turned in the other members of the mission. Dasch's cover story would be that the Coast Guard had put out a report of the landing and that "the Negro operator of the apartment house where Quirin and Heinck were staying considered them suspicious and reported it."[215] When the two were arrested and their apartment searched, they supposedly found Burger's address. Dasch was then captured after Burger's hotel manager recalled having made a reservation for him at the Mayflower in Washington. Yet telling Dasch about his cover story would entail revealing information the FBI wanted to keep from him until he finished his statement. Therefore, Traynor would have to hold Dasch's hand and string him along until the end.

By this time, the FBI was closing in on the two remaining terrorists, Herbert Haupt and Hermann Neubauer. According to Dasch, both men were supposed to travel to Chicago. The youngest, Haupt, was easy enough to track down, since he was an American citizen and his family's residence was known.

Haupt's father, Hans Max Haupt, had been a soldier in the German army during World War I; he had migrated to the United States in 1923. Herbert, or Herbie, as everybody called him, had followed

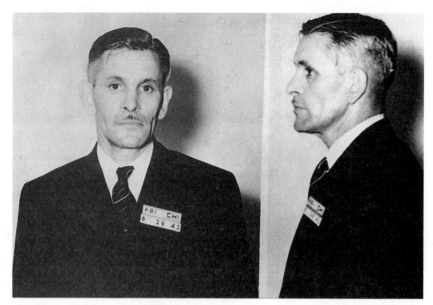

Hans Max Haupt

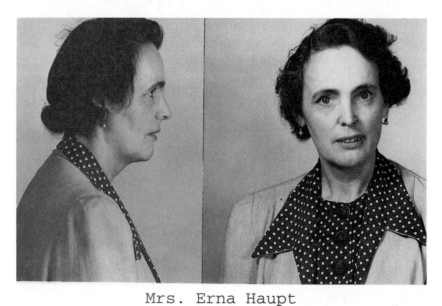

Mrs. Erna Haupt

with his mother in 1925 at age six, becoming a United States citizen five years later when his father was naturalized on January 7, 1930.

Forty-eight years old at the time, Hans Haupt was a struggling building contractor who at times during the Depression had been forced to go on relief. He was a member of several German associations, including the Schubert Liederstafel Singing Society and the Schwaben Society—a suspected Nazi front. Herbie attended public schools, completing two years at a technical high school before dropping out to go work at Simpson Optical as an optician for $25 a week—a salary he turned over to his father as a dutiful son.[216]

When young Haupt left the country, his father had given him $80 for traveling expenses. His family had not heard from him in almost a year except for a cablegram he had sent from Tokyo in September 1941. In December of that year, two FBI agents showed up at Hans Haupt's house to interview him about his son's absence. The Bureau, which supervised the selective service registration of all eligible men in the country, wanted to know why Herbert had failed to register for the draft. His father told them Herbie was out of the country, that the family's last communication with him had been the cable from Japan, and that he had no idea when he would return. That seemed to pacify the agents, who left and made no other attempt to contact the Haupts.[217]

Now, given the information gleaned from Dasch and the secret handkerchief, the FBI took special measures in apprehending Haupt. The family lived in the German section of town, where the presence of outsiders was always quickly detected. Just a few months before, in the wake of the Duquesne case, the Bureau had conducted a series of raids on Bund members and sympathizers, creating a great deal of animosity between the FBI and the resident population. Thus, on June 20, Chicago Special Agent in Charge A. H. Johnson assembled a ten-man group for continuous surveillance of the Haupts.[218]

The first day there was so little action to report, in the agents' view, that they stopped surveillance about an hour after Hans and Erna Haupt went to bed. To the agents' surprise, however, the next day they observed Herbert arriving at his parents' residence. He had just visited Walter Froehling, whose name and address had been written on the handkerchief—but whose house, inexplicably, was not under FBI watch for Haupt's whereabouts.[219]

Froehling was Herbie's uncle, his sister Erna having married Hans Haupt. A truck driver for the utility Commonwealth Edison, the 48-year-old Froehling had no idea that he had been named a contact for the terrorists or that his house had been designated a hideout by the group. In fact, Froehling had attempted to dissuade Herbie Haupt when at one point the young man discussed migrating back to Germany to join the German air force. Froehling told him living conditions in the United States were vastly superior to those in their native country and that he would be making a big mistake by returning there. The last Froehling had heard of Haupt was that he was in Japan.[220]

Froehling was therefore stunned when, on the afternoon of June 19, the very same day that Dasch had begun his long statement to Traynor at FBI headquarters, Herbert Haupt knocked at his door in Chicago. It was about 4:00 P.M. and Froehling had been dozing, contemplating the end of his vacation the following day. His wife, Lucille, was overjoyed at seeing her nephew. Froehling asked Herbie if he had been over to his parents' yet and when he said he had not, Froehling picked up the phone and called his sister Erna, asking her to come over right away because Lucille was very ill. Froehling went out to the streetcar stop a few blocks away to wait for Erna, but when after an hour she hadn't arrived, he called home and was told she was already there.[221]

At 6:30 P.M. when Hans came home from work, Froehling called and urged him to come over, too, again using the excuse that Lucille was very ill. Hans left right away, stopping only to drink a quart of beer. When he arrived at Froehling's, to his surprise, he found Lucille was not sick at all. Everyone was seated at the kitchen table.

Looking up with a smile, Froehling asked him, "What would you say if Herbert were here?"

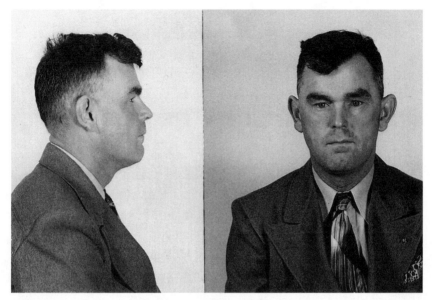

Walter Froehling

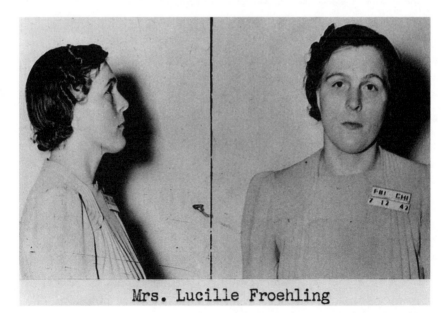

Mrs. Lucille Froehling

"Herbie?" asked an incredulous Hans.

Just then Herbert Haupt, who had been hiding behind the bedroom door, popped out and surprised his father. Hans was speechless, and just gripped his chair, unsure of what to think. Herbert, ever the good son, came over and gave his father a kiss. Hans sat down, and when they asked him if he wanted some dinner, he refused. He had no appetite, still stunned by his son's return.

Herbert was excited, talking about his stay in Germany, and their hometown, Podejuch, near Stettin. He said he had even been to France and had tried but failed to find the grave of Hans's brother, who had died during the German offensive in Verdun during World War I.[222]

Herbert said he had also been in Cologne when the Allies had firebombed it, leaving most of the city in shambles. Herbert brought them up to date on their extended family, including Froehling's mother, now senile, and his brother Otto. Hans interrupted and demanded that Herbert tell them exactly what had happened to him and what he was up to in the United States.

He and two other boys, Wolfgang Wergin and Bill Wernecke, had left town for Mexico, he said, but Wernecke's papers were not in order and he had been turned back at the border. Herbie continued, claiming that when he entered Mexico he had lived at the house of a German sausage manufacturer, who had paid for all his expenses. He had met the manufacturer through the German consul, who later got him a ticket out of Mexico to Japan. He added that when he left Mexico City, he broke four toes when he landed in Mazatlan, but in spite of that he was lucky to reach his ship, for it was the last one to sail out of Mexico for Tokyo.[223]

In Japan, he had worked at a farm for about two months. He and Wergin then left Tokyo on a boat headed for Berlin; he proudly related how he had earned an Iron Cross for spotting a warship while his freighter broke through the British blockade of France.[224]

Wergin enrolled in the German army, signing up for a twelve-year tour of duty, while Haupt joined the intelligence section of the army. He said he had been given a course in intelligence work at military school, learning how to blow up bridges, depots, and factories. After completing his course, he embarked on a U-boat, which had dropped him and three others off in Florida. He claimed that during the trip his submarine had gone on the attack: "Did you read about certain freighters that were sunk in recent days?" he asked in German.

"Yes, I read about them in the paper," answered Froehling, nodding.

"We did that," said Haupt.[225] He added that an American plane had dropped a depth bomb, which shook the U-boat and almost made it sink.

Haupt told them about the landing in Florida, the burial of the four boxes with dynamite and equipment and his trip up to Chicago. Although he didn't mention Neubauer by name, he did say his companion had checked into a local hotel, the Knickerbocker. Haupt had given him Froehling's phone number and he was expecting Neubauer's call on June 21 to coordinate their movements.[226]

Haupt made it clear to his family that the purpose of his trip was to engage in sabotage, and that he had been given a large amount of money to pay for his expenses and those of the people he worked with. He showed them a money belt holding $3,000 and a canvas bag with a false bottom, which he said contained $15,000 in cash. He hid the bag on top of an eight-foot-high dining room sideboard at Froehling's, saying it was only temporary. He explained that the infiltrators were scheduled to meet on July 6 at the Knickerbocker Hotel, where they would see the head of the mission. At that time, Haupt would turn over the money to his superior, who would take it to the president of a bank in New York to exchange it for smaller bills.[227]

No one in Haupt's family thought there was anything the least bit reprehensible about his mission—nor did they comment on the obvious illegality of his acts. The omission on their part to voice concern over Herbie's terrorist activities would soon come back to haunt them all.

Herbert enquired after his old girlfriend, Gerta Melind, who had been pregnant when he left the country. His parents answered that she was fine but that the baby had died. Herbert then announced that he wanted to buy a new car for his activities and his father agreed to help him find one.[228]

When Hans and Erna Haupt returned home that night with their son, Herbert noticed that his money belt was torn. He asked his father for an envelope, took out the money from the belt, about $3,600, and hid it under the couple's bedroom rug. Hans became very concerned about the money, knowing it was from Nazi Germany and the purpose to which it would be put, but he said nothing to his son. Only his wife suggested that perhaps Herbie should go to the FBI—and register for the Selective Service.[229]

Three days later, when FBI agents finally spotted him going to the family residence on North Fremont Street, Herbert Haupt had already made contact with Wergin's family and was in the process of buying himself a new car and getting his old job back at the Simpson Optical Company.[230]

When he had gone to visit the Wergins, Wolfgang's father was as surprised as anyone else at seeing Herbert back in Chicago. The Wergins had a female boarder at the time, and to avoid raising her

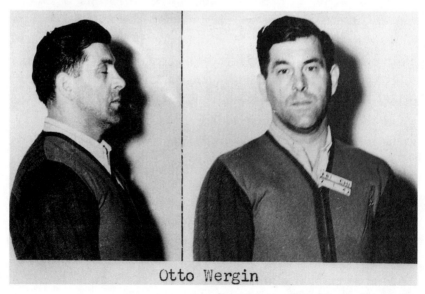

Otto Wergin

National Archives/Federal Bureau of Investigation

suspicions, Haupt and Wergin spoke in whispers. All the same, the elder Wergin's chest swelled with pride as Herbie described his Iron Cross medal and another for breaking the blockade.

"Did Wolfgang get the medals too?" he asked, and when told he had, he asked Herbert for details on how the medal looked. Wergin had been in a German submarine crew during World War I and was therefore also extremely curious about Haupt's journey on the U-boat. When the conversation turned to what Herbert was doing back in Chicago and Haupt answered that he was there to do sabotage, Wergin replied, "Oh, I see, the intelligence." Then he added, "If you need me I am willing to go along, just let me know. I am not dumb, I know how to help you out."[231]

By Sunday night Herbert's parents were growing fearful of what their son might be getting into. They insisted that Monday morning he go and register at the local FBI office, otherwise he could not stay at their home.

"Don't you like me anymore? " he asked them.

"Yes, Herbert, I like you," replied Hans, "but do me this favor and go Monday morning and do what I told you."[232]

During World War II, the FBI was in charge of compliance with the Selective Service, making sure all eligible men registered for the draft. Haupt, who had been away for over a year, reported his return with some trepidation, but if the agents who took down his name and address were aware that he was one of the most wanted men in the country, they never let on. The agent in charge asked him where he had been, and Haupt concocted a story wherein he had just returned from Mexico, where he had run into some people traveling to Japan, who had agreed to send a postcard in his name to his mother here in Chicago. The agent nodded and then asked Haupt if he was willing to fight for America. Haupt said he would but that he would rather not fight the Germans. The agent accepted his qualm without protest and issued Haupt's registration card.[233]

That evening a much-relieved Haupt showed the card to his parents, who also felt much more at ease, reasoning that if the FBI knew he was in town and did not arrest him, there was not much to be concerned about. That night Herbert again insisted he needed his own car.

"Herbie," said Hans, "take my car; I am happy with the old truck."

But Herbert would not accept his father's offer and insisted on getting his own transportation, so Hans finally broke down.

"All right," he said. "I will buy you a car, but we don't have enough money."[234]

The next day Erna went to the bank and withdrew $150. Hans added some money of his own and Herbert used part of the funds that the Abwehr had given him. He and his father looked at some cars at a Pontiac dealer and agreed upon a snazzy black six-cylinder sports coupe.[235]

Life was seemingly back to normal for the Haupts, who were not aware the FBI was constantly tracking Herbie's movements. Neither did they know that at times on Monday, Herbie, fearing the FBI might be observing him after all, engaged in an elaborate game of countersurveillance, changing subway trains and retracing his steps so well that for a few hours he managed to slip the agents tracking him.

Assistant Director E. J. Connelley, who had coordinated the arrests of Quirin, Heinck, and Burger in New York, arrived that day in Chicago and took over the final leg of the investigation. He had just flown in from Florida, where Kerling had shown him where he had buried the four boxes of explosives and equipment. Now Connelley ordered round-the-clock postings and assigned specific duties for each agent, ordering two men to constantly track Haupt across the city, taking note of all his contacts and locations. He wanted to capture both Haupt and Neubauer at the same time, if possible, but he had to measure that desire against the growing anxiety that the saboteurs might be planning an attack very soon—or that they would find out they had been discovered and flee.[236]

Agents followed Haupt that night as his father drove the family Pontiac to Edgebrook, a Chicago suburb, where they visited Andres Conrad Grunau, a superintendent at Simpson Optical. The visit was innocuous enough—Haupt wanted to get his job back, as part of his plan to blend back into American society as though nothing untoward had happened. Although surprised at seeing him back in the country, Grunau—a Nazi sympathizer—agreed to rehire Haupt the following week.[237] One can only speculate on what Connelley must have thought when he realized with whom Haupt was conferring—did that mean Grunau was also a part of the plot? If so, who else was involved? How many plants? How many more secrets?

Haupt's activities the next day did nothing to assuage the agents' concern. At 12:30 P.M. Haupt left the family residence with his mother, two agents following them as he said goodbye to her at the El. When he gave her a kiss and went on his way, one agent followed Erna as she went downtown to make some purchases at the Carson, Pirie department store while the other agent tracked Haupt on a leisurely walk to Fullerton Avenue. There, Haupt entered a radio shop, remaining inside for several minutes. Then he left and entered a nearby clothing store, where he purchased a brown sport straw hat. Afterwards Haupt had a quick lunch by himself at a restaurant, then walked curiously up and down Belmont Avenue, as though he were expecting someone. Finally he entered the Belmont Theater, where he watched *The Invaders*, a 1941 British film about a damaged Nazi U-boat stranded in a Canadian bay.[238] The agents waiting for him outside did not suspect that Haupt had chosen that theater to rendezvous with Neubauer, who sat next to him; in the dark, the two terrorists decided on a plan of action. If Kerling did not show up by July 6, as had been planned, they would strike out on their own.[239]

When Haupt came out of the theater at about 5:00 P.M., agents again shadowed him as best they could through the crowded streets back to his home. That night he and Hans returned to the auto dealership to finalize the purchase of the Pontiac and then returned home. His girlfriend, Gerta, came over to visit. The two lovers, who had not seen each other in more than a year, sat on the porch, talking about their future. When Erna fixed them some drinks, Herbie cautioned, "I don't want any whiskey in mine, I want straight ginger ale."[240]

That night Haupt asked Gerta to marry him, and although she was surprised at the suddenness of his proposal, she accepted.

The following day, Haupt took possession of the Pontiac and then began a series of drives all over town. He went to shirt shops, restaurants, and taverns, his circle of friends and acquaintances expanding by the hour. Everyone seemed surprised to see him back, yet no one questioned his return—and those to whom he confided the reason for his being in Chicago never said a word about his mission until the very end.

By Friday of that week, the FBI had rented an apartment directly across from the Haupt residence, to better observe all the comings and goings of Haupt and his friends. Haupt had made no attempt to report for work at Simpson Optical but he had made contact with his friend Bill Wernecke, who had unsuccessfully tried to accompany him to Mexico. That afternoon, agents noticed Wernecke and Haupt transporting a large guitarlike object out of a marine supply store. More and more people seemed to be cooperating with Haupt until finally, concerned that the operation was about to be exposed, or that the terrorists might strike, Connelley gave the order.[241]

On the morning of Saturday, June 27, as Haupt drove his new Pontiac six-cylinder around the El train station on Webster Street, a sedan cut in front of him and slammed to a sudden halt. Haupt rammed his brakes, barely missing a collision. Just then another car came from behind, preventing Haupt from backing away. Enraged, Haupt leapt out of his car, ready to have a good talking-to with the driver blocking him. That's when the FBI agents slid out of their sedan, flashed their badges, and informed him he was under arrest. Hours later agents took into custody his parents, his uncle, his doctor, his friend Wernecke, and dozens of other acquaintances, all swept up in a lightning-fast FBI raid.[242]

That left just one terrorist out of the eight still outstanding— Hermann Neubauer. Agents had not been able to locate him, as he had kept to himself and, aside from the meeting at the theater, had studiously avoided any public contact with Haupt. At one point they believed he had been seen with Haupt right after Haupt had

Harry Jaques

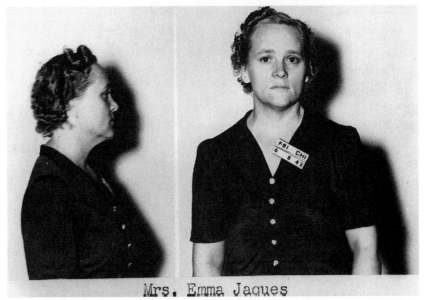

Mrs. Emma Jaques

National Archives/Federal Bureau of Investigation

registered for the draft, but that man turned out to be Bill Wernecke. So the FBI then did what it always did best: It extracted information.

Haupt gave a confession, saying the last time he had spoken to him, Neubauer had been staying at the LaSalle Hotel. When agents rushed over there, they found he had checked out. Had Neubauer left the country? Had he contacted someone in the still-active Bund and gone underground?

Within hours, the FBI had its answer. Neubauer had made contact with Emma and Harry Jaques, friends of his American wife, Alma. But that meeting had apparently been out of boredom since he had nothing to do until Kerling's planned arrival in Chicago on July 6. Neubauer had entrusted the Jaques with $3,600 of his Nazi money, but had taken no other action, save to move to more posh accommodations. Checking through the registry of all the major hotels in Chicago, searching under the name Nicholas, FBI agents found him at one of the fanciest in town—the Sheridan Plaza. He was taken into custody in his room at 6:45 P.M. Agents found among his effects, in addition to Social Security and Selective Service cards under the name Henry Nicholas, the amount of $331.86, as well as a green slicker, bathing trunks, and a small towel he had brought over from Germany on his ill-fated expedition of terror.[243]

The case had been broken. J. Edgar Hoover was ecstatic; his big gamble had paid off. Now it was time to claim the credit due him and the Bureau.

In the News Today

NEWARK, N.J., July 20, 1942—Federal law enforcement officials announced the arrest of seventy-four "enemy-aliens" here today. The F.B.I. says that as of July 1942, its New York office has searched 1,775 enemy aliens and made hundreds of arrests. Of those arrested, 365 are Germans, 43 Japanese, and 13 are Italians. E. E. Conroy, the Assistant Director of the F.B.I., said that arrests and raids are only made after the F.B.I. receives specific information that the subjects are dangerous.

STATEN ISLAND, N.Y., July 20, 1942— *Saloonkeeper or spy?* The Staten Island City Patrol Civil Defense Corp. dismissed a sergeant on suspicion of espionage today. Thirty-five-year-old Lena Guenther was removed from service after the F.B.I. alleged that the tavern her family had owned for more than fifty years has been used for Bund meetings. Guenther denies the charges.[244]

CHAPTER 6

Dinner with the Yugoslav Ambassador

United States Attorney General Francis Biddle and his wife, the poet Katherine Garrison Chapin, were enjoying dinner at the home of the Yugoslav ambassador when the call came: J. Edgar Hoover was on the line, informing his nominal boss about the arrest of the terrorists.[245] As Biddle would later recall, "I can still feel the flood of relief that poured over me when Edgar called. Yes, he had the last of them. I had a bad week trying to sleep as I thought of the possibilities. The saboteurs might have other caches hidden, and at any moment an explosion was possible."[246]

Biddle felt at home in the halls of power. Born in France in 1886 of American parents, he traced his line as one of the true blueblood Philadelphia families to William Randolph, who had come to America in 1673. Biddle had attended Harvard Law School and served as a secretary for famed Supreme Court Justice Oliver Wendell Holmes. A successful corporate lawyer before the war, Biddle had served as judge of the Third Circuit of the United States Court of Appeals and as one of the first National Labor Relations Board chairmen. He had been appointed attorney general by FDR in

August 1941. A slender, nattily dressed man, his balding pate and thin moustache gave him the starched look of a college professor.

Biddle excused himself and immediately phoned the president at his retreat in Hyde Park, New York. Roosevelt was entertaining friends when Biddle excitedly filled him in on the developments.[247] As always when hearing good news, the president was exuberant yet sarcastic, and very specific in his reply to Biddle: "Not enough, Francis. Let's make real money out of them. Sell the rights to Barnum and Bailey for a million and a half—the rights to take them around the country in lion cages at so much a head."[248]

The president's humor was both characteristic and telling. Those who worked near him knew that Roosevelt used lacerating humor to break tension and express his frustrations. But everyone involved in the case also knew that there was a tremendous amount at stake. For now that the saboteurs were in custody, the question was, what to do with them?

Although the war was taking a tremendous toll on America, it was still out of sight in strange-sounding places like Java, Benghazi, and Tobruk—worlds away to most Americans, who viewed the war through the flickering images of Movie Tone newsreels and two-dimensional black-and-white photos in newspapers and magazines. Moreover, the country had quickly grown weary of the cost of Hitler's U-boat war against the United States, the so-called *Operation Paukenschlag*—Operation Drumbeat.[249] Wolf packs of German submarines prowled off the Atlantic Coast, hunting newly minted Liberty Ships carrying raw materials, troops, tanks, and guns. Each day the newspapers were filled with terrifying stories of encounters, sightings, and sinkings by the dreaded U-boats.

The arrest and trial of the saboteurs was therefore an unprecedented opportunity to rouse the fighting spirit of the nation. Ponte Vedra and Amagansett were towns without strategic importance, devoid of military bases or wartime industries. They were backwater towns—sites renowned for their beaches and tranquility. If these places were vulnerable, any place in America was vulnerable.

The decision to make the arrests public was not universally applauded in the government. Secretary of War Harry L. Stimson *Henry* wanted to keep the arrests quiet so contacts and Nazi confederates could be rounded up and captured. But the allure of the media and the administration's desire to have the public hear of a complete American victory, especially one right at home, won out.

Hoover brought the FBI's information resources into full swing to convince the American public that his bureau was firmly in command of the home front. This propaganda campaign, not unexpectedly, made Hoover the hero of the hour, placing the ball squarely in the court of the president and his attorney general.

On Monday, June 28, the front pages of newspapers across the country were emblazoned with the news of the arrests. The *New York Times* ran the headline: FBI SEIZES 8 SABOTEURS LANDED BY U-BOATS HERE AND IN FLORIDA TO BLOW UP WAR PLANTS. Imposing a veil of secrecy on the actual details of the capture, Hoover made it look as though FBI agents had been waiting on shore to scoop up the terrorists the moment they made landfall, as the *Times* reported:

> Despite their training the two gangs of four men each fell afoul of special agents of the Federal Bureau of Investigation almost immediately and the arrest of all eight was announced last evening by J. Edgar Hoover, director of the Bureau. They were in custody within a month after they had shipped on their expedition out of a submarine base on the French coast.[250]

The issue confronting the Roosevelt administration now was how to handle the trial of the suddenly very public case. While Hoover was supremely concerned with keeping secret the actual story of the capture, Roosevelt was worried that the terrorists might actually be acquitted or sentenced to a minimal prison term. As Attorney General Biddle saw it, the eight men may not have yet committed any serious crimes by the time they were rounded up. If they were guilty of anything, it was of an attempt to commit a crime or planning to commit a crime, which would draw them at the most a few years in a federal penitentiary. They might even be found not guilty, if a sympathetic court or jury believed their unilateral claims that the Nazis had coerced them into being spies. That scenario was totally unacceptable to Roosevelt, who demanded convictions—and death sentences.[251]

In a memorandum sent to Biddle days after all the saboteurs were in custody, FDR wrote:

> I have not had the opportunity to talk with you about the prosecution of the eight saboteurs landed from the two German submarines nor have I recently read the statutes which apply.
>
> It is my thought, however:
>
> 1. The two American citizens are guilty of high treason. This being war-time, it is my inclination to try them by court martial. I do not see how they can offer any adequate defense. Surely they are as guilty as it is possible to be and it seems to me that the death penalty is almost obligatory.
>
> 2. In the case of the other six who, I take it, are German citizens, I understand that they came over in submarines wearing seaman's clothes—in all probability German Naval clothes—and that some of them at least landed on our shores wearing these German Naval clothes. I think it can be proved that they formed a part of the German Military or Naval Service. They were apprehended in civilian clothes. This is an absolute parallel to the case of Major Andre in the Revolution and of Nathan Hale. Both of them were hanged. Here again it is my inclination that they be tried by court martial, as were Andre and Hale. Without splitting hairs I can see no difference. [i.e., don't split hairs, Mr. Attorney General].
>
> FDR[252]

The President and his advisors were concerned with more than just the wartime morale of the American people. The statements of each of the Nazis told the story of a larger and more complex plot. These were men who had been recruited before the war by operatives in the United States. The school created to train them was clearly not a one-time operation. Dasch said teams like his were already operating in England, Turkey, and India, and warned the FBI to expect more saboteurs every six weeks. A third commando group was already scheduled to land in the United States in September, with the former boxer "Dempsey" or Bill Smith as its leader.[253]

Biddle found himself in an awkward position. As a Philadelphia Main Liner, a staunch Democrat, and a believer in due process, he held two things in near reverence: the presidency and the law. But at this moment, these two concepts stood in seemingly direct opposition to one another, especially since Roosevelt was painstakingly clear about his intentions. He warned Biddle, "I want one thing understood, Francis: I won't give them up . . . I won't hand them over to any United States marshal armed with a writ of habeas corpus. Understand?"[254]

As the Justice Department worked feverishly to determine the proper method and forum in which to prosecute the eight men captured by the FBI, the Bureau was embroiled in its own discussion on the topic. Hoover was concerned with the way in which his Bureau would be portrayed in the press, and how much of the true story of the events leading up to the capture of the enemy agents would be made public. In the days following the Nazis' arrests, Hoover met with officials from the Justice Department and his own lawyers. They came up with several different scenarios that would guarantee that the saboteurs were held accountable while at the same time keeping the affairs of the Bureau out of the public.[255]

The FBI's lawyers concluded that since the conspiracy to attack the United States had occurred in New York, Florida, and every other jurisdiction where an act in furtherance of the saboteurs' objectives took place, the Justice Department had a number of choices regarding the best venue for the trial. Counsel, however, contradicted the president's stated desires—this case could not be legally prosecuted in a military court. The lawyers cited an attorney general's opinion from 1918, in support of the conclusion that jurisdiction remained *solely* in the civilian courts.[256]

Hoover was additionally frustrated when the Bureau lawyers wrote that the appropriate statute under which the Nazis should be prosecuted was Section 88 of Title 18, United States Code—conspiring to commit an offense against the United States.

The language of the statute seemed to directly apply to the case at hand:

> If two or more persons conspire either to commit any offense against the United States, or to defraud the United States in any manner or for any purpose, and one or more of such parties do any act to effect the object of the conspiracy each of the parties to such conspiracy shall be . . . fined or imprisoned.[257]

The sticking point was its penalty: Title 18 U.S.C. 88, provided for a fine of $10,000 or two years of prison or both. In consolation, the attorneys suggested adding other possible prosecutions for failure to register for the Selective Service Act, failing to register as enemy aliens, and for illegally entering the country. Altogether, the government could conceivably squeeze out ten years' punishment for each terrorist.[258]

On the afternoon of June 29, Hoover was to meet with Attorney General Biddle and Secretary of War Stimson. In preparation for the meeting, Hoover called Assistant Director Connelley to discuss the problem. Connelley suggested that they obtain a secret indictment under "Section 32 of the Espionage laws." These charges would carry a potential death penalty. The indictments would allow the Bureau to "go ahead and let [the Nazis] plead on the Sabotage charge which carries a penalty of thirty years, with the idea that we could get pleas of guilty on all of them."[259]

Connelley argued that if the defendants didn't go along with a plan that would have them pleading guilty to the federal charges, the Bureau would still have an indictment that carried a death penalty. That case could then proceed to trial. Hoover said in his memo that this approach would be appropriate because "if the men want to face the issue that would be all right, as the opinion seems to be that six of them are entitled to the death penalty."[260]

* * *

The problem with this scenario was Dasch's attitude. Connelley complained that Dasch was playing the martyr and that he insisted on going to court to "tell it all, and be 'the big shot'."[261] Connelley also said that Dasch was not responding to the idea of going back to his original agreement. This was in reference to discussions that had taken place with Dasch during the course of his interrogation. Dasch had been told that if he appeared in federal court and entered his plea of guilty, he would be sentenced along with the other defendants. After a period of about six months in prison, the FBI would make an effort to obtain presidential warrant—in other words, a presidential pardon.[262]

Dasch would later testify about the promises made to him by the FBI:

> They said to me, "George, the best way for you—for your case is to go and plead guilty." So I told them, "To plead guilty to what?"
>
> "Well, you plead guilty, and you have to go in front of court, and now is your time to act. This is the biggest act in the world. You have to stay there and take the punishment and don't say nothing. Don't say, 'I have just been to the FBI'; just take it; that is all.
>
> "Then you go to prison, and after six months or three months"— Mr. Traynor said it might be only three months; the others say it might be only six months—then I would receive a presidential pardon; and to the fact—they played up the fact that my mother and the security of my parents [were in jeopardy], and I said, "Yes, sure; for the security of my parents, I am willing to do that," and so I agreed to that.[263]

Hoover's discussion with Connelley next turned to the use of a military commission. Hoover said that such a body would be secret and that the information regarding Dasch, his capture, and any FBI promises to him would remain sealed within the commission's records. Connelley seemed to agree with the Director, saying, "of course we could see that [if] all of the men were tried in such a manner [it] would result in the six men being executed and the other two placed in a military prison somewhere."[264]

The agents did acknowledge that such a result would probably have to be arranged through the president, but that it could be done in such a way that Dasch's story would only be told in the military tribunal and "nothing would be given publicity."[265]

The two justice officials had arrived at a plan that would result in an acceptable outcome: Six of the Nazis would be executed—and the proceedings would be kept quiet. Connelley added one more idea, before the Director got off the phone. He assured Hoover that if the Director wanted the case to proceed in New York, Connelley could probably arrange a grand jury hearing and have all of the men sentenced within a week.[266]

Later that evening, Hoover called Connelley back to inform him of the results of the meeting with Biddle and the secretary of war. The discussions regarding the Nazis in custody had seemed to go well. There was still no agreement or decision on the manner that would be used to prosecute the men. It seemed that a special tribunal headed by the assistant secretary of war would be formed. A panel of "two or three lieutenant generals" would hear the matter.[267]

Hoover instructed his assistant director to check on several issues before the trial. The Director was concerned over the citizenship status of the eight men. Hoover said that "a citizen could not, of course, be tried before a tribunal of this nature as a citizen could obtain a writ of habeas corpus; therefore in exploring the situation, we want to make sure that all eight men are aliens."[268]

It was clear that six of the terrorists were in fact German citizens. Burger and Haupt posed a problem, however; the evidence indicated that they were American citizens, Burger through naturalization and Haupt due to the naturalization of his parents. Hoover and the officials he met with addressed this issue. Connelley was instructed to determine if they had sworn allegiance to Germany when they had signed up for the mission in America, for it could then be argued that they gave up any claim to American citizenship.

Hoover ended the conversation by telling Connelley that they expected that the men could be tried and sentenced in about a week and that they could be executed in the middle of July. Connelley told his boss that this seemed very optimistic. [269]

President Roosevelt cut the legal Gordian knot on July 2, 1942, his sword a legal tool last seen during the Civil War. By a simple order as the commander in chief, he created a military commission to try the Nazis. From that point on, Dasch and his men would find themselves in progressively more dire legal straits, for in a stroke of rough justice they were denied the fundamental civil rights that were hallmarks of American jurisprudence they had, in essence, been sent to undermine and destroy.

> Proclamation No. 2561
> > July 2, 1942
> > By virtue of the authority vested in me as President and as Commander in Chief of the Army and Navy, under the Constitution and statutes of the United States, and more particularly the Thirty-eighth Article of War (U.S.C. Title 10, Sec. 1509), I, Franklin Delano Roosevelt, do hereby appoint as a Military Commission the following persons:
> > > Major General Frank R. McCoy, President
> > > Major General Walter S. Grant
> > > Major General Blanton Winship
> > > Major General Lorenzo D. Gasser
> > > Brigadier General Guy V. Henry
> > > Brigadier General John T. Lewis
> > > Brigadier General John T. Kennedy
> > The prosecution shall be conducted by the Attorney General and the Judge Advocate General. The defense counsel shall be Colonel Cassius M. Dowell and Colonel Kenneth Royall.
> > The Military Commission shall meet in Washington, D.C., on July 8th 1942 or as soon thereafter as is practicable, to try for offenses against the Law of War and the Articles of War, the following persons:
> > > Ernst Peter Burger
> > > George John Dasch
> > > Herbert Hans Haupt
> > > Henry Harm Heinck
> > > Edward John Kerling
> > > Hermann Otto Neubauer
> > > Richard Quirin
> > > Werner Thiel

The Commission shall have power to and shall as occasion requires, make such rules for the conduct of the proceedings, consistent with the powers of Military Commissions under the Articles of War, as it shall deem necessary for a full and fair trial of the matters before it. Such evidence shall be admitted, as would, in the opinion of the President of the Commission, have probative value to a reasonable man. The concurrence of at least two-thirds of the Members of the Commission present shall be necessary for a conviction or sentence. The record of the trial including any judgment or sentence shall be transmitted directly to me for my action thereon.

In the News Today

NEW YORK, N.Y., July 21, 1942—Federal authorities today announced the arrest of Herbert Karl Freidrich Bahr for spying for the Nazis. F.B.I. agents removed Bahr from the diplomatic exchange ship S.S. *Drottningholm* on July 9, sources said.[270]

CHAPTER 7

"A Wholesome and Desirable Safeguard to Civil Liberty in a Time of War"

The military commission created by presidential fiat on July 2, 1942, arose out of a part of American jurisprudence celebrated as one of the United States Supreme Court's first major statements regarding civil rights, *Ex Parte Milligan*.[271]

In 1864, several defendants in Indianapolis were charged with an alleged plot to assist the Confederacy, planning an armed revolt against the Union, and conspiring to free rebel prisoners held by the Union Army. One of the defendants, Lambdin P. Milligan, was a respected lawyer in Indiana and a southern sympathizer.[272] He was tried and convicted along with the other defendants by a military commission, but days before his execution, the decision was reversed and Milligan was set free.[273]

In the case of Milligan, the use of military tribunals had been authorized in 1862 by President Lincoln when he suspended habeas corpus and issued orders that rebels and those committing crimes against the United States were subject to trial by military tribunals.[274] Yet already prior to the Civil War, military commissions had played crucial roles in American military history.

On September 21, 1776, during the evening of a great fire that consumed much of New York City, Nathan Hale, a 24-year-old captain in George Washington's Continental Army, was captured by the British and held as a spy. A British commission was formed, the first use of such a tribunal in North America. Without a trial, the commission sentenced Captain Hale to death. They refused his requests for a Bible and to be allowed to speak with a member of the clergy. Hale was hanged near what is now the corner of Fifty-second Street and First Avenue in Manhattan. As he was about to be executed he uttered the now famous maxim, "I only regret that I have but one life to lose for my country."[275]

The American military's first experience with an espionage case would soon follow. John André, a major in the British army who served as the adjutant general, was a confederate of the notorious American traitor Benedict Arnold. André had received secret documents from Arnold detailing military operations as well as plans of the fort at West Point, New York. Captured by the Continental Army in 1780, André was accused of spying and being behind American lines in civilian clothing. In his defense, André argued that as a British officer caught behind enemy lines, he should be treated as a prisoner of war.[276]

General Washington convened a board of seven generals to try the British officer. The generals heard the evidence and convicted André as a spy, sentencing him to death six days after his capture.[277]

André requested that he be executed by a firing squad, a manner of death appropriate for an officer in His Majesty's Army. But in pronouncing the sentence that André was to be hanged, Nathaniel Greene, the presiding general of the commission, said, "He is either a spy or an innocent man. If the latter, to execute him in any way will be murder: if the former the mode of death is prescribed by law. . . . At the present alarming crisis of our affairs, the public safety calls for a solemn and impressive example. Nothing can satisfy it short of the execution of the prisoner as a common spy."[278]

Military commissions would be used repeatedly throughout the early part of the nineteenth century. In 1815, after the Battle of New Orleans, then-General Andrew Jackson took command of New Orleans and suspended the function of all civil authorities. He used a commission to try Louis Louaillier, a state legislator from Opelousas who had dared criticize in the local papers Jackson's imposition of martial law in New Orleans. Louaillier was arrested and jailed on General Jackson's order. In what would be one of the first jurisdictional clashes over the use of military tribunals, Judge Hall of the United States District Court granted Louaillier's writ of habeas corpus. Jackson, outraged over the order, had the judge arrested and confined to the army's barracks for nearly a week. After peace in the city was declared the judge returned to his court and held General Jackson in "gross contempt of court." The general was fined $1,000.[279] The military trial against Louaillier resulted in acquittal.[280]

During the First Seminole War in 1818, Jackson again used a military commission. The accused in this proceeding were two British traders, Alexander Arbuthnot and Robert Armbrister, accused of assisting and inciting the Seminole Indians to war against the United States. Even though their actions took place in Spanish Florida, which Jackson had invaded, the defendants were convicted. The military court sentenced Armbrister to be shot. The court then reconsidered the sentence and modified it, ordering that Armbrister was to receive "fifty stripes across the bare back and be confined with a ball and chain to hard labor for twelve calendar months."[281] The modification did not stand, however; General Jackson struck the new sentence and upon his order Armbrister was shot.[282] The military tribunal decided Arbuthnot's fate, and he was ordered hanged.[283]

During the next major conflict of the young expansionist republic, the Mexican-American War of 1847, military commissions were used extensively by General Winfield Scott, the commander of the American forces in Mexico, to try persons charged with crimes against American forces in occupied areas. General Scott established a separate judicial system in occupied Mexico to be used to adjudicate crimes involving a Mexican national and an American, as well as for crimes committed against American forces. Nonetheless, Scott was careful to keep his military justice system separate from the civil courts of the occupied territory.[284]

The military commission would not be extensively used again until the Civil War. On May 22, 1865, the United States Army convened a commission to try T. E. Hogg and several other Confederate sympathizers for "violations of the laws and usages of civilized war." Hogg and his co-conspirators had boarded a merchant steamer while it was docked in the Port of Panama in the "guise of peaceful passengers." They then attempted to seize control of the vessel and convert her into a Confederate ship of war. The military commission hearing the case found the men guilty and sentenced them to be hanged. The reviewing military authority affirmed the judgment, but modified the sentence to life in prison.[285]

In one of the most famous cases of trial by military tribunal, on May 1, 1865, President Andrew Johnson established a commission to try eight conspirators charged in the assassination of Abraham Lincoln. Johnson had declared the assassination an act of war. The crime was considered not just a premeditated murder but also an act in furtherance of the Confederacy in its war against the Union. This provided the justification and the mechanism to keep the case out of the civil courts.[286]

The War Department, charged with conducting the proceedings, entrusted the case to a panel of nine judges— most were generals who had served with the Union Army during the war and could hardly be considered impartial. None of the commission members were lawyers. The commission's procedures provided that defendants could be convicted upon a simple majority of the commission and that the death penalty could be imposed with the finding of two-thirds of the members.[287]

At first, the Johnson administration closed the proceedings to the public and the press. But after intense defense objections and

Members of the military commission that tried President Lincoln's assassins in 1865. Pictured are John A. Bingham, and generals David Hunter, Thomas M. Harris, James A. Ekin, August V. Kautz, and Lewis Wallace.

cries of unconstitutionality in the nation's newspapers, the commission consented to the presence of a few reporters and a handful of citizen spectators.

Within two months the commission had tried and convicted all the defendants. On July 5, 1865, President Johnson approved the verdicts. Lewis Powell, Mary Suratt, David Herold, and George Azterodt were informed of their sentences the next day. They were sentenced to death and were hanged on July 7. Three of the other conspirators were sentenced to life imprisonment and one was imprisoned for six years.[288]

In another episode reminiscent of the first use of the commission that tried Nathan Hale, Captain Robert C. Kennedy of the Confederate army was arrested after being seen in different parts of New York City in disguise. Accused of trying to set the city on fire,

© Bettmann/CORBIS

The military commission found the Lincoln conspirators guilty of conspiracy, and sentenced them to be hanged.

he was tried by commission and sentenced to death by hanging.[289] Also in 1865, William Murphy, a Confederate agent, was captured after he crossed Union lines and tried to set fire to a steamboat. He was tried and convicted by a military commission in 1866.[290]

But it was the case of Indiana lawyer Lambdin P. Milligan that finally focused the Supreme Court's attention on the use of military commissions. Milligan was a well-known, politically connected lawyer who favored the Confederate cause. Agents of the Union, who had infiltrated several rebel support groups, reported plans by Confederate officers and sympathizers to disrupt the Democratic Convention of 1864, scheduled to be held in Chicago. Allegedly, the sympathizers had planned an uprising to free the thousands of Confederate prisoners being held at nearby Camp Douglass.[291]

Although those plans never materialized, after a shipment of weapons was found in Indiana, several rebel activists were arrested, among them Milligan, who was taken into custody at his home on October 5, 1864, by order of the military commandant of the District of Indiana. Milligan was confined to a military prison in Indianapolis while awaiting trial by a military commission.[292]

On October 21, Milligan was charged with:

–conspiracy against the government of the United States;
–affording aid and comfort to rebels against the authority of the United States;
–inciting insurrection;
–disloyal practices; and
–violations of the laws of war.

These charges were based on allegations that he assisted a secret society known as the Order of American Knights, or the Sons of Liberty, for the purpose of overthrowing the United States Government.[293] Milligan was tried by the military commission, convicted, and ordered to be executed on May 19, 1865.[294]

Nine days before he was to be executed, however, Milligan filed an appeal, which would result in his conviction being overturned.[295] The United States Supreme Court, commenting on the powers of the president, held that the commander in chief could not order Milligan, a civilian who did not reside near any theater of war, to be tried by a military tribunal.[296]

The Supreme Court opinion that resulted from Milligan's appeal would be called a victory for civil liberties. In his history of the United States Supreme Court, Chief Justice William Rehnquist cites the following passage regarding *Ex Parte Milligan:*

> The Constitution of the United States is a law for the rulers and the people, equally in war and peace, and covers with the shield of its protection all classes of men, at all times, and under all circumstances. No doctrine, involving more pernicious consequences, was ever invented by the wit of man than any of its provisions can be suspended during any of the great exigencies of government.[297]

Justice David Davis wrote the Court's opinion in *Milligan.* Four other justices joined his majority opinion. Chief Justice Salmon

Chase authored a separate opinion in the case. Although joining with the majority in its final holding, the minority opinion criticized the majority for overreaching in discussing the authority of Congress over the issues presented in the case.[298]

The language of the Court's opinion was strong and clear. The Court was careful to acknowledge the importance of the basic rights afforded to every criminal defendant while at the same time being aware of the exigencies of war. The arguments presented by the litigants made Justice Davis well aware of the importance of the issues presented by the case:

> No graver question was ever considered by this court, nor one which more nearly concerns the rights of the whole people; for it is the birthright of every American citizen when charged with crime, to be tried and punished according to law. . . . The decision of this question does not depend on argument or judicial precedents, numerous and highly illustrative as they are. These precedents inform us of the extent of the struggle to preserve liberty and to relieve those in civil life from military trials. The founders of our government were familiar with the history of that struggle; and secured in a written constitution every right which the people had wrested from power during a contest of ages. By that Constitution and the laws authorized by it this question must be determined. . . . Those applicable to this case are found in that clause of the original Constitution which says, "That the trial of all crimes, except in case of impeachment, shall be by jury . . ."[299]

The majority's commitment to the basic rights contained within the Constitution could not be argued. The issue then became what effect a war, especially a war waged within the borders of the United States, specifically had on those rights. This nation was born out of revolution, and the founders knew well the effect that such a struggle could have on a nation. Justice Davis did not shirk from dealing with the impact that war could have on the administration of criminal justice:

> This nation, as experience has proved, cannot always remain at peace, and has no right to expect that it will always have wise and humane rulers, sincerely attached to the principles of the Constitution. Wicked men, ambitious of power, with hatred of liberty and contempt of law,

may fill the place once occupied by Washington and Lincoln; and if this right is conceded, and the calamities of war again befall us, the dangers to human liberty are frightful to contemplate. If our fathers had failed to provide for just such a contingency, they would have been false to the trust reposed in them. They knew—the history of the world told them—the nation they were founding, be its existence short or long, would be involved in war; how often or how long continued, human foresight could not tell; and that unlimited power, wherever lodged at such a time, was especially hazardous to freemen. For this, and other equally weighty reasons, they secured the inheritance they had fought to maintain, by incorporating in a written constitution the safeguards which time had proved were essential to its preservation. Not one of these safeguards can the President, or Congress, or the Judiciary disturb, except the one concerning the writ of habeas corpus.[300]

On September 24, 1862, President Lincoln had issued a proclamation which had suspended the writ of habeas corpus, imposed martial law, and authorized the use of military courts to try those accused of assisting the rebels who threatened the Union. The suspension of habeas corpus created a separate judicial response for crimes arising out of the conduct of the war. This drastic action by the president was the basic exercise of power that led to the trial of Lambdin Milligan by a military commission. The Court did not shy away from dealing with the president's action as well:

> The Constitution . . . does not say after a writ of habeas corpus is denied a citizen, that he shall be tried otherwise than by the course of the common law; if it had intended this result, it was easy by the use of direct words to have accomplished it. The illustrious men who framed that instrument were guarding the foundations of civil liberty against the abuses of unlimited power; they were full of wisdom, and the lessons of history informed them that a trial by an established court, assisted by an impartial jury, was the only sure way of protecting the citizen against oppression and wrong. Knowing this, they limited the suspension to one great right, and left the rest to remain forever inviolable. But, it is insisted that the safety of the country in time of war demands that this broad claim for martial law shall be sustained. If this were true, it could be well said that a country, preserved at the sacrifice of all the cardinal principles of liberty, is not worth the cost of preservation. Happily, it is not so.[301]

*   *   *

As the Justice Department and the FBI made preparations to try the eight Nazis who had invaded the United States, they did so in what was an obscure, but rich legal history. Dasch, Kerling, and the rest of the accused would be tried in the same manner as those who first threatened the liberty of the nation. Although the use of the military commission answered some of the immediate questions about how to deal with the Nazis in custody in the district jail, it would open other legal questions that had remained unanswered since the Revolution.

In the News Today

HAMPTON, N.J., July 22, 1942—The bodies of twenty-nine crewmen from a Nazi U-boat were buried with full military honors here today. The sailors were crew from a German submarine sunk off the Atlantic coast by a U.S. Navy destroyer.[302]

WASHINGTON, D.C., July 22, 1942—Federal naval authorities today banned all non-military shipping. Officials said this move was caused by heavy shipping losses due to U-boat attacks, which have reached the highest level of the war and have exceeded the rate of construction of new ships.[303]

CHAPTER 8

The Halls
of Justice

A t 10:00 A.M. on the morning of July 8, 1942, twenty-five days
after the first Nazi sabotage team set foot on American soil,
the military commission established by the president convened in
Room 5235 of the Department of Justice in Washington, D.C.

The only air-conditioned hall in the entire building, Room 5235
was a large, open space previously used for training FBI agents.
Blackout curtains covered the windows; save for a standard government clock above the door, everything had been removed from the
stark walls for the duration of the trial. A hastily built rail separated
the parties—the prosecutors, the defense lawyers, and the eight accused—from the commission.

For the six days between the date the president created the commission and the beginning of the trial, the fifth floor of the Department of Justice had been abuzz with the sounds of hammers and
saws building new wooden doors several feet in front of existing glass
doors. On each door in the long cold hallway, the words NO ADMIT-
TANCE were hastily stenciled in fresh paint. Armed guards stood
watch near the new construction as if to underline the warning.[304]

Solemnly, the parties took their places around large plain wooden
tables laid out along the long walls of the room. The commission

members, dressed in their khaki summer uniforms, sat in high-backed leather chairs on a raised platform. The president of the commission sat in front of an American flag, which, besides the ribbons on the officers' uniforms, lent the only color to the room. To the commission's right sat the eight defendants, in alphabetical order, each one separated from the other by vigilant military guards.

New procedures had been put in place to assure security and secrecy. For the first time since the war began, passes were demanded of all persons entering the Department of Justice. One corridor of FBI offices was sealed to anyone without proper identification, while fifty soldiers stood guard outside.

For Dasch, the opening of the trial affirmed the realization that he was not about to be given his freedom by the FBI. Dasch would write that, "[t]he eight days of cooperating with the FBI were really my last happy ones."[305] Dasch spent the days as he confessed to the FBI between a hotel room and the FBI headquarters. His feelings of comfort did not last, however; he soon found himself in jail-issued clothing sitting alone in a cell.[306]

The Nazi saboteurs were held in the Washington, D.C. district jail for the duration of the trial. On the evening of July 4, 1942, while the rest of the country celebrated Independence Day with picnics and parades, Dasch and his cohorts had been transferred from FBI custody. Shortly after 6:00 P.M., a detachment of soldiers had arrived at the jail in a convoy of trucks under the personal command of Brigadier General Albert L. Cox, the district's provost marshal. As soon as the trucks pulled into the courtyard of the jail, the fully armed soldiers piled out and double-timed to predetermined positions around the courtyard and the driveway leading to the jail.

About an hour later, a line of ten dark sedans sped up the driveway. The soldiers snapped to attention and the gates were flung open as the first car approached the gate. Each of the cars pulled into the courtyard and stopped, the last car blocking the entrance to the jail. Each contained one of the terrorists, handcuffed to an FBI agent.

District jail officers opened the door to the newly constructed women's division of the jail. Veteran officers would later tell re-

National Archives/United States Army Signal Corps

Each day of the trial, the eight Nazi prisoners were taken by U.S. Marshal vans, escorted by armored cars manned by heavily armed soldiers, from the Department of Justice to the district jail. The curious lined the streets hoping to catch a glimpse of the terrorists.

porters from the *Washington Times Herald* that this was the first time there had been armed officers inside. The Nazis were taken down a long corridor lined with FBI agents and soldiers to a part of the building that at one time had housed the infirmary. They were walked past heavily barred doors into the section that contained the solitary cells. Each of the prisoners was then placed in an individual cell. The men sat alone, waiting for the first military commission trial in seventy years.[307]

As the trial was about to begin, the nation learned the names of the officers chosen to serve as members of the commission selected by the president. None of them were trained in the law but all of them were generals. These men were considered some of the brightest stars in the United States military, each of them boasting decades of decorated service.

Major General Frank R. McCoy, the president of the commission, was a West Point graduate who had served as an aide to the military governor in Cuba and to Teddy Roosevelt during the Spanish-American War. He had also commanded the Sixty-third Infantry Brigade in France and Germany during World War I.[308]

Major General Walter S. Grant had won the Distinguished Service Medal and served in France during World War I from 1917 until after the Armistice. He had served as the Commander of Third Corps in Baltimore in 1940; shortly before the case, he had been assigned to the Army Chief of Staff.

Major General Blanton Winship was a former judge advocate general. He had a long and distinguished army career, having served

National Archives/United States Army Signal Corps

Five of the members of the military commission. From left to right: General John Lewis, General Lorenzo Gasser, General Walter S. Grant, General Frank E. McCoy, and General Blanton Winship.

in Veracruz, in France during World War I, and in Puerto Rico for a term as the appointed governor, before that island colony was granted the right of self-determination.

Major General Lorenzo D. Gasser had retired as the deputy chief of staff of the army in 1939. His career included service chasing Pancho Villa with General Pershing in Mexico, as well as combat in the Spanish-American War in Cuba and at Château-Thierry in France during World War I. He had returned to army service following Pearl Harbor.

Brigadier General Guy V. Henry, a Nebraskan, was a famous cavalry officer who had commanded Fort Myer, Virginia, and the Army Calvary School at Fort Riley, Kansas.

Brigadier General John T. Lewis was a career coast artillery officer with service in France and Hawaii.

Brigadier General John T. Kennedy was the final officer selected to the commission. He had been awarded the Congressional Medal of Honor for his valor during the brutal pacification campaign in the Philippines at the turn of the century. He had seen combat in World War I in France and was in command of the garrison at Fort Bragg, North Carolina, at the time he was selected to serve on the commission.

The lawyers chosen for the case came from the elite of the military and government legal circles. To underline the gravity of the case, the prosecution was to be undertaken by the two top prosecutors of the country, Attorney General Biddle and Judge Advocate General of the Army Myron Cramer. Aiding them was a junior counsel fresh from New York, Lloyd Cutler, who would later rise to prominence as leader of the Democratic Party and advisor to Presidents Jimmy Carter and Bill Clinton.

In a move that today would draw an immediate legal challenge, none of the men, except for Dasch, were appointed their own individual attorneys. Instead, the president named four prominent lawyers to represent the seven terrorists. Lead counsel were Colonel Kenneth Clairborne Royall, who would later become secretary of the army, and Colonel Cassius M. Dowell. Joining them were

Captain William G. Hummel and Major Lauson H. Stone—the son of Supreme Court Chief Justice Harlan F. Stone. Dasch, the FBI's star informant, was represented by Colonel Carl L. Ristine, who served as a lawyer in the office of the army's inspector general.[309]

Colonel Royall was a native of Goldsboro, North Carolina. During the legal proceedings he would wield his considerable southern charm to emphasize points during his arguments to the commission. Royall had entered the army in May 1917. After completing Officer's Training Camp at Fort Oglethorpe, Georgia, he had served as a field artillery officer until his discharge in February 1919. Following his World War I service, Royall had established a successful law practice in Goldsboro. After a turn as a member of the North Carolina State Senate, he had reentered the United States Army with the rank of colonel in June 1942, just weeks before Dasch and his comrades set foot on American soil.

The defense lawyers selected to defend the saboteurs were proceeding in the face of overwhelming public opinion against their clients. On July 6, 1942, the *Los Angeles Examiner* ran an editorial entitled "Death for Spies: Justice Demands Prompt Action."[310] The paper was very direct in stating its opinion as to what should happen to Dasch and his comrades:

> Nothing seems clearer than the FACT that six of these men are guilty of spying and that two American citizens among them are guilty of treason to the country to which they swore to be loyal.
>
> They came here, besides, for the deliberate purpose of murder, arson and dynamiting great public utilities and to organize a ring designed "to take America from within" as Hitler has expressed it.
>
> The penalty for treason and spying is death.
>
> This is not a question of vengeance.
>
> It is a question of CARRYING OUT THE LAW TO THE LETTER."[311]

The editorial went on to quote a congressman and a senator who had each gone on the record saying that the Nazis should be immediately shot. The paper urged that "anything less than the death penalty . . . would stamp us as 'softies.' "[312]

The rage against the eight terrorists was not limited to the newspapers. In an internal FBI memorandum by J. Edgar Hoover dated August 4, 1942, Hoover recounted that Colonel Dowell of the defense team informed him that he and other defense counsel had been receiving a large number of letters during the course of the trial. Most of the letters condemned and threatened the lawyers for defending the Nazis, but a significant number of the letters were from pro-Nazi groups and individuals who voiced support and encouragement. These letters were turned over to the G-men for investigation.

Before the daily proceedings, the defendants were transported to court from the district jail through the streets of Washington in somber black vans, each with an armed soldier riding on the back running boards. A team of nine motorcycle police officers led the jail convoy. Although police shut traffic down along the route of the vans, the streets along the convoy's route and near the court were lined with the curious and those hoping to sell them drinks, treats, and souvenirs.[313]

Upon arrival in the utilitarian basement, the vans were met by the sight of two armored cars, each equipped with machine guns and crewed by four soldiers equipped for combat. When the defendants alighted, each was handcuffed to an individual FBI agent. Once at Room 5235, more than a half-dozen military guards manned the doors.

From the outset Colonel Royall challenged the constitutionality of the president's order creating the commission, arguing that as long as the civil courts were open and ready to try the defendants, only the civil courts could be used to prosecute them. Moreover, he pointed out that several of the specific charges levied against the eight saboteurs were technically deficient.[314]

Attorney General Biddle framed the government's position clearly and succinctly. First, he argued that as the commission was composed of officers of the United States Army, it would not be appropriate for them to override or challenge an order issued by their commander in chief. Biddle buttressed his argument by alleging that the eight Germans were "exactly and precisely in the same position as armed forces invading this country. I cannot think it conceivable," he said, "that any

National Archives/United States Army Signal Corps

United States Attorney General Francis Biddle, assigned by FDR to personally prosecute the military commission trial.

commission would listen to an argument that armed forces entering this country should not be met by the resistance of the Army itself under the commander-in-chief or that they have any civil rights . . ."[315]

These arguments laid out in a matter of minutes the basic positions each side would take. It was clear from the evidence collected by the FBI and by the statements from the defendants themselves that they had in fact landed on the shores of the United States with cash, the implements of sabotage, and a specific target list. The only factual question, at least as to Dasch and Burger, was their intent the moment they first lowered their feet over the side of the rubber landing boats and stepped into the waters of the United States. That was of paramount importance, for intent—or the lack thereof—could mean the difference between a prison sentence and a death sentence.

The case proceeded with the defendants being arraigned of the charges against them. The government had filed four separate charges against each defendant under the authority of the Articles of War. Charge I alleged that the saboteurs, "being enemies of the United States and acting for and on behalf of the German Reich, a belligerent enemy nation, secretly and covertly passed, in civilian dress . . . through military and naval lines . . . and the defenses of the United States . . . for the purpose of committing acts of sabotage, espionage and other hostile acts." The charge further alleged that the defendants assembled explosives, money, and other supplies in the United States for the purposes of sabotage.[316]

Charge II alleged that the defendants attempted to assist enemies of the United States and held intelligence for those persons who were in the United States.

Charge III alleged that the defendants, enemies of the United States, were found lurking or acting as spies in or about the fortifications, posts, and encampments of the armies of the United States and secretly and covertly passed behind the lines of the United States for the purposes of espionage and sabotage.

Charge IV alleged conspiracy to commit the acts charged in Charges I–III. It is interesting to note that upon reciting this charge, the attorney general stated that this first crime would not be a crime recognized by any civilian court.

Then, in arguing for the jurisdiction of the Commission, Biddle said,

> . . . I cannot conceive of anyone successfully arguing that in time of war and in time of actual invasion by enemies, charged to be enemies, or by spies, charged to be spies . . . by persons coming in to commit sabotage with that intention, changing their uniforms and putting on civilian garb or civilian dress, in order to get behind the military and naval lines established to prevent that very invasion—I cannot imagine any military tribunal holding that you have no jurisdiction.[317]

Colonel Dowell for the defense responded that the acts committed by the defendants, if proven, would constitute crimes under civil statutes and should be tried in the civil courts. He argued that one of the reasons that colonists fought the Revolutionary War was to throw off the yoke of military rule and that military courts should only be resorted to when the civil authority is unable to operate.[318]

The trial had begun with the peculiar mix of mystery and spectacle that would mark its entire run. General McCoy issued orders to everyone involved in the case that they were sworn to not disclose anything that happened in the commission. The secrecy of the trial was immediately assailed by the press. The *New York Times* reported that after the first day of the trial, the only thing Attorney General Biddle would say to the press upon leaving the building was, "We will resume tomorrow. I think it is fair to state that."[319]

Each day, at the end of the testimony, General McCoy would issue a cryptic summary to the hungry press outside. As the country ached to know what was going on behind the blackout drapes in Room 5235, the government would send only messages similar to the following communiqué from July 20:

> The commission reconvened at 10:00 A.M.
> This morning's session was primarily devoted to the arguments on certain motions. The defense then recalled certain FBI agents for further cross-examination.
> It is anticipated that the defense will open the defense of its case during the afternoon session.

The commission recessed at 12:45 P.M. and will reconvene at
2:00 P.M.

The commission reconvened at 2:00 P.M. The prosecution formally
rested the government's case at 2:36 P.M.

The remainder of the afternoon session was devoted to argument
upon various motions made by the defense.

The commission adjourned for the day at 4:30 P.M. to reconvene at
10:00 A.M. tomorrow.

It is anticipated that the defense will start introducing its evidence
tomorrow.

The government presented its case piece by damning piece. Each
of the FBI special agents who had taken part in the case was called to
testify. They spoke of explosives and tools found on beaches, of secret
ink used to write on handkerchiefs, of plans for sabotage, and large
amounts of cash. Every detail of the case as related to the Bureau by
the defendants and the witnesses they discovered was presented.

The prosecution opened its case with one of the most dramatic
pieces of evidence. The man who had discovered the Nazis, John
Cullen, was called to the stand and sworn in to testify. The young
sailor sat facing the four men he had encountered on the beach and
recounted each detail to the members of the commission. He described being on patrol on a "dark and very foggy" night on the Long
Island beach.[320] As the attorney general questioned him, Cullen
stood and pointed to the Nazi who had threatened him, identifying
Dasch as one of the terrorists in the court that would decide the German's fate. Biddle walked Cullen though the identification:

"Do you recognize the man in court who walked towards you?"

"I think so, sir."

"Will you stand up and identify him, if you see him in court?
Stand up please. Now, do you see the man?"

"Yes, sir."

"Right here [indicating], sir."

"Go and point to the man that you have in mind. It won't hurt
you. Just go ahead and point at him. Point at him. Which is he?"

"Yes, sir; right here" [indicating].

"Will you stand up please?"[321] Biddle ordered Dasch to stand
and approach the witness stand.

"Is that the man that you remember seeing?"

"Would he mind saying a few words?"

The attorney general tried to clarify Cullen's hesitation in making a positive identification. "Do you want to identify him by his voice? Is that what you mean?"

"Yes, sir."

The Commission ordered Dasch to ask Cullen one of the questions asked on the beach. "What is your name?" Hearing the Nazi's voice sealed it—Dasch was identified.[322] Yet Cullen, the only witness who actually saw any of the terrorists as they landed, could not identify any of the other Nazis.[323]

The first clash between the lawyers over the rules of evidence to be used during the commission trial took place during Cullen's testimony. The attorney general asked Cullen about observations made

National Archives/United States Army Signal Corps

Heinrich Heinck encounters prosecution witness John Cullen outside of the courtroom.

by another witness. Colonel Royall made one of the most basic trial objections: "We object to that . . . [it] is hearsay."[324]

The president of the commission overruled the objection, noting, "I have to pass on the admissibility of evidence, and I take it, from the president's proclamation, that there is unusual freedom for both sides in the term 'probative value for a reasonable man.' So I want to make it perfectly clear that the rulings will be to give full and free presentation of evidence that would fit into the statement."[325]

This first evidentiary objection would mark the tenor of the entire proceeding. The attorney general would rely on the "reasonable man" language of the proclamation throughout the trial. At one point, he argued that although the admission of a defendant's statement would probably violate the law, it still should be admitted. ". . . I do claim that any reasonable man confronted with this evidence—not a reasonable lawyer, but a reasonable man—any reasonable man—would say, 'Why, of course, this shows that that fellow was guilty!' "[326]

Some of the most dramatic arguments in the trial revolved around the prosecution's use of the defendant's statements to the FBI. It is a long-standing legal rule that an out-of-court confession by one defendant cannot be used against another. The Constitution provides that every criminal defendant has the right to confront and cross-examine those who present evidence against him. Cross-examination of a prosecution witness is the most powerful tool in a defense attorney's arsenal. When damning testimony is presented through an investigator who heard the incriminating statement, the defendant against whom the evidence is presented has very little room to maneuver. He cannot impeach the person who made the declaration, explore the intent and mindset of the witness, and in fact, the judge or jury receiving the evidence cannot even measure the demeanor of the person who provided the actual evidence.

The only general exception to this rule is in the case of a conspiracy. When a statement is made during the course of a conspiracy, it can be introduced against any of the charged co-conspirators. But there is a catch: the statement must be made in furtherance of the conspiracy. The confessions that the FBI obtained from Dasch and

Burger were the cornerstones of the government's case. Yet, using these well-established legal rules, the defense forcefully argued that the statements were inadmissible.[327]

As the lawyers argued over the admissibility of the defendant's confessions, Biddle became even more forceful in his arguments that the commission should disregard the rules of evidence:

> But the main point, it seems to me, where the Commission should not rule unfavorably to these admissions is found in the direction of the Commission itself, and this I emphasize particularly. You are directed as follows:
>
> "Such evidence shall be admitted as would in the opinion of the President of the Commission have probative value to a reasonable man."
>
> Is it not the very purpose and essence of that clause in the Commission creating this body to disregard the highly technical and complicated rules of evidence . . . ?[328]

Colonel Royall vigorously countered the attorney general's argument:

> One thing we are proud of in this country—and I am not trying to get oratorical about it, but I think it is so essential that I want to make this point—is our system of administering government. We are proud of it particularly in times like this, when it stands out in sharp contrast to other systems which we are fighting—and we are fighting presumably and, I think, actually to protect our system of government.
>
> Perhaps in the case of pure technicalities this question does not arise; but when we deal with a fundamental principle or trying seven other men upon an unsworn, unexamined, and uninvestigated declaration of an eighth, we are approaching in our humble opinion, upon a fundamental element of our administration of justice.[329]

However vigorous, Royall's argument did not persuade the commission; they overruled the defense objections and allowed the statements of the eight defendants into evidence.

Biddle built the prosecution's case in textbook fashion. He approached the case chronologically, calling the FBI special agents who discovered the Nazis' equipment in Long Island and Florida.[†] Each

---

[†]For a complete list of the property recovered by the FBI, see Appendix 2.

General Cramer, one of the prosecutors, examines evidence during the trial.

piece of damning evidence was brought into the court, explained, and left for the commission to consider. The FBI agents who interrogated Dasch were called as witnesses. After fierce arguments over the admissibility of Dasch's statement, the commission ruled that it could come into evidence.[330] It took three days and several shifts of agents to read the Nazi's 254-page statement into evidence.[331]

Each of the eight accused men would also testify, his testimony a retelling of the story he told the FBI. Each would also speak of his dissatisfaction with Nazi Germany and his lack of intent to harm America. Always desirous to stand out, Dasch, in his testimony, tried to paint himself more as a refugee than a soldier.

Throughout the trial, the prisoners were kept well away from the public and the press. During the noon recess each day, they were taken to a guardroom and given the same sandwiches and coffee that the

National Archives/United States Army Signal Corps

Camera crews were allowed into the trial on July 9, 1942, to record some of the proceedings. Here, a movie crew films members of the commission. The accused Nazis are seated on the left side of the room.

guards ate.[332] The FBI basked in its role as the heroic agency, with the Senate Judiciary Committee giving unanimous approval to award Hoover an "appropriate medal."[333] In an effort to quell some of the clamor over the secrecy of the trial, several select reporters were allowed into the commission for one day. Pictures from the makeshift courtroom would appear the next day in papers throughout the country.

The trial ran through the sticky, hot days of July. The commission continued to work in secret, with the papers chomping greedily at any tidbit that was tossed to them. Each small detail glimpsed by the reporters prowling outside the trial was reported. On July 20, 1942, a woman was seen walking into and then later out of the court. Gerta Melind, Haupt's ex-fiancée, was called to the commission to testify about her relationship with Haupt. She stated that she saw him after he had returned to the United States—and that she "had a hunch that something was wrong."[334] Papers ran stories on her appearance at the commission and featured pictures of the pretty twenty-four-year-old, and even described what she was wearing— "[a] white suit, flowered blouse, and white turban."[335]

The defense case consisted primarily of the testimony of the eight accused men. The only one of the saboteurs who did not try to portray himself as lacking the nerve or commitment to carry out their orders was Kerling. He did not disparage the Nazis nor did he shy away from the fact that he knew the nature of the mission.[336] Kerling described himself "as a loyal German."[337]

As the trial wound down with the lackluster testimony of the accused, the makeshift courtroom went dark for three momentous days between Monday, July 27, and Thursday, July 30. The commission recessed for the parties to present their case before the United States Supreme Court, which would decide in an unusual emergency session issues that went to the heart of the country's constitution—and the foundation of its system of justice.

In the News Today

NEW HAVEN, CONN., July 22, 1942— Yale University officials today disclosed their cooperation with federal law enforcement authorities in the investigation of what are considered "seditious" post cards. Students at this Ivy League school have received a number of cards with messages critical of the United States war effort.[338]

CHAPTER 9

The Meeting
at the Farm

For Colonel Royall and the defense, the United States Supreme Court truly became what the founding fathers intended it to be—a court of last resort—yet paradoxically it would be also the *first* court to examine the legal issues in the case.

From the opening minutes of the commission, the defense had argued that the order establishing that military judicial body was illegal.[339] The only court with authority to overrule the presidential decision, however, was the Supreme Court. Typically, in American jurisprudence, the Supreme Court hears a case only after a long and arduous journey through the halls of trial and appellate courts. But in *Ex Parte Quirin*, as the Nazi case would come to be known in legal parlance, defense lawyers would have only one opportunity to argue their case. Even then, there was no guarantee that the High Court would hear the case. The justices could turn down without comment the defense request for a ruling on the constitutionality of FDR's order by simply denying it. Supreme Court review was discretionary.

By July 27, after the prosecution presented all of its evidence to the commission, the defense attorneys turned back to their first and original argument. In preparation for a meeting to ask to be allowed to argue their case before the Supreme Court, the defense had applied to the district court for leave to file petitions for habeas corpus.[340] As expected, Justice James W. Morris immediately denied the application.[341] But the motion did have the effect of getting the case ready for the first and final legal recourse.

At an unusual meeting at Supreme Court Justice Owen J. Roberts's farm in Chester Springs, Pennsylvania, Justice Roberts and Justice Hugo L. Black, as well as Colonel Dowell, Attorney General Biddle, and Judge Advocate General Cramer heard Royall plead for a hearing by the Supreme Court.[342] In that bucolic setting, distant in miles and atmosphere from the packed concrete halls and chambers of the tribunal, it became clear to the two justices that there were indeed very important issues to be decided. The Court would be called back from its summer recess as the chief justice announced that the case should be heard "in view of the public importance of the questions raised, and of the duty which rests on the courts, in time of war as well as in time of peace, to preserve unimpaired the constitutional safeguards of civil liberty."[343]

Biddle, always conscious of his image and political position, would later write that he flew to the farm with Colonel Royall to make a joint request for the Supreme Court hearing.[344] The day after the meeting the papers would report, however, that Attorney General Biddle had vigorously opposed the move, appearing only as an opponent to Colonels Dowell and Royall.[345] Whatever his true motivations, Biddle was acutely aware of the consequences of defeat. He warned FDR, "We have to win in the Supreme Court or there will be a hell of a mess."[346]

The country received notice of the unusual move when Nelson Potter, the superintendent of the Supreme Court pressroom, addressed the members of the press corps that evening. At 5:45 P.M., in a sleeveless sweatshirt, having been called away from gardening at his home, Potter made the announcement from the imposing court building, which was otherwise closed. Reporters watched scrub-women working in the marble halls as Potter intoned, as solemnly as he could in his stained clothes, the court's decision.[347]

Seven of the Nazi saboteurs on trial, all but George John Dasch, would seek relief from the United States Supreme Court. For the first time in twenty-two years, the justices of the Court would be called in session during a summer recess from scattered points around the country back to their chambers in Washington.

Justice Frank Murphy was reached through a field telephone hanging off a tree. At the time of the summons back to the Court, he was on maneuvers with his unit in Dilworth, North Carolina, as a lieutenant colonel in the army.[348] The next day readers of the *New York Times* would wake up to the unusual photograph of a sitting Supreme Court Justice in full Army regalia under the headline SUPREME COURT IS CALLED IN UNPRECEDENTED SESSION TO HEAR PLEA IN NAZI CASE.[349] The other justices came from points scattered around the country—Justice Black from Alabama; Justice Felix Frankfurter from New Milford, Connecticut; Justice Stanley F. Reed from Tuxedo Park, New York; Justice William O. Douglas from Oregon. Justices James F. Byrnes and Robert H. Jackson were already in Washington.[350]

The intervention by the Supreme Court was a controversial move. From the president down to the common defense plant worker, the country wanted a quick resolution and a severe punishment.[351] Editorial pages in the nation's newspapers recognized the duty of the defense to demand all possible rights for the terrorists, but all the same, they wanted the commission to get the job done.[352]

In Congress the next day, Representative Emmanuel Celler, of Brooklyn, was much more forthright: "The eight Nazi saboteurs should be executed with all possible dispatch . . . [Our people] are confident that the military tribunal will decree their death. Any interference with that trial by civil court would strike a severe blow to public morale."[353]

Celler was not wrong in his reading of the public pulse. Polls published as the Supreme Court readied to hear the case showed that Americans, by a margin of ten to one, wanted the eight Nazis simply taken to the gallows or the firing squad for execution.[354]

* * *

The stakes were high, as an adverse ruling against the president might not only spare the Nazis but strip away some of the commander in chief's powers during a time of war. Nonetheless, the Supreme Court had committed to hear the case. The American legal system, built upon the inspiration of the English Common Law system, is a living, evolving entity. Its course is always shifting and minor moves can have dramatic impact for hundreds of years— much more in a case such as *Ex Parte Quirin*, which addressed issues at the very foundation of the country's justice system.

The writ of habeas corpus is one of the basic elements in both American and British law. The term is from the Latin "you have the body." The writ is an order for a prisoner to be brought before a judge to make a determination if the detention of the prisoner is lawful. The term, and arguably the protection of habeas corpus, first appeared in England in 1215 with the signing of the Magna Carta. The right was codified in England with the passage of the Habeas Corpus Act of 1679.

The right at that time commanded the jailer to bring the applicant before a court "with the day and cause of his taken and detained . . . [so that the court] may then and there examine and determine whether such cause is legal."[355] Habeas corpus became the safety valve, the insurance policy built into the system to check that the individuals and agencies charged with enforcing the law do so within constitutional boundaries.

Habeas corpus is enshrined in the United States Constitution, which provides that, "The privilege of the Writ of Habeas Corpus shall not be suspended, unless when in Cases of Rebellion or Invasion the public Safety may require it."[356]

By contrast, the Bill of Rights—the cornerstone of most modern criminal procedure—was not passed until 1791, some three years after the Constitution was fully ratified. Citizens of the United States have lived under the protective blanket of habeas corpus since the country won its independence. Only during one dark period of American history was habeas corpus in danger—the Civil War, when President Abraham Lincoln suspended habeas corpus to allow him to battle insurgents and rebels unimpeded. So it would be to the Civil War–era case of *In re Milligan* that the parties, and the Supreme Court, would turn for guidance.

"The echoes of centuries of Anglo-Saxon struggle for civil liberties, from the Magna Carta onward will be heard in the Supreme Court chambers tomorrow when the justices will be asked to decide whether they will entertain habeas corpus pleas from seven of the eight defendants charged with sabotage and now on trial before a military commission."[357]

On the morning of July 30, 1942, the day the Supreme Court was scheduled to hear the case, requests for passes to the Supreme Court building far outnumbered the three hundred seats that were available. Those who managed to obtain one of the coveted passes

National Archives/United States Army Signal Corps

J. Edgar Hoover, Director of the FBI, seated behind Attorney General Biddle during the trial.

walked into the air-cooled courtroom, leaving the sweltering heat of a Washington, D.C., summer day behind. Most of the observers probably did not notice the two dozen or so FBI agents who had taken up strategic positions around the courtroom.[358] Many had come in the hope of being part of history and others for a chance to ogle the Nazi invaders. They didn't realize that the Supreme Court, the highest appellate court in the land, was not a trial court and that no witnesses would appear at this hearing. Tight security was put in place, however, despite the fact that the seven petitioners, the accused Nazis whose story was blazing across the headlines of papers around the country, would not appear, either.

As the parties approached the court, they were greeted by the now familiar press contingent, which clamored in vain for comments from the attorneys. Colonel Royall wore a "wound stripe" on the sleeve of his uniform tunic, the insignia a reminder of his service in World War I as a lieutenant in the 317th Field Artillery of the Eighty-first "Wildcat Division."[359] In addition to the lawyers arguing the case, FBI Director J. Edgar Hoover was seen confidently climbing the stairs in a light suit and white fedora, accompanied by his aide Clyde Tolson.[360] Hoover, who had sat in every meeting of the commission, made sure the justices registered his personal interest in the case.

Every seat in the court was occupied. Several of the audience members were officers in uniform who were allowed to attend only after receiving special permission.[361] Colonel Royall's wife and daughter, who had come from North Carolina to see him argue before the highest court in the country, sat in the gallery.[362] Seven justices, wearing the black robes of their office, walked out into the courtroom as the Court was called to order, "The Honorable, the Chief Justice and the Associate Justices of the Supreme Court of the United States!"

Nine justices comprise the full court, but Justice Murphy had recused himself because of his service in the army, while the seat of Justice Douglas, who was en route from Oregon, remained empty. Now the justices stood behind their high-backed chairs as the crier completed the call to order. "Oyez! Oyez!! Oyez!!! All persons having business before the Honorable, the Supreme Court of the

United States, are admonished to draw near and to give attention, for the Court is now sitting. God save the United States and this Honorable Court!"

The hearing in the venerable halls of the Supreme Court started with an unusual twist. Justice Stone began on the record: "I am informed that my son, who is an officer in the army, was assigned to participate in the defense. Of course if that fact were regarded as ground for my not participating in the case, I should at once disqualify myself [sic]. In order that I may be advised and that the Court may be advised whether he has participated in this proceeding and what his connection with this case is, I will ask you, if you are so advised, to state, so that it may become of record."[363]

Each side assured the chief justice that the service of his son, Major Lauson Stone, should not disqualify him from hearing the case. Spectators leaned forward to hear what was being said in the Court—the imposing Supreme Court building, in service only seven years at the time of this hearing, was known for its bad acoustics. A legal hush fell on the hall as the chief justice announced that the Court's usual one-hour-per-side time limit on arguments would be lifted due to the importance of the issues involved in the case.[364]

The two lead lawyers were a study in contrasts. Biddle was a lean and tan figure in a light-colored vested suit, showing his customary air of aloofness and noblesse oblige, a blueblood in service to his country.[365] The attorney general was assisted by Major General Myron C. Cramer.

Royall was in almost every way Biddle's polar opposite. He may have only worn his officer's uniform for two months since returning to the army, but it perfectly fit his powerfully built frame. Tall and deep-voiced, he gave an impression of power and commitment to a cause. But, to mute a self-confidence that might otherwise skirt self-righteousness, Royall accentuated his southern drawl and sprinkled his speech with homespun references to his North Carolina country roots to ingratiate himself to his listeners.[366] Royall was assisted in the Supreme Court by Colonel Cassius Dowell and Colonel Carl L. Ristine.

Although this was his first appearance before the Court, Royall was already known to one of the justices. The noted scholar and proponent of judicial restraint, Justice Frankfurter, had been Royall's law professor at Harvard. Time and again during the hearing he would pepper Royall with questions, pressing his former student to define his terms and expand convincingly on the legal ramifications of his arguments.[367]

Taking care not to offend the Court, but stating his case as decisively as he dared, Royall devoted a large portion of the opening phase of his presentation to arguing that the Supreme Court did have jurisdiction to receive the defendant's petitions for habeas corpus. As Royall made his arguments explaining his rush to get the case before the Court, he treaded carefully because he did not want to voice his true fear—that the defense lawyers would not learn of the final decision of the military commission until after the president had made his order and the sentences carried out.[368]

The themes of his case were the same as those he had advocated before the generals of the commission. He argued that first and foremost, the seven petitioners had the same rights to apply for a writ of habeas corpus as any other person in the United States, for the president's order of July 2, establishing the military commission to try the eight men, was illegal and unconstitutional on several grounds. First, the order depriving them of the right of access to the courts made the order unconstitutional. Second, the use of a military commission to try the eight men was contrary to the law and therefore illegal, and any crime that the men might be culpable of could only be prosecuted in the civil courts.[369]

As Royall built his arguments concerning the jurisdiction of the commission, Chief Justice Stone interrupted the defense lawyer with a question to Biddle:

"Does the attorney general challenge the jurisdiction of the Court?"

Biddle replied without hesitation, "I do not."

The chief justice moved the argument from this point by saying that the Court did not have to deal with the issue at once.[370]

Justice Jackson—who would later serve as the Chief Prosecutor for the Nuremberg Tribunals and argue his case before Biddle, who would serve as a judicial officer of that tribunal—stated that, in his opinion, if the men invaded America and had been shot while landing, it would not have been murder. Colonel Royall quickly responded that all the same, once the men landed and mingled with members of the public, they were entitled to access to the civil courts.[371]

The exchange between Jackson and Royall continued, with Jackson asking from the bench: "Why are not these men all members of an invading force and subject to the law of war?"

Royall was quick to respond, "Because they do not admit they were an invading force, but only used this as a means to get out of Germany."

Jackson did not hesitate to challenge and push the defense attorney. "They did not report to any authority and say, thank God, they were from Germany?"

Royall could only respond, "No."[372]

The argument then turned to one of the more technical points of the defense, the contention that the Articles of War, upon which the prosecution was premised, only applied to activities in a theatre of operations, or in other words, a war zone. Royall argued that a review of the War Department's paperwork did not reveal a declaration that the East Coast of the United States was a theatre of military operations.

Justice Jackson swiftly challenged Royall, asking, "Where is this war if it is not along the Atlantic seaboard?"

The North Carolinian unfurled his southern charm, hoping to change the tack of the questioning. "I have heard it is across the water," he replied.

Justice Frankfurter pursued his old student on this point. "Cannot the enemy determine the theatre of operations?" Before accepting an answer, Frankfurter pressed on. "Suppose parachutists were to land in the building, wouldn't that make this a theatre of operations?"

"Yes, sir," was Royall's response.

"Why didn't this landing [then] create a theatre of operations?" asked the justice.

"Because they came unarmed and did not engage in combat operations."

Frankfurter seized upon Royall's answer, bearing in mind the host of explosive devices the Nazis had brought into the country. "I am glad to know what 'unarmed' is," he said. The courtroom broke into laughter.

Jackson reentered the fray expressly to highlight the point that the intent of the Germans could not be innocent, since they landed with TNT. In a foreshadowing of his decision, he asked if the authorities had to "wait until the explosives are set off."[373]

By the end of the first day's session, the discussions turned to the differences between spying, sabotage, and espionage. The justices asked if there was in fact a great need to determine the difference between the terms, as they are, in many cases, used interchangeably. Royall answered that the difference was indeed very important to the seven petitioners, as it could mean the difference between thirty years in jail and mandatory death.[374]

Royall's line of argument was in reference to the statutes of the day, which had been written with spying as the greatest fear. The main concern of the legislation to that date had been the loss of key information—military secrets. The notion that Nazis would ever be walking through the streets of New York or Washington, D.C., with TNT and plans of destruction had never been contemplated.

The arguments continued the next day in a courtroom only half as full as the day before. Perhaps it was the broiling summer heat outside that drove spectators away. Perhaps those who were hoping to catch a glimpse of the Nazi invaders lost interest when they learned the defendants would not be in court. Or perhaps it was just that, as the arguments turned toward technical legal points, those who craved the sensational departed, seeking more lurid entertainment elsewhere.

Biddle continued advancing the theory that the eight men were Nazi soldiers, nothing more and nothing less. He pointed out that all of them were German-born and had lived in the United States, only to return to their homeland, where they chose to join the German army and train for their mission. He argued that, "[t]rained in a German sabotage school, they came here wearing fatigue clothes of the German marines so that if arrested as they landed, they could make the claim they were prisoners of war. They forfeited that right when they changed to civilian garb."[375]

Royall touched on every point he could make in his attack on the commission. He argued that the appointment of Major General Cramer, the judge advocate general, made the commission invalid as the law provided that appeals to decisions made by military judicial bodies were to be made to the judge advocate general. He also attempted to portray the Nazis in a more sympathetic light, reminding the justices that the Germans had thrown Burger in a detention camp and that Haupt was just a boy who had gotten into trouble with a girl in Chicago and had fled to Mexico, where he was persuaded to return to Germany.

Justice Jackson stepped back into the argument regarding the Germans' intent in coming to America. He ruled that those decisions could not be made on the "cold record" and must be made by the seven men, the generals on the commission, who sat across from the accused and watched and listened to the evidence presented.

The questions and replies continued up until five minutes to four that afternoon when Colonel Royall, having exhausted all his possible arguments, took his seat at counsel table, closed his books, and put away his legal pads. Chief Justice Stone then announced that the Court would be in recess until the next day at noon and the justices filed out of the room.[376]

Columnists and legal scholars across the country debated and predicted what the court would do. Some cited the discussion of the Civil War precedent as conclusive evidence that the justices would agree with the government's position, while others would not even venture a guess.

On July 31, 1942, the third day of the hearing, the line of those waiting to see and hear the Nazis' lawyers was the shortest it had been all week. Precisely at noon, Chief Justice Stone took the bench with his brethren after the crier called the court to order. He picked up several typewritten sheets that had been on the bench and began to read.[377] Justice Stone delivered the opinion of the court after a preamble detailing the origins of the motions:

> The court has fully considered the questions raised in these cases and thoroughly argued at the bar, and has reached its conclusion upon them. It now announces its decision and enters its judgment in each case, in advance of the preparation of a full opinion which will require a considerable period of time for its preparation and which will be filed with the clerk.
>
> The court holds:
>
> (1) That the charges preferred against petitioners on which they are being tried by military commission appointed by the order of the President of July 2, 1942, allege an offense or offenses which the President is authorized to order tried before a military commission.
>
> (2) That the military commission was lawfully constituted.
>
> (3) That petitioners are held in lawful custody, for trial before the military commission and have not shown cause for being discharged by writ of habeas corpus.
>
> The motions for leave to file petitions for writ of habeas corpus are denied.
>
> The orders of the District Court are affirmed. The mandates are directed to issue forthwith.[378]

Chief Justice Stone laid the papers back down on the bench at 12:04 P.M., and adjourned the court. The seven Germans' last effort to have their cases heard in the civil courts had failed.

Biddle, in a rare public display of emotion, was visibly elated by the affirmation of the president's decision. A glum Colonel Royall packed to go back and finish the case before the commission. To the end of his days Royall would consider this appearance before the Supreme Court the high point of his legal career—"his failure to get a group of reviled Nazis a fair American trial."[379] But his only comment on that unforgiving summer day in Washington was, "The Court has acted."[380]

In the News Today

DETROIT, MICH., July 26, 1942—Federal agents today raided the homes of sixty enemy aliens in the Detroit area, seizing guns, cameras, binoculars, and short-wave radio sets. This operation was part of one hundred and twenty raids conducted by G-men in this area to find spies.[381]

INDIANAPOLIS, IND., July 27, 1942—Fascist Silver Shirt leader William Dudley Pelley issued a surprising number of subpoenas today in his sedition trial. The anti-Semitic publisher subpoenaed noted aviator Charles Lindbergh, Federal Reserve Board Chairman Marriner S. Eccles, Major General Van Horn Moseley-United States Army Retired, and former United States Senator Rush D. Holt as witnesses sympathetic to his cause.[382]

CHAPTER 10

Invaders or Refugees?

The prosecution, through Judge Advocate General Cramer, began the summation of the case at 10:00 A.M. on Friday, July 31, 1942. The general framed his arguments plainly and simply, acknowledging that this was the first military commission to be held in seventy-one years.[383]

There was no question that Ernst Peter Burger, George John Dasch, Herbert Hans Haupt, Heinrich Harm Heinck, Edward John Kerling, Hermann Otto Neubauer, Richard Quirin, and Werner Thiel had entered the United States by stepping onto a beach after crossing the Atlantic in the belly of a U-boat. The question that each of the defendants posed was, why had they come back to America?

Every criminal trial has its own rhythm and feel; the mix of defendant, prosecutor, defense counsel, and judge always comes together to create a separate being that is a combination of them all. But this trial was marked from the start by its main character, one that overshadowed all the other players and every argument, witness, and piece of evidence: World War II.

The fractures that war causes in the foundation of a nation are the reason why military commissions are constituted. In 1942, those fissures were evident in cities and towns throughout the country,

National Archives/United States Army Signal Corps

From left to right: Thiel, Quirin, army guard, Neubauer, and Kerling in court.

where small white flags decorated the windows of many cottages, houses, and apartments. A blue star in the center of a flag let everyone know a man from that home was in the army, navy, or air corps fighting for America and her allies. With greater frequency, those flags were being exchanged for others that bore a gold star—the grim symbol that meant the serviceman had given his life for his country. Not unexpectedly, newspaper editorials and opinion polls blared the public's lust to convict and execute the defendants.[384]

As General Cramer took up the prosecution's cudgel, he acknowledged that the case was unusual because the eight defendants stood accused primarily on the weight of their own statements. Yet he also pointed out that there were mounds of evidence in the case. The question was how to interpret that evidence in light of the statements of the defendants. As Cramer phrased it, "they claim that instead of being invaders, they are refugees."[385]

In the movies, trials most often turn on the question of identity: *Who* committed the crime? In real life, however, most trials hinge on intent: *Why* was the crime committed? A convincing snapshot of the mind of the defendant at the moment of the commission of the crime can make the difference between manslaughter and murder, acquittal and death.

Any good prosecutor weaves a powerful story in his opening argument. Cramer's story was a compelling one—a tale of betrayed countries, Nazi High Command, sabotage schools, and submarines. He concluded by arguing, "The prosecution submits upon the evidence that we have made out a case for which we ask on each of these charges and specifications a finding of guilt and a sentence in these cases of death."[386]

Colonel Royall rose on behalf of the defense. He began by noting the challenge the lawyers faced in representing seven defendants at the same time. In many multi-defendant criminal cases, the best defense for one may be antagonistic to the interests of the others on trial. Effective representation was not possible in this trial— to paraphrase a popular Benjamin Franklin adage, either they would all hang together or they would each hang separately.

Royall reminded the commission of its unique position as the court of first and last resort. Since the United States Supreme Court rejected the appeals of the saboteurs, the general officers sitting in judgment of the eight men would hear their final arguments. If the commission reached a verdict of guilt on the defendants, only the President of the United States could alter their ordained fate.[387]

Royall argued that the eight defendants—eight Germans, two of whom were American citizens—had been captured through the "very excellent preventative work which had been done by the Federal Bureau of Investigation . . . [which] makes it impossible for any similar plan to succeed in the future. Therefore it is not necessary to punish these men as a preventative measure for any probable repetition of this offense."[388] Royall urged the generals not to reflect on the preventative merit that the conviction of the defendants would achieve, but to reflect instead upon the precedent that the commission would achieve with its decision.

In an argument that would bring shock to a current courtroom and invite accusations of intolerance and anti-Semitism, Royall reasoned that Americans might learn how to treat their prisoners from the way Germans treated theirs.

> It was true in the last war, as all of you know better than I do, that the Germans, in their treatment of Englishmen, adopted a much higher standard and a fairer standard than they did as to any other nation. There may be something in the Teutonic origin of the race; I do not know. It may be an inherent feeling of similarity in our heredity. The same thing was true of their treatment of Americans; and history and common knowledge show today that the matters with which Germany is charged, that is, atrocities, do not concern the English people nor the English-speaking people, but concern the Slav races largely and, to a lesser extent, the Latin races of occupied France.[389]

Royall then turned to an argument of prevention and circumspection, stressing that the manner in which the commission treated these defendants would affect American soldiers. "I think it is legitimate for this commission to take it into account, when we will probably send ten boys on similar missions for every one that Germany has or can send, realizing the fact that the decision in this case may establish a criterion which will be applicable, ten to one, to our own boys who are going overseas," he argued. "That is a legitimate consideration in this matter."[390]

From that point on, the two sides positioned themselves in the classic posture of a criminal case. The prosecution focused on the basics of the defendants' conduct and the external ramifications of the results of the case. From that perspective, when the eight men clambered out of the steel hatch of the U-boat and paddled onto American beaches, they had sealed their fate.

The defense concentrated on the men's intent and on the process used to convict them. Placing the importance of process above the facts is one of the riskiest moves in the criminal justice system. The notion that legal procedure can be as important to the interests of a free society as the impact of the criminal acts of a defendant, if not more so, can be a difficult pill to swallow. This difficulty is compounded when the country is in a state of war and the accused come wearing the uniform of a nation sworn to destroy the United States.

The defense argued that at worst the men had attempted to commit a crime. Colonel Royall pointed out that, "These men may have planned something, but they have not done any terrible thing. They prepared to do some things, which, if accomplished, might have been terrible. But they have not done it."[391]

Royall's argument takes a very limited view of the crimes of terror and sabotage. The defense wanted the members of the

National Archives/United States Army Signal Corps

Peter Burger sitting in the commission hearing room.

commission to focus only on the physical targets of the Nazis' mission: the stores, plants, and railroads. Terrorism, however, carries with it a psychological component that can be nearly as damaging to a nation as the destruction of bricks and mortar. Experts define terrorism and sabotage as unique crimes, with definite political and military purposes.[392] The obliteration of an enemy's resources is only part of the motive behind these acts. The famed historian Carl von Clausewitz, when discussing the definition and purpose of war, wrote: "If we desire to defeat the enemy, we must proportion our efforts to his power of resistance. This is expressed by the product of two factors which cannot be separated, namely, the sum of available means and the strength of the Will."[393]

The mission assigned to the terrorists of Operation Pastorius by the German High Command addressed each of von Clausewitz's goals. They were sent to attack the light metal industry of the United States, so critical to the construction of aircraft—the same aircraft that would rain thousands of tons of bombs down on the German homeland and reduce Dresden to rubble.

Yet Dasch, Kerling, and their teams also had been ordered to bomb department stores and other high-profile targets, locations that had little, if any, military significance, yet targets that if destroyed would strike fear into the heart of the enemy—America. Terrorism, it can reasonably be argued, is the one crime that in most cases is accomplished as soon as the terrorist ventures out of his door. This is because the intertwined goals of terrorism—the physical act of destruction and the psychological attack on public morale—can exist independently. When the terrorist leaves his home, if he completes his act and is successful, he has accomplished both of his goals. If the saboteur is captured along the way, the news of his intent and capture can infect his enemy with nearly the same result as if he had been successful. The mere fact that he exists, is prepared, and has begun his mission can instill great fear in his enemy. Only if the terrorist's acts are kept secret from the public can the psychological effect of the crime be greatly diminished.

The president, FBI director, and the attorney general, who approached the case as part of the war effort—and kept details of it a secret until well after the end of the war—recognized this dynamic.

The defense countered by declaring that when the eight men shed their Nazi uniforms on the beaches of Long Island and Ponte Vedra, they also shed their status as soldiers, and should therefore be subject to the same system of justice as any other criminal. The defense focus was clearly on the role of the individual men and their conduct over the short weeks they were in the United States. Royall argued,

> We believe that these men have done nothing, if we take every word and every inference of the prosecution's contentions to be correct, that warrants the infliction of the death penalty. They did not hurt anybody. They did not blow up anything. They did not affect the conduct of the war, except by the fact that they came over here and enabled us to take preventative measures, which will help our conduct of the war. But if it be said that their intentions were bad, according to the prosecution, the law has always drawn a distinction between what a man intends and what a man does.[394]

Colonel Ristine then rose to argue for Dasch. He echoed themes present in Dasch's statements from the moment that he first spoke to Traynor at FBI headquarters. Ristine told the impassive commissioners that Dasch was not committed to the mission, that he had planned to give himself up to the Americans, and would never have carried out his instructions.

Ristine reminded the commission of the promises the FBI had made to Dasch—if he pled guilty and remained quiet, he would receive a presidential pardon after three to six months. FBI agents had testified that Dasch was told if he cooperated with the government, his father and mother would be cared for if found in Allied-controlled territory.[395] Ristine read the following testimony from Agent Wills into the record:

> Q: And what did you say to him with reference to if he would plead, what would happen, what was told to him exactly?
> A: As I recall the substance, he was told that if he appeared in federal court and entered his pleas of guilty and be sentenced along with

the other defendants, that after a period of about six months, efforts would be made to get a presidential warrant, or that he would get a presidential warrant [sic]—a presidential pardon.

Ristine turned to another portion of testimony:

Q: Did anybody promise him anything?
A: Yes, sir. Mr. Donegan, on the afternoon of Saturday, June 27th, told defendant Dasch that he would be indicted and appear before a federal court, that at that time he should enter his plea of guilty, or if he entered his plea of guilty and he was sentenced to prison along with the others that through the FBI a presidential pardon would be obtained for him.[396]

Colonel Royall finished the argument for the defense by seizing on the promises made to Dasch as it related to the FBI's evaluation of the case. It was a well-established method of argument in a criminal trial, where every piece of evidence can be simultaneously a sword against an opponent's case and a shield to defend against his arguments. The promises made to Dasch not only afforded an opportunity to argue a reliance on an agreement with the government, it was also an evaluation of the worth of the case by the investigators of the primary law enforcement agency. Royall pressed forward with the classic legal gambit:

The suggestion of the FBI as to the plea of guilty was not made to this Commission; it was made in connection with a civil court. . . . I think, however, it is very material that the FBI was of the opinion that Dasch ought not to have any material punishment. They had studied the case very carefully. It was brought out on cross-examination that they had studied it for eight days. They had the statements of practically all of these defendants at that time, and they knew the thing from top to bottom, and they certainly were diligent on behalf of the government and they felt that Dasch ought not be punished in any material degree at that time, to such extent that that promise was made, according to Mr. Wills.[397]

Royall then pressed the promises made to Dasch into service to justify lesser punishment for Burger, who had given the FBI a great deal of information without the seeming manipulations that filled Dasch's self-serving statements. Royall argued that, with the promise of six months of jail time to Dasch as the benchmark, Burger should receive even less time in jail.[398]

National Archives/United States Army Signal Corps

Herbert Haupt and George Dasch in the courtroom guarded by Lt. Meekin, United States Army.

Before addressing the plight of his other clients, Royall told the commission he had compiled a list of thirty-seven inconsistent statements made by the FBI agents who testified during the trial. He cleverly argued that the existence of so many holes in the FBI testimony should not be taken as a condemnation of the Bureau. If men surely as dedicated and well trained as the agents of the Federal Bureau of Investigation could amass such a large number of inaccuracies in their testimony, then any mistakes and inconsistencies in the testimony of the eight defendants could be well understood if not

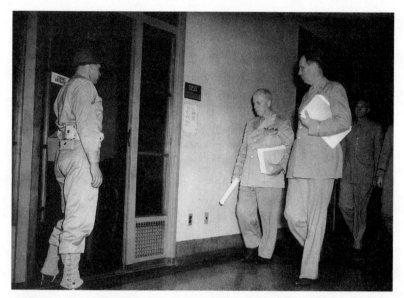

Defense counsel Colonel Cassius Dowell (left) and Colonel Kenneth Royall (right) enter the courtroom.

expected. Referring to inconsistent statements between several of the special agents, Royall argued: "That does not mean that either one of these men is untruthful or subject to censure. It just means that they understood it [referring to promises made to Dasch] differently. But if that can occur with an agency as careful as the FBI certainly is, it can occur with men of this type."[399]

Royall turned back to familiar themes in an attempt to mitigate the characterization of the men as invaders and terrorists. He argued that since Neubauer's wife was an American and had never become a German citizen, it was evidence that they planned all along to settle down and live in the United States.[400]

With regard to Haupt, the youngest of the invaders, Royall suggested that his "difficulty with a girl" precipitated his later mistakes. "She became pregnant, and he did what many other 21-year-old boys would have done: he left and went down to Mexico." The defense lawyer elaborated this theme further: "You see, we were not at war with Germany when he went. He landed there the day war was declared and was immediately viewed with suspicion. He was a young boy, and all his ties were here. He tried to get back to America, and this was the only way in which he could do so."[401]

Royall continued, "Well, he had two motives. He did not want to go to [sic] concentration camp, and he wanted to get back to America. That was where his mother and father were, and most 21-year-old boys want to be with their parents if they have no family of their own." Royall was hammering the point that Haupt was young and naïve. "He did not know a boy his age in Germany except for the boy who came with him. He did not know anybody else his age. He did not have any close family connection of any kind. So, he took this up with no intention of carrying out the plan."[402]

The North Carolina lawyer took a different tack with Peter Burger. This was not a young and immature man, but a strong and frank person of substance who helped convict the real saboteurs.

> Burger is in this situation. He is a proven man of character in this country. He served two enlistments in the national guard in different states. Not only did each of his commanding officers give him a character of excellent, but they went out of the way to add a note, and one of them said, "Exceedingly reliable and trustworthy. . . ." Not only is that true, but when he was leaving they wrote him a special letter commenting upon his integrity. After he had gone to Germany his commanding officer wrote him there and told him the high regard in which he was held by his comrades and commanders, and he stated to him, "I am sorry that you were out [of] work and had to go on that account. Conditions have now improved. It looks like you picked a bad time."[403]

The defense lawyer noted that Burger had testified fully in the case, taking the stand during the Prosecution's case-in-chief. He described Burger as a

> soldier, a soldier in his personal and family relationships and in every relationship. He was a soldier over here, and as long as they were treating him decently and treating him like a soldier, he was a soldier in Germany. But as soon as they started killing his soldier friends— friends he had served in the street fightings [sic] and skirmishes that started the Nazi party, and he had been decorated for it—after they

killed his comrades and his leader, then he had the natural desire that anybody would have to get out of Germany and get away from it.[404]

One can only speculate what must have been the expressions of the commissioners as they heard this improbable argument, which tried to turn the brutal terror of the Storm Troopers into a soldier's duty. As if sensing their disbelief, Royall hurried to paint Burger's life in a concentration camp and his desire to flee from the Nazis and come to America. He then turned to each of his other clients, once more referring to Haupt's youth and inexperience, and the others' ties with the United States.

Royall closed his argument by again reminding the commission of the challenge he and the defense team had in being assigned to represent multiple defendants with conflicting defenses. "Now, it has been a difficult task to argue all these defendants. It is difficult to be fair to all of them and present the case of one. We have sought to do it. We are convinced that they are different. We are convinced that none of them should receive the severe penalty. With that remark we leave the matter to the commission."[405]

This argument has to be considered within the context of modern criminal law practice. The right to the effective assistance of counsel is one of the most revered principles of American criminal law. The Sixth Amendment provides, "[i]n all criminal prosecutions, the accused shall enjoy the right . . . to have the Assistance of Counsel for his defense."[406]

With that, Royall sat down, and for a moment only the hum of the newly installed air conditioners could be heard. The saboteurs' side of the case was done.

As is customary in criminal cases, the prosecution rose for the last word and to rebut the defense arguments. The judge advocate general was first to address the commission. General Cramer walked them carefully through the case, reiterating the prosecution theory—these men came to the United States as an invading force with the objectives, uniforms, and equipment of soldiers and saboteurs. They had many opportunities to give themselves up, but it was only

Dasch and Burger who turned themselves in. The rest never stopped acting as Nazi soldiers, trained and sent across the ocean, waiting only for the right time to start killing Americans.[407]

Aristocratic Attorney General Biddle would be the last lawyer to argue in the case. This case would not be the last major trial that Francis Biddle would be involved in, however. In 1945, he was appointed a member of the tribunal at Nuremberg. He served as one of the judicial officers to hear the trial and pronounce judgments in the first modern criminal case to consider and litigate crimes against humanity and war crimes.

Nuremberg was another trial in which the theory of conspiracy was a foundation of the prosecution's case. There, Biddle was wary of the Nuremberg prosecutors' efforts to convict the defendants on a conspiracy theory. "I had learned to distrust conspiracy indictments, which in our country were used too often by the government to catch anyone however remotely connected with the substantive crime. I had seen them resorted to, particularly when I was an Assistant United States Attorney in Philadelphia, far too casually and without any clear sense of responsibility," he recalled.[408]

The defendants in the Nuremberg Tribunal were the architects of the Reich—infamous names such as Hermann Göring, Rudolf Hess, and Albert Speer. Biddle, one of the judicial officers who delivered the sentences in the tribunal, wrote of that experience, "[s]tanding there before us they behaved like men. I felt sick and miserable. We had seen them day-in and day-out for a year. What right had I . . . I knew they deserved it."[409]

Yet, in the case of these eight men, Biddle showed no hesitation, urging the commissioners that,

> You must remember that these defendants were not men who were caught in the war and were seeking to get back here. They, with their past associations with the Bund, their German citizenship, their background and action in the German army, all went, except one, before the war between us and Germany broke out. They went over to join Germany.
>
> Perhaps they are soldiers. Perhaps they are young. Perhaps they are neurotic. But, nevertheless, they came over here and went behind

our lines as spies and saboteurs. To say that you cannot find that because they now tell you, without any corroboration, that they never intended to do any of this—it seems to me that if every essential fact is considered, all the talk about details is highly unnecessary.[410]

A few administrative details were then attended to, and the trial was recessed for the lunch hour. The commission reconvened for the last time at 2:24 P.M. on August 3, 1942. The hearing lasted one minute, with the president of the commission stating: "The prosecution and defense having nothing further to offer, the Commission is closed."[411]

The defense filed a request with the commission that before any verdict in Burger's case was rendered, the president consult with the attorney general and the judge advocate general of the army. Seven of the Nazis filed a three-page application for clemency for the president's review. The petition, signed by Haupt, Heinck, Kerling, Neubauer, Quirin, and Thiel was a request to "respectfully petition your Excellency for clemency or leniency in connection with such sentence (in case of conviction) as may be imposed by the Military Commission."[412] Dasch did not join in the application for clemency. Ristine told the commission that if convicted, Dasch wanted to be shot.

General McCoy, General Cramer, and Oscar Cox then carried the original transcript of the commission to the White House, along with the sealed recommendations and verdicts of the members of the commission. They were delivered to Marvin McIntyre of the president's staff with the understanding that they would be taken to Roosevelt at Hyde Park.

The fate of the eight Nazis was now in the hands of the president of the United States.

CHAPTER 11

"We're Here
to Help!"

The clanging thunder and the pounding, almost viscous rain the evening of August 7, 1942, could not muffle the loud and persistent bell heard deep inside the Washington, D.C., district jail. The FBI and the army had carefully scripted the day's critical events, and unannounced visitors were not in the plan. Armed guards responding to the main door were surprised to encounter John Martin, a demanding British seaman far from his usual duties in Her Majesty's Royal Navy. Dripping wet and more than a little tipsy, he explained that he'd spent that Saturday walking through the heavy rain along with three American soldiers he knew from Bolling Field.

Prison guards hear many extraordinary requests, but John Martin was the first man who'd ever shown up asking to be admitted so that he could execute condemned men. Specifically, he wanted permission to come in and serve on a firing squad to execute the eight Nazis who had been convicted by the military commission. Allowing him and his friends to shoot the men, he explained, would save the American government some electricity. Seeing the surprised reaction of prison officials, Martin said he'd take his request to Winston Churchill, or if need be, even to FDR. Eventually Martin was made to understand that his offer could not be accepted and he walked away with his GI buddies, disappearing into the mists of history.[413]

Inside their individual cells, Dasch and his team were unaware of the commotion at the prison gates, the throng of reporters standing in the rain, even of the rain itself. As their guards brought them plates heaped with fried fish and cabbage, corn on the cob, and bread and butter, they must have suspected the verdict would not be a favorable one; nonetheless, their plates were returned clean to the army guards.

After the president took the findings of the commission under submission, the days that followed had been tense and full of speculation. While the army and FBI prepared to carry out whatever plans were decided, the president deliberated in his retreat in the Catocin Mountains of Maryland. Now, as always, he remained in full control of the proceedings, waiting for the right moment to announce what had always been a foregone conclusion.

Even the German government had commented on the trial. Nazi-controlled Rome Radio broadcast the following story, which was recorded in New York:

> Habeas corpus or real democracy: It is useful to stop from time to time and to consider the moral aspects of this war between two worlds and two principles, the democratic and the totalitarian one. These are at least as important as the material aspects.
>
> The democrats reproach the totalitarians with having suppressed the so-called civil guarantees, which protect the individual liberty of the citizen, but no guarantee has been suppressed in the totalitarian countries, where prosecution of political crimes has been entrusted to the regular courts, whose jurisdiction is clearly defined and regulated, while in the democratic countries there does not exist any rule or any limit.
>
> Let us see, instead, what the famous democratic guarantees are worth. In the United States a decision by the Supreme Court has denied the right of habeas corpus to eight persons arrested by military authorities on the accusation of planning premeditated sabotage.
>
> This would not be possible in a country with Roman law, where the crime under consideration does not exist, to begin with. No crime here can be considered in that way unless there is at least the beginning of consummation, but it is not enough.

By suppressing the habeas corpus for these eight individuals, they have legally abolished the habeas corpus for all American citizens of the United States for the duration of the war. But the habeas corpus is the only civil guarantee which can prevent the arrest and arbitrary killing of the people with Anglo-Saxon law. . . .

From now on all Americans who love their country will be persecuted without pity. Roosevelt, in his folly for bloodshed, has already contrived to have found by his G-men, a police force made up entirely of gangsters, a plot which would have as an aim to turn over the entire Pacific coast to the Japanese. He has his press state that the guilty number is 100,000. One can thus already foresee that each defeat he suffers at the hands of the tri-partite powers will cost the lives of further innocents.[414]

At 10:00 A.M. on Tuesday morning, August 4, Brigadier General Albert L. Cox, provost marshal of the military district of Washington, received a call from one of the lead prosecutors in the German saboteur case, Major General Myron C. Cramer, the United States judge advocate general. He asked Cox to meet him at his office as soon as possible. Fifteen frantic minutes later, General Cox and Major Thomas Rives of the provost marshal's staff walked into General Cramer's office. There they found Cramer with Colonel John Wier, Oscar Cox from the White House staff, Assistant FBI Director Ladd, Assistant Solicitor General Townsend, and a stenographer.

Mr. Cox, who was assistant to the president, informed General Cox that the president was going to order that six of the Nazis be executed by electrocution; the remaining two prisoners were to be sentenced to prison. The saboteurs scheduled to die were Haupt, Heinck, Kerling, Neubauer, Quirin, and Thiel. This order was consistent with the findings of the commission and recommendations by the attorney general. The commission had found all of the defendants guilty and had recommended that they all be executed. The attorney general had recommended lighter sentences for Dasch and Burger because of their cooperation.[415]

Cox said the president would not issue the orders imposing the sentences until sometime after Thursday afternoon, August 6—the executions would be carried out sometime after midnight. General Cox was thereby instructed to make the necessary preparations.

General Cox and Major Rives returned to their offices to begin their task, mindful of instructions to keep the matter secret. The country was waiting for the verdict. Every day since the commission had submitted its findings to the president, the papers had been carrying stories speculating on the future turn of events in the case. Cox and Rives had no intention of being the ones who leaked the secret to the hungry press.

The following day, General Cox called the White House to obtain the actual order of execution from the president. He was asked to wait, that he would receive it presently. General Cox ordered everyone else in place and remained in his office all day. Major Rives was sent to the prison with six chaplains, the executioners, and the medical personnel necessary to immediately carry out the commander in chief's orders—whenever they came in.

By 6:00 P.M., still not having received the order, General Cox packed up his things and left for home. He called the White House the moment he got there to inquire what had happened. Again, he was told to wait.

At 7:10 P.M., General Cox's phone rang. He picked it up, expecting to be told to proceed with the executions, but the White House staffer told him the earliest the executions would now take place would be Friday. General Cox called Major Rives and ordered the team to stand down, but again reminded Rives to make sure everyone involved knew that the matter required the utmost secrecy and that they should all go home to await further orders.

General Cox did not have to wait long. The following day he received a call from Captain J. L. McCrea, naval aide to the president, summoning him to the south entrance of the White House. Shortly after 1:00 P.M. on Friday, August 7, 1942, the provost marshal of the district of Washington made his way to the south entrance of the White House past the guards and military presence that had been a fixture since the war began. Captain McCrea walked out of the president's residence and toward the spot selected to meet the general.

The four gold embroidered stripes on his sleeves told Cox that he had found the right man. Captain McCrea handed Cox the president's orders and instructed him that he would receive the exact time of execution later.

Once again all the personnel necessary to carry out the executions were gathered at the district jail. They were told to report at 7:00 A.M. on Saturday morning, August 8. Late Friday night, Captain McCrea called the General with the exact time—the executions would be held the next day, at noon.

At 6:45 A.M. on August 8, Brigadier General Cox, wearing his crisply pressed summer khaki uniform, decorated by the stars of a general officer and by the ribbons signifying a career of distinguished service to his country, was escorted by a cadre of guards and men of God as he took an elevator to the Nazis' cells. The group walked gravely down the long cold corridor of the section of the jail that had been cleared to house the Nazi terrorists. Armed soldiers wearing

National Archives/United States Army Signal Corps

Heinrich Heinck waiting in the guardroom to enter court.

webbed ammo belts and steel helmets continually patrolled the corridors. The group spoke in low, hushed tones as it approached the prisoners' cells.[416]

The youngest Nazi was the first to receive the news. Herbert Haupt had been extremely nervous from the moment the commission had adjourned, which only emphasized his relative youth and inexperience. When Cox entered the cell, Haupt's agitation increased. He stood as the General pronounced the sentence: He would die with his comrades in the electric chair. Haupt froze, stunned and speechless. With a curt nod the general walked out of the room, leaving chaplain W. B. Adams behind to give Haupt his last rites.

Heinrich Harm Heinck had been calm throughout the trial. He had quietly listened to the evidence, watching the government's witnesses give their damning testimony one after another. Heinck had befriended his guards throughout the trial and even while awaiting sentence, telling them the proceeding had been fair and that he had been treated well in custody. He said he understood why they were being tried and that he really only wanted to know beforehand the day he would be shot. When Cox finally told Heinck the time and manner of his death, Heinck did not say another word.

The entourage then moved to the cell of the second team leader, Edward Kerling. In a manner befitting a good Nazi, Kerling had been self-possessed during the final week of the trial and in the days awaiting the verdict. He rose as Cox entered the cell and stood at attention while the General opened the sheaf of documents. Cox informed Kerling that it was the pronouncement of the Commission, as ratified by the president of the United States, that he die in the electric chair. Kerling listened, displaying no emotion, his implacable reserve still in place as Cox turned and left the cell.

In contrast to Kerling, Hermann Neubauer had been extremely jittery throughout the entire trial. He was visibly upset and anxious during the testimony before the seven generals. But now, on hearing that he would die in the electric chair like most of his team, Neubauer showed little emotion, other than a visible trembling.

The slap of the officer's hard-soled oxfords against the cement floor resounded down the corridors as the group marched on, its number reduced by one clergyman at each cell.

Richard Quirin was next to be told of his fate. He had remained stoic since the commission had adjourned. Again he displayed no emotion as Cox told him when, where, and how he was to die. Quirin's rage toward Dasch for turning in the teams to the FBI only manifested itself when he tried to convince a guard to smuggle out a letter before the execution. Quirin never did write the letter, but he told the young army guard he wanted to get the word out to his contacts in the United States that Dasch had "ratted" them out. That way, Quirin could die knowing Dasch would be taken care of when he was released from prison.

Cox continued his walk down the long hall. Werner Thiel had been very quiet from the moment the commission had adjourned, as if preparing himself for the inevitable. When his sentence was read, he stiffened as though the electric current were already coursing through him, but he said nothing. The Nazi only lowered his head and closed his eyes as Cox departed.

Dasch, on the other hand, had talked about this one moment more than any of the other prisoners. He was sure that his deal had finally come through and that the FBI would make good on its promise. Dasch would not have been surprised if J. Edgar Hoover himself had stepped into his cell, but instead it was General Cox who now entered.

Dasch rose to face the general. Very nervous, he wrung his hands and fidgeted about, but remained silent while the general opened the file and read him the sentence. He would not be executed but would spend the next thirty years of his life at hard labor. Dasch then began to speak very quickly, almost incoherently, babbling of the promises made to him by the FBI and Mr. Hoover, of his intent to help America, and once again asserted that he was, in fact, a very bad German and a very good American. Cox indulged Dasch for a few moments, and then lifted his hand to silence him. The sentence would stand.

Ernst Peter Burger was the last in line. As expected of a good soldier, he had been calm and reserved during the entire trial. Now, he stood as Cox entered his cell. The general read aloud the sentence of the commission. Burger would spend the rest of his natural life in prison working at hard labor. The prisoner listened to the sentence with the same unsettling calm that he had exhibited during the trial. He was silent as the general exited, his dreadful task completed.[417]

The plans for the executions were now put into action. Secrecy was the primary goal. The electric chair had been chosen, as it could be used under the most clandestine of circumstances. Hanging and death by firing squad had also been considered, but ultimately rejected; it was feared that a hanging or shooting at some military reservation might provoke a disturbance.

Every guard on shift at the district jail the night before was held over for double shifts. Ambulances were moved from Walter Reed Hospital to the jail so that the bodies could be rushed directly to the hospital morgue. Guards were stationed at each of the phones to prevent anyone from calling the press to tip them off about the impending executions.

The stark, empty execution chamber was prepared for the arrival of spectators. General McCoy and J. Edgar Hoover would be among those to witness the executions.[418] Twenty-four plain aluminum chairs were placed behind a large glass panel separating the electric chair from the rest of the assembly. The room had not been used in a while and it reeked of dust and must. Several large fans were brought in to clear the musty smell, which would soon be replaced by an odor more foul.

The executioners had been identified and their fees agreed to. There would be a principal executioner and three assistants. The executioner received $50 for each prisoner he electrocuted. The principal assistant received the same fee for each death, and the other assistant received $25 for each prisoner. Their identities would not be disclosed.

Early that morning, reporters clustered outside the old massive jail, looking up at the windows, waiting for the ominous dimming of the lights that signaled the chair was being used. As the reporters kept vigil, the prisoners were prepared for their sentences.

First, they were marched to their death cells one at a time. It was a long walk from the cells they had lived in during the trial to the death cells. They had to walk through several long halls and up and down several flights of stairs, which concerned General Cox. One or more of the prisoners might collapse on the harrowing walk. But the six condemned men made the trip without assistance. Each was escorted by two guards and the chaplain assigned to him.

Then the Germans were allowed to write letters to their families. As priests and ministers stood by, they were given a substantial meal with wine. The prisoners then had their heads shaved, and were bathed and given fresh clothing. The right leg of their trousers was slit to accommodate the straps from the chair.[419]

While the prisoners were eating their final dinner, 57,305 baseball fans in New York watched the Brooklyn Dodgers beat the Yankees 7 to 4 at the Army Relief game played at Polo Field. Shortly ~~Grounds~~ after 9:00 P.M., Umpire George Magerkurth signaled the game to end before the ninth inning, to comply with Army blackout regulations. Fans could be heard booing above the strains of "The Star-Spangled Banner." Some of the fans rose to their feet and lit matches as the national anthem resounded through the park.[420]

The execution chamber was ready, and the prisoners were again escorted one at a time.

As Haupt was being prepared for his death, he broke down and cried. Yet, when the guards came to his cell and swung open the heavy door, he quietly followed them to the execution chamber. At 12:01 P.M., Haupt was seated in the electric chair, strapped around the waist, hands, and ankles.

At 12:03 P.M., the current was applied. When the executioner threw the switch and the voltage hit him, Haupt stiffened and seemed to rise out of the chair. He then slumped down and his head leaned down to the left. Haupt was pronounced dead at 12:11 P.M. by Dr. A. Magruder MacDonald, the District of Columbia coroner who had been brought to the jail early that morning. FBI witnesses would later say that he had "walked to the chair like a real man."

At 12:18 P.M. the current was applied to Heinck, the calmest of the six who died. He talked to the guards up to the time of the execution and seemed outwardly collected, encouraging FBI witnesses to comment that he "exhibited a lot of courage." Perhaps his calm was actually resignation and a bit of relief—he had told all of those around him that he had expected to be executed for his crimes. He was pronounced dead at 12:21 P.M.

Kerling was next. At 12:27 P.M. he was walked to the electric chair. Standing ramrod straight, he declared he was proud to be a German. His only regret was that the mission had not succeeded and that he would do the same thing all over again if given the opportunity. After his death, Kerling was quickly removed from the chair and placed on an army cot that had been laid out for him. Even as Kerling was being covered by a sheet, the next man, Neubauer, was brought to the chair.

Unlike the other defendants, Hermann Neubauer was visibly nervous before his execution. He ate very little of his final meal. Instead, he smoked, his hands shaking so much he had a difficult time holding on to his cigarette. But as he walked out of his death cell, he regained his composure and marched quietly to the chair. Neubauer was electrocuted at 12:38 P.M. and pronounced dead at 12:41 P.M.

Quirin remained outwardly calm as he prepared for death, although his hands too were shaking. He collected himself and coldly stared at the spectators as he was escorted into the execution chamber and strapped into the chair. At 12:47 P.M., 10,000 volts surged through him for six seconds. A second shock was not necessary. At 12:54 P.M. the coroner pronounced Richard Quirin dead by electrocution.

Thiel was the final prisoner to be led into the room. To the end he was as inconspicuous in death as he had been in life. He walked quietly to the chair and remained calm as he was strapped in. The time of death was 1:04 P.M.[421]

At 1:20 P.M., just sixteen minutes after the last of the executions, the White House released the following statement:

> The President has completed his review of the findings and sentences of the military commission appointed by him July 2, 1942, which tried the eight Nazi Saboteurs.
>
> The President approved the judgment of the military commission that all of the prisoners were guilty and that they be given the death sentence by electrocution.
>
> However, there was a unanimous recommendation by the commission, concurred in by the Attorney General and the Judge Advocate General of the Army, that the sentence of two of the prisoners be commuted to life imprisonment because of their assistance to the government of the United States in the apprehension and conviction of the others.
>
> The commutation directed by the President in the case of Burger was to confinement at hard labor for life. In the case of Dasch, the President commuted the sentence to confinement at hard labor for thirty years.
>
> The electrocutions began at noon today. Six of the prisoners were electrocuted. The other two were confined to prison.
>
> The records in all eight cases will be sealed until the end of the war.

As the White House released this statement, President Roosevelt was entertaining guests at Shangri-la, his retreat in the Catocin Mountains of northern Maryland. The compound, which had been constructed on the site of a WPA project built to provide recreation for federal employees, would later be renamed Camp David by President Eisenhower, in honor of his grandson.

Roosevelt seemed calm and in fact joked with his guests. He told stories of appeals for clemency he had received when Governor of New York. He didn't speak of the Nazis' fates, however, until asked by one of his guests. He then joked that he had wanted a public hanging, as it would have been good for the morale of the country. All in all, Roosevelt seemed relieved and in a rather good, if morbid, mood.[422]

As the president's statement was being read to the press, two black ambulances pulled into the jail courtyard. The bodies of the executed Nazis were quickly loaded into the vans. Sirens sounded as the vans sped out, followed by several trucks loaded with armed soldiers. Reporters tailed them all the way to the grounds of the army hospital, where the gates were closed on the frustrated newshounds.[423]

After the executions, General Cox ordered that none of the people in the execution area of the jail be allowed to leave until he gave further notice. The staff was then assembled and told in no uncertain terms that they were to keep the events of the day under the utmost secrecy, as per the direct orders of the president of the United States. This obligation of secrecy would remain with them until the president himself lifted the order.

The night of the Nazis' execution, a group of people in New York stood and sang in the Nazis' honor—Germans being held in a detention camp on Ellis Island.‡ As news of the executions was announced to the country over the radio, the detainees gathered in the open area of the compound. They listened to speeches by activists Erich Fittkau and Adolph G. Schickert praising the terrorists as heroes and calling for revenge. Next, in defiance of the guards, they lit matches and began to sing:

Die Fahne hoch die Reihen fest geschlossen
S.A. marschiert mit ruhis festrem Schritt
Kam'raden die Rotfront und Reaktion erschosen
Marschier'n im Heist in undern Reihn mit

Die Strasse frei den braunen Batallionen
Die Strasse frei dem Sturmabteilungsmann
Es schau'n auf's Hackenkruez voll
Hoffung schon Millionen

Zum letzen Mal wird nun Appell geblasen
Zum Kampfe steh'n wir alle schon bereit
Bald flattern Hitler-fahnen Uber allen Stassen
Die Knechtschaft dauert nur mehr kurze Zeit.

---

‡Information regarding the internment of Germans and Italians can be found in Appendix 4.

It was the Horst Wessel song, the anthem of the Nazi party. Few if any of the army guards watching them probably knew—or cared—what the words of the song meant or how many of the saboteurs fervently believed in them.[424]

> Hold high the banner! Close the hard ranks serried!
> S.A. marches on with sturdy stride
> Comrades, by Red Front and Reaction killed, are buried,
> But march with us in image at our side.
>
> Gangway! Gangway! now for the Brown battalions!
> For Storm Troopers clear roads o'er the land!
> The Swastika gives hope to our entranced millions,
> The day for freedom and for bread's at hand.
>
> The trumpet blows its shrill and final blast!
> Prepared for war and battle here we stand.
> Soon Hitler's banners will wave unchecked at last,
> The end of German slav'ry in our land![425]

The Ellis Island detainees were not the only ones to react to the executions. That evening the British and American radio stations in London broadcast the news in several different languages to Europe that six of the agents sent to the shores of the United States had been swiftly found, captured, tried, and executed.

Herbert Haupt's parents, Hans Max Haupt and Erna Haupt, were confined in the Cook County Jail on $50,000 bail when their son was executed. United States Marshal William H. McDonnell told reporters that they would not be officially told of their son's death, but he was sure that they would learn of it through the jail "grapevine."[426]

Attorney General Francis Biddle made the most direct comment of any government official regarding the executions and sentences. He announced his plan to seek stiffer penalties for those convicted of conspiracy to commit sabotage and for those who harbored or assisted spies. Biddle said, "The proposed legislation would provide severer penalties for conspiracy to commit sabotage and for harboring or assisting saboteurs. In addition, the proposed legislation may establish machinery for speeding up prosecution of such cases and may provide [that] appeals be allowed only upon direction of the Supreme Court."[427]

The German government at first had little comment on the executions, merely saying that the deaths of the six Germans forfeited the rights of those who sought to condemn Nazis for the security measures adopted by the German army in occupied areas.[428]

In private, though, Hitler was furious at the failure of his pet project. He called in Canaris and the head of the Abwehr-II, Colonel Erwin van Lahousen, then railed at them in front of Himmler, for masterminding such a fiasco. They had chosen men who were obviously not qualified for the mission.

Ever sly, Canaris let his leader vent, and then he offered the excuse that the terrorists really had not been Abwehr men but untrained Nazis picked by the SS. This further enflamed Hitler, who screamed, "Why not use criminals or Jews?"

Canaris would later use Hitler's words to spirit Jews out of Germany, and from the grip of the Gestapo, under the cover of service for the Abwehr, arguing that it was being done under the orders of the Fuehrer himself.[429]

On August 12, the *Deutsche Diplomatisch Politische Korrespondence*, a part of the Nazi propaganda arsenal, condemned the American executions as the conviction and execution of men who had not even attempted sabotage. The broadcast went on to say that the United States was using measures at least as "rigorous" as those used by the German army and that the accusations of inhumanity leveled at the Nazis were pure hypocrisy.[430]

The reaction of the American public was strong and loud. Telegrams and letters arrived at the White House from all over the country, praising the president and the government for the swift retaliation.[431] As always, Roosevelt had correctly gauged the feelings of the average American. Even Special Agent Duane Traynor felt the right thing had been done—clemency had been shown to those who had cooperated, and stern justice had been meted out to those who sought to destroy the American fighting spirit.[432]

The morning after his comrades had been executed, Dasch was taken to breakfast in the old jail. He had been morose and bitter the entire day of the executions, complaining that the FBI had not kept its promise that he be given a clean slate after the trial. When told that the six men had died, Dasch dug into his hearty breakfast and spoke openly to his guards. He asked them over and over if they thought he had done the right thing by turning in the others to the FBI. With each forkful of food, he tried more vigorously to justify his conduct.

Later, a confidential FBI informant in the jail would write that Dasch had said that, on the evening of the executions, he died six deaths thinking about the ill-fated mission.[433]

The six agents of the Reich, Herbert Hans Haupt, Henry Harm Heinck, Edward John Kerling, Hermann Otto Neubauer, Richard Quirin, and Werner Thiel were buried in a potter's field in the District of Columbia, their graves marked only by numbers.

Less than a week later, on August 14, the first anniversary of the Atlantic Charter, President Roosevelt sent the following message to British Prime Minister Winston Churchill:

> When victory comes, we shall stand shoulder to shoulder in seeking to nourish the great ideals for which we fight. It is a worthwhile battle. It will be so recognized through all the ages, even amid the unfortunate peoples who follow false gods today.
>
> We reaffirm our principles. They will bring us to a happier world.[434]

In the News Today

NEW YORK, N.Y., July 27, 1942— The need to conserve has hit the home front. While Federal authorities today warned housewives of an alarming shortage of sugar supplies on the East Coast due to U-boat attacks in the Caribbean, the nation's homemakers are being urged to fight back. In the upcoming issue of *Ladies Home Journal* readers are being told that sugar cane is needed to make molasses. Molasses is used to make industrial alcohol, which is needed to make explosives. Explosives are needed to sink the Axis.[435]

CHAPTER 12

Writings from Sugar Hill

The *per curiam* opinion delivered to Biddle, Royall, and those who looked on from the gallery of the Supreme Court was not the full opinion of the court. The task to draft the full opinion in *Ex Parte Quirin* would be undertaken by Chief Justice Harlan Fiske Stone well after the executions had taken place.

President Calvin Coolidge had appointed the liberal justice to the Supreme Court in 1925, after Stone had served his administration with honors as the attorney general. When Stone took over Justice, the department was in deep disarray, racked by scandal and graft. He authorized a series of dramatic reforms, charging its execution to an ambitious lawyer in the FBI named John Edgar Hoover. The young bureaucrat—who would soon shorten his first name to an initial to avoid confusion with a criminal of the same name—did such an outstanding job that his interim appointment as director was made permanent and Hoover became a fixture of Washington life.[436]

President Roosevelt had expended considerable effort in building a Court that would embrace the New Deal, as well as support his dramatic new social programs. Despite the fact that he had not been one of FDR's selections for the court, Roosevelt appointed Stone to chief justice in 1941. He would continue to serve his country from the bench until struck with illness in 1946, just as Justice Douglas read the Court's opinion in *Girouard v. United States*, a case concerning the question of whether a conscientious objector was eligible for citizenship.[437] Stone was helped down from the bench by his brethren and died shortly thereafter.[438]

Having left Washington shortly after the special session of the Court that heard the end of the Nazi's appeal, the senior justice packed the necessary materials and documents he would need to draft his opinion and traveled by train in a cold Pullman car to his summer retreat at Peckett's in New Hampshire.[439]

Nestled in New England's White Mountains, Peckett's was an exclusive lodge decorated with fine antiques. Chief Justice Stone had even once said, "Sugar Hill is attractive and Peckett's comes as near as being a perfect place as any I ever saw."[440]

Stone knew that sorting through the law, politics, and facts of this case would be a formidable task. The chief justice complained about the job. In writing the case's briefs, he said that the lawyers "have done their best to create a sort of legal chaos." And of the litigants, he grumbled, "I hope the military is better equipped to fight the war than it is to fight its legal battles."[441]

Although he was in a serene environment and out of the bustle of wartime Washington, Stone was uncomfortable as he worked. He was in constant pain, suffering from a severe attack of lumbago.[442] Despite his physical discomfort, Stone was even more uncomfortable with the case he was working on. In crafting his opinion, Stone was forced to reconcile several statutes, well-established legal principles, and the Constitution. At times it seemed an impossible task, so much so that the Justice would call the effort a "mortification of the flesh."[443]

Stone was not only concerned with the legal precedent that would be established by his opinion—he was also very aware of the political impact of his decisions. He would later write of this struggle to Justice Frankfurter, saying, "My most serious difficulty, I passed over *sub silento*, in order to avoid indecent exposure of some very worthy gentlemen."[444]

In finding an approach to these issues, Stone wrestled hardest with some of the more technical, procedural, but all-important issues in the case. The arguments raised by the seven petitioners regarding the makeup of the commission and its rules of operation under the Articles of War particularly concerned him. He was unsure if the Court should even address the arguments surrounding the construction of the Articles of War because they raised serious questions about the procedures put in place by Roosevelt's order. The case could be adjudicated without becoming enmeshed in these thorny issues, but avoiding them also raised some troubling concerns.

Stone wrote:

> But whenever the facts do become known, as they ultimately will, the survivors, if still in prison, will be in the position to raise the question. If the decision should be in their favor it would leave the present Court in the unenviable position of having stood by and allowed six men to go to their deaths without making it plain to all concerned—including the President—that it had left undecided a question on which counsel strongly relied to secure petitioners' liberty.[445]

His challenge was to weave together an opinion that supported the Court's decision, while at the same time avoid the numerous legal minefields created by the case. In the end, Stone was not completely satisfied with his final product. "There were so many eggs in the case which I felt it necessary to avoid breaking that I am afraid the opinion was not good literature," he would later comment. "I hope you noticed that the opinion flatly rejected (as unobtrusively as possible) the president's comment that no court should hear the plea of the saboteurs."[446]

Justice Stone found himself dealing with an area of the law that had remained static since the Civil War—one that, with the stroke of his pen, might weaken the powers of a president charged with guiding the nation through the most terrible war in world history. Or, on the other hand, one that would limit the basic constitutional guarantees afforded to those charged with crimes by the government of the

United States: It was truly a Hobson's choice. Support the president in his fight against fascism or limit the rights of American democracy.

As Cicero said, "*Inter arma silent leges*"—Laws are silent in times of war.[447] Yet, the chief justice knew that in this case, Cicero may have been wrong. In the final analysis, Stone's opinion, which was to be joined by the entire Court, carefully limits and defines the issues involved to arrive at its desired result: upholding the commission as well as the president's order, but without creating broad new exceptions to basic civil liberties.

In the Court's opinion, Chief Justice Stone stated the issue clearly and directly: "The question for decision is whether the detention of petitioners by respondent for trial by Military Commission, appointed by order of the President of July 2, 1942, on charges preferred against them purporting to set out their violations of the war and the Articles of War, is in conformity to the laws and Constitution of the United States."[448]

In beginning his review of the procedural and factual history of the case, Justice Stone did not shy away from the consequence of the matter:

> In view of the public importance of the questions raised by their petitions and of the duty which rests on the courts, in time of war as well as in time of peace, to preserve unimpaired the constitutional safeguards of civil liberty, and because in our opinion the public interest required that we consider and decide those questions without any avoidable delay, we directed that petitioners' applications be set down for full oral argument at a special term of this Court."[449]

The question had been phrased squarely and the significance of the opinion was clear. Not mentioned in the opinion, however, was the fact that six of the seven petitioners had already been executed.

Much of the argument in the case had turned on the status of the seven men, both by citizenship and through their relationship with a military force. In many ways the case would become a question of who they were as much as what they had done. The justices took time to make it clear that all eight of the men were born in Germany, and that, with the exception of Herbert Haupt and Peter Burger, they were citizens of the German Reich.[450]

It was argued by the government that, even though Haupt's parents had become naturalized citizens of the United States—making him a citizen—he lost those rights when he pledged his allegiance to Germany, as did Burger. Although the Court makes the arguments clear regarding Haupt, the opinion states that the case can be decided without answering this question. If the Court had rendered an opinion on this issue, it may have had an effect on the thousands of people classified as "enemy aliens"—Italians, Germans, Romanians, Hungarians and, of course, the more than 100,000 Japanese who were being detained by the government while the opinion was being written.

The Court then undertook the task of discussing President Roosevelt's proclamation of July 2, 1942. The executive order had two primary components: first, to establish and order the use of military commissions to try those charged with offenses against the law of war and in violation of the Articles of War; second, in a phrase that at first blush seems in opposition to the Court's holding in *Milligan*—to deny persons charged with these crimes access to the courts.[451]

The lawyers for the seven charged men in *Quirin* argued that the President's proclamation, directing criminal cases out of the civil courts to military commission, ran afoul of numerous legal safeguards, including the Fifth and Sixth Amendments of the Constitution.

These Amendments, in many ways the cornerstones of American criminal justice, provide that:

Amendment V
No person shall be held to answer for a capital, or otherwise infamous crime, unless on a presentment or indictment of a Grand Jury, except in cases arising in the land or naval forces, or in the Militia, when in actual service in time of War or public danger; nor shall any person be subject for the same offense to be twice put in jeopardy of life or limb; nor shall be compelled in any criminal case to be a witness against himself, nor be deprived of life, liberty, or property, without due process of law; nor shall private property be taken for public use, without just compensation.[452]

Amendment VI

In all criminal prosecutions, the accused shall enjoy the right to a speedy and public trial, by an impartial jury of the state and district wherein the crime shall have been committed, which district shall have been previously ascertained by law, and to be informed of the nature and cause of the accusation; to be confronted with the witnesses against him; to have compulsory process for obtaining witnesses in his favor, and to have the Assistance of Counsel for his defense.[453]

The seven defendants had argued, however, that under the protections afforded by the Constitution, they must be tried in the courts and must be given all of the procedural protections provided for by the Bill of Rights.

The government's response revolved around the question of character and conduct. The government's position was that, if the defendants fell within a certain class of offenders and if their crimes could be prosecuted under the Articles of War or the laws of war, then there was absolutely no bar to the use of a military commission to try them, irrespective of the Bill of Rights.[454]

The court opened its response to these questions with a clear statement of the stakes involved in the resolution of the positions of the parties to the lawsuit:

We are not concerned here with any question of the guilt or innocence of petitioners. Constitutional safeguards for the protection of all who are charged with offenses are not to be disregarded in order to inflict merited punishment on some who are guilty [quoting *Ex Parte Milligan*]. But the detention and trial of petitioners—ordered by the President in the declared exercise of his powers as Commander-in-Chief of the Army in the time of war and of grave public danger—are not set aside by the courts without the clear conviction that they are in conflict with the Constitution or laws of Congress constitutionally enacted.[455]

With the issues defined and the importance of the case clear, Stone's opinion then turned toward a resolution. The members of the Court had struggled and argued about many aspects of the case. Although Justice Stone had completed much of his initial work before he returned to Washington, he returned to his Supreme Court chambers on September 14 and finished the first part of the opinion.[456]

Stone's intense work on the case gave rise to doubts that the president had followed procedures in accordance with the Articles of War when he established the military commission in this case.[457] The questions that Stone harbored regarding the propriety of Roosevelt's proclamation struck to the heart of the most fundamental provisions of the executive order. The president's order provided that the commission could impose the death penalty if five members of the panel agreed. Under the Articles of War, a verdict of death could only be made by a unanimous decision.

Justice Stone was also concerned with the burden of proof that was established for the commission. In this case, the presidential order allowed the commission to consider "such evidence . . . as would, in the opinion of the president of the commission, have probative value to a reasonable man." This rather low burden of proof was not found in the law governing the administration of courts martial or criminal trials.[458] In American criminal cases the prosecution bears the highest burden of proof—proof beyond a reasonable doubt.

The problems with the procedural aspects of this case gave the justices great concern. As the appeal had been taken before there was a conviction in the case, Stone had considered labeling the procedural objections as "premature" in order to avoid ruling on them. He wrote, however, that it seemed "almost brutal to announce this as grounds for the decision after six of the petitioners had been executed." In the end, he would reject this approach.[459]

The chief justice was not alone in his hesitation on this point. Justice Frankfurter would write: "If a legal right exists, to say that it is prematurely presented when as a practical matter there would be no later time for presenting it—for dead men can present no legal claims—is to bring the law into disrepute and make a mockery of justice."[460]

The fact that judgment had already been rendered in the case, the defendants had been sentenced, and the executions had been carried out, put the Court in the position of having to consider the impact of the opinion on the public and the facts that had occurred outside of the record before the court. In the end, the Court did not directly answer the questions that Stone posed regarding defects in the process. Instead, the Court found that, under two different theories, the Articles did not prevent a procedure of the type used in this case. The Court in the final opinion in the case held:

> We need not inquire whether Congress may restrict the power of the Commander in Chief to deal with enemy belligerents. For the Court is unanimous in its conclusion that the Articles in question could not at any stage of the proceedings afford any basis for issuing the writ. But a majority of the full Court are not agreed on the appropriate grounds for the decision. Some members of the Court are of the opinion that Congress did not intend the Articles of War to govern a Presidential military commission convened for the determination of questions relating to admitted enemy invaders and that the context of the Articles makes clear that they should not be construed to apply in that class of cases. Others are of the view that—even though this trial is subject to whatever provisions of the Articles of War Congress has in terms made applicable to "commissions"—the particular Articles in question, rightly construed, do not foreclose the procedure prescribed by the President or that shown to have been employed by the commission in a trial of offenses against the law of war and the Eighty-first and Eighty-second Articles of War, by a military commission appointed by the President.[461]

The primary issue now dealt with the classification of the petitioners and the characterization of their conduct. The Court had distinguished *Milligan* by holding that the Court in that Civil War case had focused on a case and a petitioner who was not a part of, or associated with, the armed forces of the enemy—that he was in fact a non-belligerent.[462] This approach allowed the Court to support its initial opinion without striking the heralded opinion in *Milligan*.

The Court, finding that each of the petitioners was not a citizen of the United States and were members of an enemy military power meant that they could in fact be tried for violations of the laws of war and Articles of War. The Court interpreted the plain language of the Fifth and Sixth Amendments, which excepted cases "arising in the land or naval forces" as removing the issues of the protections afforded citizens by the Amendments from consideration. The Court went further to find that, in drafting and adopting the Fifth and

Sixth Amendments, the Congress had exempted offenses committed by enemy belligerents against the law of war.[463]

Having found the petitioners to be members of the armies of the Third Reich who had come to the United States with the aim and purpose of waging war against America, they were now placed within a group of people who could be tried by military commissions without running afoul of the holding in *Milligan*. The Court found a path of analysis that supported the president's action without having to examine the specific procedures used in the trial of the eight saboteurs.

After all of the analysis, argument, and soul-searching done in conference and by each of the jurists, the chief justice penned an opinion that each of the justices who heard the case would adopt. On October 29, 1942, the Court handed down its opinion affirming the district court and denying the petitions for writs of habeas corpus—a decision supporting the president, almost three months after the executions.

Chief Justice Stone had been uncomfortable with the manner in which the case had reached the Supreme Court, the timing of the appeal, and the secrecy that shrouded the commission. As a result, he did not feel comfortable openly endorsing the proceedings. But, Stone was also clear about the outcome. While drafting the opinion he would say, "I have no doubt of the correctness of our decision not to sustain any of the petitions for habeas corpus." He went on to write, "The precise ground on which it should be put presents a question of some delicacy for the Court . . ."[464]

Even though the opinion had been difficult for the chief justice and the entire court, Stone would receive great praise for how he handled the case from inside the court and from observers in the legal community.

"The picture of the highest court in the country convening specially to hear and pass upon the lawfulness of the trial of avowed enemies of the nation presents a sharp contrast to the practices prevalent in the land whence they came," fawned one legal writer in the *Michigan Law Review*.[465] Professor Robert Cushman of Cornell University would similarly flatter the opinion: "The Supreme Court stopped the military authorities and required them, as it were, to show their credentials. When this had been done to the Court's satisfaction they were allowed to proceed."[466]

The Supreme Court had successfully affirmed the convictions and had done it in a manner that was described at the time by one legal scholar as "a wholesome and desirable safeguard to civil liberty in a time of war . . ."[467]

The difference between the opinions of the Supreme Court in *Milligan* and *Quirin* are remarkable—perhaps as remarkable as the conflicts in which they were decided. *Milligan*, after all, arose during a struggle in which a young nation was tearing at itself, a war fought in the name of freedom and to determine the role of the government in state affairs. Viewed through the filter of the times it is understandable that a court would adopt the passionate language that characterizes the dicta of the *Milligan* opinion.

World War II, however, was a very different kind of war. It saw Americans from all over the country banding together as one nation, united in purpose and principle, which is why it has often been called the "last popular war." In such a conflict, the law being used as a weapon against those who would slip though the shadows to cause destruction in the name of fascism is, in a term so often used in the law, *foreseeable*.§

---

§For the full text of the opinion in *Ex Parte Quirin* 317 U.S. 1; 63 S. Ct. 2; 87 L. Ed. 3 (1942), see Appendix 3.

In the News Today

PORTLAND, ME., July 30, 1942—Dock workers in this port city were shocked today by the sight of a crazed would-be Nazi saboteur in their midst today. Federal officials arrested a twenty-nine-year-old German man who emerged from the woods and made his way to a local waterfront. The man had been living in New York at the outbreak of war in Europe. He had fled to the woods of Maine and had lived there as a hermit since 1939. He was found wandering about the shipyards and docks looking for a way to get back to the Fatherland to fight for Hitler. He was arrested by the F.B.I. and sent to the German-Italian-Japanese colony on Ellis Island.[468]

CHAPTER 13

Plaques, Condos, and Porcupines

Dasch was a man with plans. Burger waited and did what he was asked. That was the FBI's conclusion after agents visited Dasch and Burger in the district jail on August 21 to evaluate the use of the two prisoners as witnesses and informants.

In a secret memorandum to Hoover, Special Agent C. F. Lanman reported that Dasch was still working the angles—he spent his days writing a complete history of his time in Germany, including names of people working there who had lived in the United States or who were American citizens. Dasch planned to send the statement off to Hoover in hopes that this additional information might be enough to secure his freedom. Dasch seemed calmer and more content as he was writing and he complained less about his sentence.[469]

Burger proved eager to cooperate with the FBI and supplied them with information regarding U-boat bases in South America and in the Gulf of Mexico.[470] Hoover would forward this to the War Department and the OSS so that the information could be used to show the FBI's skill in counterespionage. Burger even tried to persuade the agents to let him work for the FBI in South America to uncover Nazi spies there—he suggested that it would be best if it could be arranged to make it look like he had escaped from federal custody.

Since there were still a large number of influential people in the United States in league with the Nazis, his escape would be a good cover for his spy work for the FBI.[471]

Yet, the FBI still worried that Dasch and his men had been only the first of many landings of spies from U-boats. Burger reassured his questioners he didn't think that there would be any further expeditions to America. He was convinced that their case had demonstrated to the Nazis that the American coast was too well guarded. He was certain, however, that there would be future landings in Mexico.[472]

As if to support this theory, Burger related the story of an ultra-secret unit of the German army, the *Lehrregiment*—a unit that had been formed to undertake missions of sabotage and espionage. The regiment's main camp, *Regenwurm-Larger*, was in the town of Baden near Vienna. In German it meant Rain-Worm Camp—a reference to night crawlers, the earthworms that slither from the ground in foul weather. Burger said that the villages around *Regenwurm-Larger* were emptied and the men training there were kept under the highest levels of security and secrecy. The men selected for this unit were recruited from all parts of the Reich and countries occupied by the Germans. Then, he described the Third Company of the Third Battalion of the unit, which had been set aside for men with knowledge about the United States.[473]

At the end of the interview, Burger echoed Dasch in his complaints about the uncomfortable district jail and reminded his captors that he and Dasch should be moved to more comfortable quarters if they cooperated with the Department of Justice in other trials.[474]

Burger and Dasch were not the only ones left with a connection to the case, however. On July 13, 1942, FBI Director Hoover announced that the Bureau had taken into custody fourteen people who had assisted the saboteurs after they had landed. The FBI recommended that the majority of those held be charged with treason, conspiracy to commit espionage and sabotage, and aiding and abetting a felony.[475] Those detained in the sweep included:

Ernest Herman Kerkof: A resident of Eighty-eighth Street in New York, he became a naturalized citizen in 1932 after coming to the

United States from his native Hanover, Germany. Kerkof was a close friend of Kerling's wife and served as one of the primary contacts for the Nazis while they were in New York.

He had made preparations through the Swiss Consulate to return to Germany on July 2, 1942, aboard the SS *Serpa Pinto*. He was arrested on June 23, however, and was turned over to the Immigration and Naturalization Service.

Marie Kerling: Married to Edward Kerling, the leader of the Florida team, Marie was born in Munich and came to New York in 1926. She married Kerling in 1930, and was listed as a non-resident member of the National Socialist Party. She had been scheduled to sail to Germany on June 13, 1942, aboard the SS *Nyassa*—although she did not use her ticket.

During the military commission trial she was held in Washington, D.C., as a material witness for the defense. She was then placed in the custody of the Immigration and Naturalization Service and held in detention on a presidential warrant.

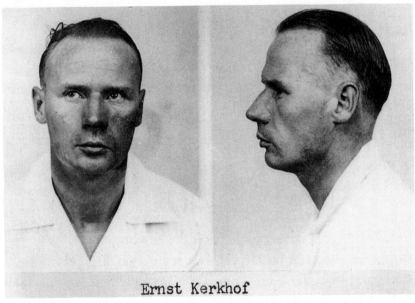

Ernst Kerkhof

Walter Otto Wilhelm Froehling: Herbert Haupt's uncle was considered one of the saboteurs' primary contacts and was the first person that Haupt reached in the United States. His name was printed with invisible ink on Dasch's handkerchief. Froehling's house on North Hipple Street, Chicago, was a hideout for the terrorists and a location where they could safely exchange information.

The bricklayer admitted to the FBI that Haupt contacted him upon his arrival and hid $9,500 in a secret compartment in his house. Froehling had come to the United States in 1926 and had become a naturalized citizen in 1931. At the time of his arrest he worked as a truck driver for a Chicago public utility.

Lucille Froehling: Married to Otto Froehling, Lucille was present when he discussed the mission with Haupt. She told FBI agents that she knew about the money hidden in her house. She came to the United States from her native Berlin in 1923 and she became a naturalized citizen in 1935. She and Otto had two young children.

Hans Max Haupt: The father of Herbert Haupt, Hans Max lived in the same home where he had raised Herbie on North Fremont Street in Chicago. Herbert had gone directly to his parents' home after separating from the other agents in Florida. Hans told FBI agents that he knew about his son's landing and mission. He hid more than $3,000 of the saboteurs' money under a rug in his house. Hans Haupt was active in many organizations supportive of the Reich, including the Association of German World War Veterans, the German Day Association, and the Schwaben Society, and he served as the secretary of the *Deutscher Veteren Unterstutzungs*. The 48-year-old bricklayer was born in Labes, Germany, in 1894. He served in the Kaiser's army in World War I and came to the United States in 1923, where he became a naturalized citizen.

Erna Froehling Haupt: Herbert Haupt's mother, Erna, also lived in the family home in Chicago. She admitted to the FBI that she knew of her son's landing and mission and that he returned with a large sum of money. She was born in Podejuch-Stettin, Germany, in 1899.

She came to the United States with her husband after marrying him in Germany in 1919. She became a naturalized citizen in March 1941.

Harry Jaques: Jaques, a resident of Chicago, was a friend of Neubauer's through his wife, Alma. FBI agents found $3,600 of Neubauer's money hidden in a coffee-bean jar in his house on West North Avenue in Chicago. Jaques's true name was Andreus Heinrich Jans. He entered the United States in 1924 or 1925, as a seaman on the SS *Hamburg* and jumped ship when it made port in New York. At the time of his arrest, Jaques was working as the manager and coach of the Chicago Kickers soccer team.

Emma Jaques: Emma was a close friend of Alma Neubauer, Hermann Neubauer's wife. She and her husband were the first contacts for the team that had landed in Florida. Born in Stuttgart, Germany, in 1901, she came to the United States in 1925 with her then-husband, Adolf Weik. That same year she left him in New York and moved to Chicago with Harry Jaques.

Hermann Heinrich Faje: A resident of Astoria, Long Island, Faje was a friend of Heinrich Heinck, one of the Nazis who landed in

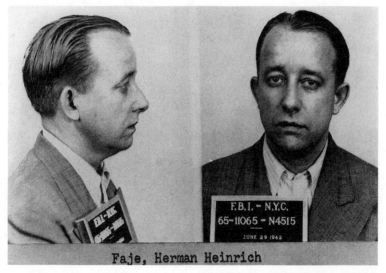

Faje, Herman Heinrich

National Archives/Federal Bureau of Investigation

New York. Faje and his wife were the first people Heinck contacted in America. The Fajes hid $3,600 for Heinck behind their radiator cover. Faje came to the United States in 1928 from his native Hamburg, Germany. He was working as a hairdresser in New York when he was arrested.

Faje's wife, Hildegard, was arrested, but no case was filed since she was pregnant.

Hedwig Engmann: Hedwig "Hedy" Engmann of East Fifty-sixth Street in New York was Edward Kerling's mistress and his first contact in the United States. She admitted to the FBI that she knew that Kerling had landed in the United States on a U-boat, but that she had not come to authorities because of her affections for Kerling. She was born in Brooklyn in 1907, of German parents.

Anthony Cramer: A member of the Friends of Germany, Cramer was a close friend of Werner Thiel. After Thiel landed in Florida, he had gone directly to Cramer's home in New York. The FBI recovered $3,670 of the Nazi's money in Cramer's safe-deposit box in a New York City bank.

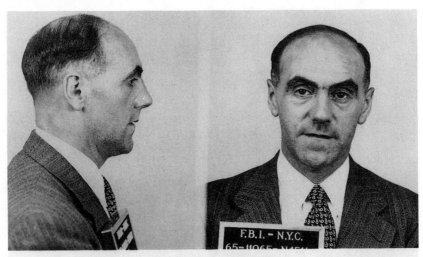

Anthony Cramer

National Archives/Federal Bureau of Investigation

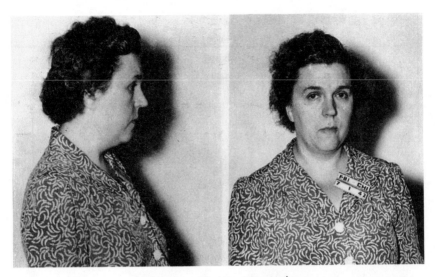

Mrs. Kate Wergin

National Archives/Federal Bureau of Investigation

Kate Martha Wergin: Mrs. Wergin lived on South Wood Street in Chicago and was a close friend of the Haupt family. Her son, Wolfgang, had left Chicago for Mexico with Herbert Haupt. At the time of her arrest, the FBI believed that Wolfgang Wergin was in Germany.

Mrs. Wergin admitted that she knew the Haupt family, but denied any involvement in the case. She entered the United States in 1927 and became a naturalized citizen in 1934. She was a member of the *Reichsdeutsche Vereingung*—a pro-German organization in Chicago—with her husband.

Otto Richard Wergin: Otto Wergin—a fervent pro-Nazi member of the German American-Bund, the Germania Club, and the *Reichsdeutsche Vereingung*—was contacted by Herbert Haupt after Haupt's arrival in the United States. Wergin admitted that he knew about Haupt's mission and had offered to assist him.

Born in Aranswalde, Germany, in 1896, Wergin worked as a machinist. He had served in the German navy in World War I, had come to the United States in 1926, and had become naturalized in 1936.

Helmut Leiner: Leiner was identified as one of the men approved by the German High Command as a contact for the Nazis and his name was written on Dasch's handkerchief in invisible ink. A close friend of Kerling, Leiner lived in Astoria on Long Island, and after his landing in the United States, Kerling contacted him. He helped Kerling change money from large denominations and assisted him in contacting other Nazi sympathizers in the States.

Leiner came to the United States from Germany in 1929. Having joined the Nazi party in 1928, he never became an American citizen. He was an active member of the Bund and met Kerling through those meetings.[476]

The initial charges against the sympathizers were only the beginning of a long and hard legal battle that would find six of the defendants charged and convicted of treason—three of them ultimately receiving sentences of death.

On July 9, 1942, Special Agent "Mickey" Ladd wrote a memorandum to Hoover with his recommendations. The fourteen held in custody for helping the saboteurs should be tried for treason.[477]

The United States obtained an indictment charging Hans Max Haupt, Walter Otto Froehling, Otto Richard Wergin, Erna Emma Haupt, Lucille Froehling, and Kate Martha Wergin with one count. The crime was a violation of 18 U.S.C.A. 1—Treason. This statute provided that, "Whoever, owing allegiance to the United States, levies war against them or adheres to their enemies, giving them aid and comfort within the United States or elsewhere is guilty of treason."[478] The issue of American citizenship once again would come to the forefront. Unlike the eight Nazis who were tried by the military commission, most of these defendants were naturalized American citizens, and they would be tried in the civil courts.

The trial started in the federal courthouse in Chicago—a city with a large German population.[479] It was also a city in which many of the windows were decorated with the flags bearing stars that signified a loved one was serving in the armed forces or had been killed in the line of duty.

On October 26, 1942, the trial began. The government alleged that the defendants' conduct in contacting and meeting with the eight terrorists before they were captured served as overt acts that justified conviction for the crime of treason. The case was built primarily upon statements made by the defendants when they were taken into custody and the testimony of Ernst Peter Burger.[480]

The defense argued vigorously that the defendants' statements should not be allowed into evidence—they were coerced and too prejudicial to be allowed into the case. The defense also argued that the statements were not voluntary, in that they had been obtained before the defendants were brought before a magistrate as required by the law. The court rejected the arguments, however, and admitted the statements.[481]

On November 14, 1942, the jury returned guilty verdicts against all six defendants after six hours of deliberation.[482] Hans Max Haupt, Walter Otto Froehling, and Otto Richard Wergin were sentenced to death. The women charged and convicted in the case—Erna Emma Haupt, Lucille Froehling, and Kate Martha Wergin—were sentenced to prison for twenty-five years and ordered to each pay a fine of $10,000.[483]

The lawyers for the six convicted Nazi sympathizers appealed the case on three grounds. The statements introduced into the trial were inadmissible, as they were involuntary and the defendants had not been taken before a federal magistrate for an initial hearing as required by law; their cases were prejudiced when their motions to sever the trials were dismissed and they were tried together; and the judge gave improper instructions to the jury.[484]

On June 29, 1943, the Seventh Circuit Court of Appeals reversed the convictions, agreeing with the defendants on all stated grounds. In its opinion, the court of appeals declared it was concerned over the defendants' statements for two reasons. First, federal law provided that, upon arrest, the arresting agency had the duty to bring the person before a magistrate for an initial hearing and bail setting. This was not done for any of the defendants.[485]

The government's position was that each of the defendants had forfeited the right to an initial hearing when they signed a waiver before being interrogated by the agents. One of the waivers produced by the FBI read:

> I, Walter Otto Froehling, do hereby consent to remain under the continuous physical supervision of the Special Agents of the Federal Bureau of Investigation, U.S. Department of Justice, without immediate arraignment, and at such place as may be designated by the said agents, while information furnished or to be furnished by me regarding violations of the laws of the United States is being verified.
>
> This I regard solely as a step necessary for my protection during the progress of this investigation and my consent to this arrangement is, therefore, freely given by me without fear of threat or promise of reward. It is, however, not to be construed as an admission of guilt on my part.

The court rejected the government's argument. Judge Major, who wrote the opinion, noted that the six prisoners were not advised of their right to counsel or informed of what rights they were being deprived of by signing the waivers.[486] The requirement to provide defendants with the now-familiar *Miranda* warnings before conducting an interrogation would not be the law for many years to come.[487] Yet the court held the statements inadmissible since the government could not show that the defendants had knowingly and voluntarily waived their rights.

The defendants had also argued that by being tried together, they were not afforded a fair trial, that the jury was unable to keep prejudicial evidence limited to the person it was being introduced against. Since much of the evidence produced in the trial was specific to individual defendants, the defense alleged that by trying them together, the prosecution had painted them all with the same broad brush.

In concurring with the defense, the court again made clear that issues surrounding fairness in trials must be extended to all people under the threat of criminal penalty. The right to a fair trial, said the court,

. . . is all inclusive; it embraces every class and type of person. Those for whom we have contempt or even hatred are equally entitled to its benefit. It will be a sad day for our system of government if the time should come when any person, whoever he may be, is deprived of this fundamental safeguard. No more important responsibility rests on the courts than its preservation. How wasted is American blood now being spilled in all parts of the world if we at home are unwilling or unable to accord every person charged with a crime a trial in conformity with this constitutional requirement.[488]

The Court also found that the trial judge's instructions to the jury had been confusing, unclear, and inaccurate statements of the law.

The government was in a difficult position regarding the six sympathizers. To retry them without the evidence provided by their statements would be next to impossible, yet the evidence had been ruled inadmissible by the court of appeals. In the end, only Herbert Haupt's father would be tried again. The other five defendants would see their cases come to an end.

Lucille Froehling and Kate Wergin were released from federal custody. Otto Wergin and Walter Froehling entered pleas of guilty to misprision [to conceal another's crime] of treason and were sentenced to five years in prison. Under the law, they were given credit for the time in custody that they had already served. Erna Haupt's citizenship was revoked; she remained in detention for the duration of the war and was then deported back to Germany.[489]

Hans Max Haupt was retried for treason by giving aid, comfort, and assistance to his only son, Herbert. The jury heard evidence from FBI agents, Herbert's ex-fiancée, inmates who had been in custody with the elder Haupt, and his coworkers and supervisors. Even Peter Burger testified, as did members of pro-German organizations. Hans Haupt did not testify in his own defense.

Hans Eric Poppe, a Chicago resident, testified that in 1939, Haupt said, "that if war would break out with the United States and Germany, he would never permit his boy to join the American army. He would send him to Mexico and from there he could go to Germany and join the air force. He told me that if war broke out, that if the country would take him in the army, he would crawl over to the enemy lines and tell them our position."[490]

A parade of other witnesses swore that Haupt had told them of his son's mission and his assistance to Herbie, that he admired and lauded Hitler, and that Germans in America should feel shame if they didn't contribute to the German cause.[491]

Haupt was convicted and sentenced to life in prison and ordered to pay a fine of $10,000.[492] At his sentencing on June 14, 1944—only a few days after D-Day—Judge Peter Barnes described Haupt as a "fanatical Nazi."[493]

Haupt's case was appealed to the Seventh Circuit Court of Appeals. This time the reviewing court rejected the claims of error and affirmed the conviction. The convicted Hitler sympathizer had only one route of appeal left open: the United States Supreme Court. Once again, the High Court ruled against a party involved with the Nazi landings in Florida and New York.

In affirming the ruling of the lower court and upholding the conviction, Justice Jackson said:

> Haupt has been twice tried and twice found guilty. The law of treason makes and properly makes conviction difficult but not impossible. His acts aided an enemy of the United States toward accomplishing his mission of sabotage. The mission was frustrated but the defendant did his best to make it succeed. His overt acts were proved in compliance with the hard test of the Constitution, are hardly denied, and the proof leaves no reasonable doubt of the guilt. The judgment is affirmed.[494]

There was a dissenting opinion, however, filed by Justice Douglas, who stated that the parental feelings of Hans for Herbert could not be separated from his political feelings for the Nazis:

> The indictment alleged the petitioner committed an overt act of treason by sheltering and harboring his son for those six days. Concededly, this was a natural act for a father to perform; it is consistent with parental devotion for a father to shelter his son, especially when the son ordinarily lives with the father. But the Court says that the jury might find, under appropriate instructions, that petitioner provided this shelter, not merely as an act toward a disloyal son, but as an act designed to injure the United States. A saboteur must be lodged in a safe

place if his mission is to be effected and the jury might well find that petitioner lodged his son for that purpose.

But the act of providing shelter was of the type that might normally arise out of a petitioner's relationship to his son, as the Court recognizes. By its very nature, therefore, it is a non-treasonous act. That is true even when the act is viewed in light of all the surrounding circumstances. All that can be said is that the problem of whether it was motivated by treasonous or non-treasonous conduct is left in doubt. It is therefore not an overt act of treason, regardless of how unlawful it might otherwise be.[495]

Hans Haupt was sent to the federal prison in Danbury, Connecticut. After the war he was released and sent to Germany to be reunited with his wife who had already been deported.[496]

Anthony Cramer was also prosecuted for treason. The government alleged that Cramer, who had lived in the United States since 1925, had provided assistance to Kerling and Thiel before the FBI took them into custody. Cramer stashed the $3,600 given to him by Thiel in his safe-deposit box. The evidence produced at the trial showed that Cramer met Thiel at New York's Grand Central Station after finding a cryptic note on his door from the Nazi saboteur.[497] The FBI arrested Cramer after his second meeting in New York with Kerling and Thiel.

Much of the evidence in the trial came from the testimony of Peter Burger and Norma Kopp. Kopp, a laundry and kitchen maid, had known both Cramer and Thiel intimately. She became engaged to Thiel less than a week before he left for Germany. The maid knew that Thiel was a Nazi and was told of the terrorist mission by Thiel when he returned to America. She provided some of the most damaging testimony in the trial, describing clandestine meetings between Cramer and the Nazi agents.[498]

As a result, Cramer was convicted of treason. At the time of sentencing, the trial judge stated:

I shall not impose the maximum penalty of death. It does not appear that this defendant, Cramer, was aware that Thiel and Kerling were in possession of explosives or other means for destroying factories and property of the United States or planned to do that.

From the evidence it appears that Cramer had no more guilty knowledge of any subversive purposes on the part of Thiel or Kerling than a vague idea that they came here for the purpose of organizing pro-German propaganda and agitation. If there were any proof that they had confided in him what their real purposes were, or that he knew, or believed what they really were, I should not hesitate the death penalty.[499]

In what would be the last of the cases involving the failed Nazi landings, the United States Supreme Court heard Cramer's appeal. Justice Jackson, who would soon be the chief prosecutor in the Nuremberg Tribunals, delivered the opinion of the Court, which found it clear that Cramer was pro-Nazi and supportive of his native country. The Court noted that Thiel and Cramer had been very close before the saboteur left for Germany. In fact, the two men had been roommates and partners in a failed and "luckless" delicatessen. Cramer kept close ties with friends and family in Germany before the war and attended the 1936 Olympics held in Berlin.[500]

In the opinion, the Court engages in a very thorough discussion of the law of treason. The Court notes that the law required two witnesses to provide evidence proving the acts that constitute the high crime. Justice Jackson quoted an apt warning to courts regarding cases of treason from Chief Justice Marshall in 1807:

> As there is no crime which can more excite and agitate the passions of men than treason, no charge demands more from the tribunal before which it is made, a deliberate and temperate inquiry. Whether this inquiry be directed to the fact or to the law, none can be more solemn, none more important to the citizen or to the government; none can more affect the safety of both.[501]

Despite a strong dissent joined by three justices, the United States Supreme Court held that the evidence produced at the trial was insufficient. Cramer's conviction for treason was reversed.

Only the two saboteurs now remained in custody. In July 1947, Dasch and Burger's appeals for clemency began to attract serious consideration from government officials. Already in 1945, *Newsweek* magazine had carried a story chronicling the details of the arrest—but also the promises made to Dasch and Burger.

*　*　*

The warden of the federal penitentiary in Atlanta, where both men were housed, wrote to the FBI recommending a pardon for Burger, extolling his exemplary conduct and cooperation with law enforcement.

> Somewhere along the line I believe that sight has been lost of the tremendous job this man did for our country in reporting the presence of these groups of saboteurs in this country and then by giving full cooperation to the FBI throughout the war. . . . Furthermore, he testified in a number of court cases which resulted in convictions of saboteurs and espionage agents practically on his testimony alone.[502]

Dasch, however, failed to impress the warden as favorably as the former Storm Trooper had. He labeled Dasch a bitter Communist troublemaker and predicted that, ". . . if released to Germany, [Dasch] will not be in the American zone any longer than necessary than it takes him to traverse the border to the Russian zone."[503]

Although President Truman was poised to grant clemency to Burger and Dasch—in spite of J. Edgar Hoover's *sotto voce* opposition—the White House feared that the president could be subject to a great deal of criticism unless the release was handled properly.

In a memorandum dated February 11, 1948, the judge advocate general's office urged caution, reminding the administration that "the president's action will occasion widespread interest and it is important that all the mitigating circumstances which justify clemency be recounted. Otherwise, a storm of press criticism may result from a bare announcement of the release of prisoners convicted of such a heinous offense."[504]

On March 20, 1948, President Truman commuted the sentences. United States Army Chief of Staff Dwight D. Eisenhower issued the order for the release of Burger and Dasch from prison. They were to be deported to Germany with restrictions on their travel, employment, and political activities as determined by the commanding general of the United States Army's European Command.

The White House explained that the men would remain prisoners until they were safely in the American zone of occupation in Germany, at which time the remainder of their sentence would be suspended. To justify its action, the administration quoted the joint recommendation made by the attorney general and the judge advocate general:

> It is the view of the undersigned that Burger and Dasch have now been sufficiently punished for their offenses against the United Sates. In fact, their services in revealing the details of the conspiracy, and later in disclosing valuable information as to conditions in Germany, as well as in assisting the Department of Justice in obtaining convictions of disloyal persons in the United States, seem amply to justify clemency. It may also be desirable to indicate to the world at the present state of affairs that persons who have been employed by foreign powers for espionage or sabotage have everything to gain by coming to the proper offices of this Government and disclosing details of the conspiracy. It is accordingly our recommendation that Burger and Dasch be returned to the custody of the Department of the Army and be transported to Germany . . .[505]

On April 27, 1948, in a classified message to the War Department, Lieutenant Colonel Bradlee of the Military Police Division of the United States Army's headquarters in Europe confirmed that the American authorities had no objection to the failed spies being released in their jurisdiction. The fallen heroes of the Reich were on their way home.[506]

Far from the spotlight, Burger melted into the rebuilding German countryside. He fell out of the public eye and would live and die in anonymity. Dasch returned home, not as the conquering hero but as a traitor.

In 1953, a series of articles about the case was published in the German magazine *Der Stern*. The stories told of Dasch's cooperation with the FBI and the executions of his six comrades. The articles incited a backlash against Dasch as a traitor throughout Germany. In his book, Dasch described carloads of people coming to his home looking for him and threats from all quarters. A local newspaper headline that was published after the *Der Stern* articles blared:

EX-AGENT SOUGHT: DID HE BRING SIX
GERMANS TO THE ELECTRIC CHAIR?
EX-AGENT DASCH SAYS "MY CONSCIENCE IS CLEAR"
SHOW YOURSELF MR. DASCH! THE GAME IS UP![507]

Reviled now in two countries, in 1959 he wrote and published *Eight Spies in America*, giving his side of the story.

Dasch never wavered in his assertion that he always had America's interest at heart. In his book he reflected on the events leading up to his arrest and conviction:

> As the troubled years go by I often wonder at the strange course my life followed, making it possible for me to render that one wartime service for the United States. . . . Despite all that has happened since the landing at Amagansett, despite all the disappointments and frustrations, I still have the hope justice will win out.[508]

For years he tried to return to the United States but was blocked at every turn by Hoover's unremitting opposition. Dasch's true motives remain an enigma. He can be viewed as a true opportunist and con man, loyal to no one but himself, or he can be painted as a failed spy—an operative who started a dangerous and deadly mission and simply lost his nerve. To believe Dasch, he was an American patriot caught in unlucky circumstances, but still trying to help his adopted country. To some involved in the investigation and trial, Dasch's true motivations were not as important as the fact that he was the key to solving the case. The unfulfilled promises made by Hoover rest uneasy to this day. In the words of FBI Agent Traynor, who welcomed Dasch to the arms of the Bureau, "It wasn't fair."[509]

Dasch died in 1991.

After the failure of the Pastorius mission, there was only one other confirmed case of Nazi saboteurs landing in the United States. On November 30, 1944, *Kapitänleutnant* Hans Hibig, commander of the U-1230, discharged two passengers at Hancock Point in Frenchman's Bay, Maine—German-born Erich Gimple and American-born William Colepaugh.[510] The two men formed *Unternehman Elster*, Operation Magpie, a mission to spy on shipyards, airplane factories, and rocket-testing sites. They had come with $60,000 in cash and ninety-nine diamond chips in case they ran out of money—this at a time when the average yearly salary for an American family was $2,378.[511] As they stumbled off the beach onto the nearby highway, a Boy Scout spotted them hailing a taxi to Bangor. The scout reported his sighting to the police, but nobody believed him.[512]

The two Nazi agents were taken into custody in New York after Colepaugh, like Dasch, turned himself in to the FBI. Colepaugh claimed to be a distant relative of President Roosevelt. That did not help his case at all, since he and Gimpel were tried by a military tribunal and sentenced to death on Valentine's Day, 1945. Their sentences were later commuted to life imprisonment. Gimpel was deported back to Germany in 1955 and Colepaugh was freed in 1960.[513]

Today, a brass plaque hangs in the Department of Justice, commemorating the trial of the Nazi terrorists in Room 5235. Another plaque stands on the beach in Amagansett, pointing out the place where the saboteurs first landed. Ponte Vedra has grown into a bustling resort and retirement community known for its lush golf courses and beautiful beaches. Few of the golfers teeing up there suspect that they are standing on ground that was once the sight of a failed Nazi attack on the United States.

Throughout his remaining years, Attorney General Biddle occasionally carried one of Dasch's lucky porcupine amulets on his watch chain, given to him by an ironical Hoover as a souvenir. Biddle wrote that he never understood why the Nazis had picked the unapproachable animal as their mascot. In his case, he said, the piece had never given him any luck, good or bad. He felt that perhaps the charm's powers were lost on him, as he was an American, "on whom such occult mysteries do not appear to work."[514]

APPENDIX 1

William Dudley Pelley and His Silver Shirt Legion

Although the German-American Bund sank beneath the waves of American history, William Dudley Pelley, a lesser-known figure of the time, with a smaller number of followers and greatly reduced resources, has left his sorry mark on our nation's zeitgeist to this day.

Novelist, screenwriter, mystic, failed presidential candidate, and rabid anti-Semite, Pelley is the spiritual father of today's Aryan Nation, Posse Comitatus, and so many other right-wing extremist groups who pine for and often, as did Oklahoma City bomber Timothy McVeigh, try to bring about Armageddon. Pelley's story is a uniquely American one, born out of the delusions, xenophobia, and religious fanaticism that have long been the lot of the white American underclass.

In 1937 Pelley advocated the overthrow of the United States government, saying, "The time has come for an American Hitler and a pogrom."[515] In the pages of his magazine, *Liberation*, he castigated what he called the diabolical, Bolshevik machinations of the

Roosevelt administration. He fancied himself the savior of America, chosen by God to prepare for the Last Day—which he described as coming, precisely, on September 17, 2001, when Christ and the Silver Shirts would finally wrest the country from the domination of the Jews and the Devil. Yet during World War II Pelley would wind up accused of sedition, and would be sentenced to fifteen years in a federal prison.[516]

It was a long and strange transformation for the son of an itinerant Methodist preacher from Lynn, Massachusetts. Born in 1885 into abject poverty, Pelley remembered that in his childhood he was "perpetually hungry and shabbily dressed." Self-educated, he dreamed of becoming like that other famous autodidact of American literature, Jack London. Pelley became a newspaper reporter and contributed to magazines such as *Colliers* and *Redbook*; he also covered World War I for the *Saturday Evening Post*. In 1917 he traveled to Japan and Siberia as a foreign correspondent. In the 1920s he moved to Hollywood, where he had middling success as a screenwriter at MGM and Universal Studios, crafting scripts for stars such as "The Man of a Thousand Faces," Lon Chaney, and sex goddess Theda Bara. He also wrote novels, among them *The Greater Glory* and *The Four Guardsmen*.[517]

But by the mid-1920s that measure of accomplishment had been taken from him. His wife had deserted him and several of his businesses ventures had failed. Then, in 1928, in a bungalow above Los Angeles, he died. Unlike most of the deceased, however, he came back to tell the world about it—for the rest of his remaining natural life.

Pelley never gave many details of how or where his death took place, leaving one to wonder whether his passing was the sort of transfiguration experienced by St. John of the Cross or St. Theresa when they too died to the world—or whether his death experience was just another way to capitalize on the craze for mysticism then rampant in American society.

It was the time of Christian revivalists like Aimee Semple McPherson and Billy Sunday; of metaphysical prophets like Manly

P. Hall, Gurdjieff, and Kahlil Gibran; as well as Eastern mystics like Swami Yogananda and Krishnamurti. Pelley was of a kind.

In an article he wrote in 1928 for the *American Magazine*, "My Seven Minutes in Eternity," Pelley described how, when he died, he journeyed to heaven or a place like it, where he met with God the creator and Jesus Christ; they urged him to bring about a deep spiritual and political transformation in American society.[518]

Years later he called the visit a "hypo-dimensional experience," a vague esoteric term, rather than an actual death.[519] No matter, the story gave Pelley a cult-like fame, with thousands of people writing to him to echo his beliefs. That particular issue of the magazine sold over two million copies. Afterwards he claimed to have developed other mystical faculties, such as levitation, x-ray vision, and willed out-of-body experiences.

Following the collapse of the stock market in 1929, Pelley joined with other conservative critics who blamed President Hoover and "Jewish bankers" for the crash. His anti-Semitism, which had been a minor ingredient of his bizarre philosophical ramblings, now took center stage.

Pelley claimed to have been told by Jewish commissars during the Russian Revolution that Communism was not an ideology but a cover for Jewish world conquest; Jews, motivated by greed, power, and revenge, were intent on destroying Western civilization. "After Russia, then Europe, then later, America!" one of them reportedly told him.[520]

Pelley argued that even the word *Jew* as we know it was wrongly applied to the Jews, for they are not the true Israelites of the Bible. His thinking was closely allied to British or Anglo/Israelism, which posits that Anglo-Saxons are the true chosen people, lineally descended from the Ten Lost Tribes of Israel. In Pelley's view, it was the duty and obligation of the white race to stop the so-called Jews from taking over the world.[521]

By 1930 Pelley was attracting more and more followers, and he moved his base of operations to Asheville, North Carolina. There he founded a number of spiritualistic companies, among them the

Galahad Press, Galahad College, and his magazine, *Liberation*. He continued to write extensively about his conversations with God and Jesus and the approaching Day of Reckoning. Like today's survivalists and right-wing extremists, he urged his readers to store food and ammunition, to drill in military fashion, and to prepare for the upcoming end.

Pelley, who had kept abreast of the rise to power of the fascists in Italy and of the Nazi Party in Germany, became convinced that January 30, 1933, the day that Hitler officially became Chancellor of Germany, was a "pyramid date" of enormous historical significance. This was a reference to the Great Pyramid of Gizah, a touchstone of many metaphysical cults. As a writer of the time put it, "Pelley and his followers believe that if the hieroglyphs that cover the corridor of the pyramid are correctly interpreted, they will foretell all events in world history down to Judgment Day."[522]

Following Hitler's ascension to power, Pelley became even more perfervid in his preaching that the end was near. He started his own Storm Troopers and named them The Silver Shirt Legion, dressing them in a uniform of khaki shirt, black tie, and riding breeches, with a silver "L" embroidered on the chest pocket. Pelley staged marches throughout the nation, hobnobbed with Charles Lindbergh and Fritz Kuhn. Using colorful language borrowed from Protestant fundamentalism, he elaborated on the literal existence of the Devil, the nearness of Armageddon, and the Jewish cabal of bankers and intellectuals who battled his Silver Shirts, Christ's own Soldiers of Light. (He also claimed that the Jesuits were a hidden Jewish organization and that its founder, Ignatius of Loyola, was actually a Jew.)[523]

Pelley's way of managing the growth of his movement was in a diffuse style that presaged the "leaderless-cell" style of the radical right in the 1990s. The Legion had no central headquarters; instead, Pelley himself would be constantly on the move, visiting all the posts, staging outdoor rallies and mass meetings along the way. He would regularly cover more than 100,000 miles in his car every year.

Pelley, like many extremist leaders, was reported to have been a very personable man in private. His legionnaires, perhaps not taking his message of hatred very seriously, called him "Captain Bob."[524] Most of these followers were lower-middle-class people looking for an answer to the economic turmoil that had so radically shaken up their lives. Many of them were also former Ku Klux Klan members. They were primarily Protestants, with a large female component— 28 percent—and of what Pelley called "Old Stock"—the assorted British, Scottish, Irish Protestants, and Germans who had settled the country long before the troublesome waves of southern and eastern European migration at the turn of the twentieth century.

Unlike the Bund, whose membership was concentrated on the East Coast, Pelley's Silver Shirt Legion was centered on the West Coast, where his odd combination of politics, metaphysics, and anti-Semitism found fertile soil. More than half, twenty-seven, of all the Silver Shirt outposts were located in California, with ten others in the West and the Midwest, respectively, and only five chapters on the East Coast.[525]

Federal authorities did not take Pelley's message so benignly. The same congressional committees that investigated the Bund and other fascist groups such as the Italian Black Shirts—10,000 strong in the United States, another 100,000 under their influence—turned on the Silver Shirts with as much vigor as they had with the Bund. Perhaps they feared that native-born Americans would join these made-in-the-USA extremist groups, which could be much more difficult to isolate or disparage than immigrant- and foreign-controlled organizations like the Bund.

The Dies Committee called Pelley in to testify about his writings, which in the committee's opinion encouraged "the forcible removal of Jews from office" and advocated the use of violence against the government. Pelley defended himself claiming he was exercising his First Amendment rights and that he was only being forceful, not instigating violence.

Pelley insisted that his "Christian militia" had been organized to take action only in case the legitimate government of the country was to collapse. In apologetic, almost servile tones, Pelley said he had changed his mind about the work of the Dies Committee. While earlier he accused it of persecuting patriots like himself, he now saw that it was actually rooting out the Bolshevik Communist menace. He eulogized the work of the Dies Committee so lavishly that Dies ordered him to stop giving them so much praise, so transparent was his intention of deflecting the work of the committee.

There was no mistaking Pelley's anti-Semitism, however, as the Committee was quick to point out, reading from his published material:

> I feel exactly as the Nazi Party in Germany felt in regard to Germany, regarding the Jewish element in our population. . . . We are the inalterable foes of the Russian-Jewish form of communistic government, against which Adolf Hitler is making such a gritty and successful stand at the present time.[526]

Pelley claimed that there had been an influx of four million Jews into the United States between 1917 and 1918 and that 90 percent of them were Communist. His answer to the "Jewish problem" would have been to strip Jews of all their money, positions of authority, and civil rights and confine them in ghettoes where they couldn't cause the rest of the population any more trouble.

There was no doubt that some of the Silver Shirt chapters were actively preparing for an armed conflict of some kind. According to the Dies Committee, the San Diego chapter had purchased rifles and a machine gun, preparing for a Communist revolt instigated by Jews, who were going to take over the city on May Day, 1934. When they did, the Silver Shirts would fight back and take over City Hall, then go out and exterminate all the Jewish officials who had caused the ruckus. And in Cleveland, Ohio, a Silver Shirts group leader told his members to be prepared to fight an impending communist revolution.[527]

Silver Shirts staged numerous marches and demonstrations around the country as well, engaging in street fights with Jewish groups opposed to the organization, in imitation of Hitler's Brown Shirt tactics in Germany. One of the Silver Shirt Legion marchers was Henry Beach, a

Portland, Oregon, dry cleaner—and the founder, in the 1960s, of the right-wing revolutionary organization Posse Comitatus.[528]

In 1936 volunteers had placed Pelley's name on the presidential ballot under the name of the Christian Party in Washington State, where he garnered 1,598 votes out of 700,000 cast. Pelley had hoped to make a better showing in 1940 since he had received so much publicity in the intervening years, but it was not meant to be.

In 1939 FBI agents raided Pelley's headquarters in Asheville, North Carolina, upon direct orders of Attorney General Francis Biddle. They were reportedly looking for evidence of embezzlement of funds; in the process, they seized all of the organization's office equipment, books, and records. When Pelley complained to the local federal judge who had signed the warrant, the magistrate told him he could always sue the government to get his property back.

Ultimately, the federal government took Pelley to court for tax evasion, but he defeated the charges. Nonetheless, the time and effort it took for him to clear himself derailed his 1940 presidential campaign. So Pelley again shifted gears and changed the direction of the Legion, from running for elective office to actively opposing the Roosevelt administration.

The Silver Shirts joined up with other right-wing organizations such as the Bund, the Christian Front, the Christian Mobilizer, the Social Justice, and the Knights of the White Camellia, which, together with such isolationist groups as the America First Committee, Father Charles Coughlin's National Union for Social Justice/Christian Front, the Mothers of America, and others, clamored for the United States to stay out of war unless physically attacked.

The Japanese attack on Pearl Harbor devastated the Silver Shirts and Pelley personally. He dissolved the Silver Shirts and walked away from politics. Remarried, he moved to Indiana with his new wife, reportedly wanting to forget his past. Within months, however, he had started a new magazine, *Roll Call*, which was unapologetically pro-fascist and against United States intervention in the war. In 1942 he was arrested on charges of sedition and insurrection for alleged preparation for the overthrow of the government. He was found not guilty of the sedition charge but was convicted of the others and sentenced to fifteen years in federal prison.[529]

The mystic who claimed he could levitate and see through walls was unable to escape the grip of the federal government. Pelley remained imprisoned until 1952, when he was released on parole. He died in 1965; reportedly, while he was lying in state, a cross was burned on the lawn of his funeral parlor. Authorities could not determine if an enemy or an admirer had set the fire.

Pelley's precise political ideas died in America years before he did, but his doomsday approach to society, his anti-Semitism, and his paranoid ramblings about the United States government would haunt the country for decades.

Material and Evidence Recovered by the Federal Bureau of Investigation from Amagansett, Long Island, and Ponte Vedra, Florida

Material Recovered in Amagansett:

On June 13, 1942, members of the United States Coast Guard located material and evidence buried on the beach near Amagansett. The Coast Guard gave the agents two military foldable shovels and a German *Kriegsmarine* cap. Four wooden boxes were also delivered to agents of the FBI. These boxes contained numerous German naval uniform items and the following material:

- Two small bags containing ten fuse lighters. These bags were marked "C. Heinrich Anton Dusberg Reissbanzunder."
- One small paper bag containing five fuse lighters.
- Twenty-five .30-caliber electric blasting caps.
- Brass tube containing fifty electric match heads.
- Twenty-five small wooden boxes, each containing five detonators.

- A small paper bag marked "25 Brand Kapseln" containing five wooden boxes, each containing five detonators.
- A cardboard box containing eleven glass capsules. Each capsule contained what appeared to be sulphuric acid.
- A box containing ten brass and plastic devices holding a small charge of a chlorate mixture protected by a paper diaphragm. The box was wrapped in brown paper which was labeled in German "For F.O. Miuntan [sic] H2SO4 EBOINT"
- A box containing:
  - Two leatherette cases each containing two mechanical pen and pencil sets. These items were actually time-delayed detonators marked with pink tags indicating "6 to 7 hours."
  - Two leatherette cases each containing a mechanical fountain pen and pencil sets. These items were time-delayed detonators labeled with a blue tag indicating "2–3 hours."
  - One leatherette case containing a mechanical fountain pen and pencil set. This time-delayed detonator was labeled "11–13 hours."
  - Five small brown tablets rolled in tissue paper and labeled "*Rhiz Rhei 0,5—Wehrpresseissanitatspark X.*"
  - Several scraps of paper with German writing.
- One box containing:
  - Ten clockwork-timing devices.
  - Ten sets of buttons to set firing pins and fasteners for the timers.
- One tin box containing:
  - Eight demolition blocks of TNT, drilled with holes for a cap or fuse.
  - Three rolls of black safety fuse.
  - A cardboard box containing four bombs shaped to look like lumps of coal. Each of these blocks had a hole drilled in one end for a fuse or cap. Also in this box were a roll of safety fuse and a roll of detonating fuse.
- Two tin boxes, each containing 18 - 3″ × 2⅝″ × 5⅝₆″ demolition blocks.
- One tin box containing two blocks of TNT.

Items recovered from Ponte Vedra, Florida:

On June 25, 1942, Edward Kerling accompanied FBI agents to the beach of Ponte Vedra. The location pointed out by Kerling was 4.3 miles from the town of Ponte Vedra. FBI agents dug in the place pointed out by Kerling—which was halfway between the waterline and Florida Route 140. The agents discovered four wooden boxes buried in the sand. The boxes each had two metal strips wrapped around the outside. Inside of the wooden boxes the agents found packing material and smaller sealed metal containers. The following items were found inside the containers:

- Forty-six blocks of TNT, individually wrapped in paper.
- Four blocks of TNT shaped like coal.
- One coil of detonating fuse.
- Four small coils of detonating fuse.
- A small round paper box containing approximately one pint of Thermite.**
- Ten clockwork-bomb timing devices.
- Ten brass and plastic timing devices marked *"70 Minuten."*
- Five leather cases containing:
  - Timing devices marked "11–13 hours."
  - Timing devices marked "6–7 hours."
  - Timing devices marked "2–3 hours."
- Eleven sealed glass vials containing sulphuric acid.
- Twenty-five fuse lighters, marked, *"C Heinrich Anton, Dulsburg, Beissanzunder 6. 1939."*
- Fifty electric match devices.
- Twenty-five electric blasting caps.
- Fifteen wood blocks containing blasting caps.
- Ten wood blocks containing detonators.
- Five wood blocks marked with red lines containing detonators.

**Thermite is a mixture of powdered aluminum and iron oxide. It was commonly used in incendiary bombs.

Ex Parte Quirin et al.; United States ex rel. Quirin et al. v. Cox, Provost Marshal

Supreme Court of the United States
317 U.S. 1; 63 S. Ct. 2; 87 L. Ed. 3

July 29–30, 1942, Argued
July 31, 1942, Decided. Per Curiam decision filed,
July 31, 1942. Full Opinion filed, October 29, 1942.

OPINION: MR. CHIEF JUSTICE STONE delivered the opinion of the Court.

These cases are brought here by petitioners' several applications for leave to file petitions for habeas corpus in this Court, and by their petitions for certiorari to review orders of the District Court for the

District of Columbia, which denied their applications for leave to file petitions for habeas corpus in that court.

The question for decision is whether the detention of petitioners by respondent for trial by Military Commission, appointed by Order of the President of July 2, 1942, on charges preferred against them purporting to set out their violations of the law of war and of the Articles of War, is in conformity to the laws and Constitution of the United States.

After denial of their applications by the District Court, petitioners asked leave to file petitions for habeas corpus in this Court. In view of the public importance of the questions raised by their petitions and of the duty which rests on the courts, in time of war as well as in time of peace, to preserve unimpaired the constitutional safeguards of civil liberty, and because in our opinion the public interest required that we consider and decide those questions without any avoidable delay, we directed that petitioners' applications be set down for full oral argument at a special term of this Court, convened on July 29, 1942. The applications for leave to file the petitions were presented in open court on that day and were heard on the petitions, the answers to them of respondent, a stipulation of facts by counsel, and the record of the testimony given before the Commission.

While the argument was proceeding before us, petitioners perfected their appeals from the orders of the District Court to the United States Court of Appeals for the District of Columbia and thereupon filed with this Court petitions for certiorari to the Court of Appeals before judgment, pursuant to § 240(a) of the Judicial Code, 28 U. S. C. § 347(a). We granted certiorari before judgment for the reasons which moved us to convene the special term of Court. In accordance with the stipulation of counsel we treat the record, briefs and arguments in the habeas corpus proceedings in this Court as the record, briefs and arguments upon the writs of certiorari.

On July 31, 1942, after hearing argument of counsel and after full consideration of all questions raised, this Court affirmed the orders of the District Court and denied petitioners' applications for leave to file petitions for habeas corpus. By per curiam opinion we announced the decision of the Court, and that the full opinion in the causes would be prepared and filed with the Clerk.

The following facts appear from the petitions or are stipulated. Except as noted they are undisputed.

All the petitioners were born in Germany; all have lived in the United States. All returned to Germany between 1933 and 1941. All except petitioner Haupt are admittedly citizens of the German Reich, with which the United States is at war. Haupt came to this country with his parents when he was five years old; it is contended that he became a citizen of the United States by virtue of the naturalization of his parents during his minority and that he has not since lost his citizenship. The Government, however, takes the position that on attaining his majority he elected to maintain German allegiance and citizenship, or in any case that he has by his conduct renounced or abandoned his United States citizenship [citations omitted]. For reasons presently to be stated we do not find it necessary to resolve these contentions.

After the declaration of war between the United States and the German Reich, petitioners received training at a sabotage school near Berlin, Germany, where they were instructed in the use of explosives and in methods of secret writing. Thereafter petitioners, with a German citizen, Dasch, proceeded from Germany to a seaport in Occupied France, where petitioners Burger, Heinck, and Quirin, together with Dasch, boarded a German submarine which proceeded across the Atlantic to Amagansett Beach on Long Island, New York. The four were there landed from the submarine in the hours of darkness, on or about June 13, 1942, carrying with them a supply of explosives, fuses, and incendiary and timing devices. While landing they wore German Marine Infantry uniforms or parts of uniforms. Immediately after landing they buried their uniforms and the other articles mentioned, and proceeded in civilian dress to New York City.

The remaining four petitioners at the same French port boarded another German submarine, which carried them across the Atlantic to Ponte Vedra Beach, Florida. On or about June 17, 1942, they came ashore during the hours of darkness, wearing caps of the German Marine Infantry and carrying with them a supply of explosives, fuses, and incendiary and timing devices. They immediately buried their caps and the other articles mentioned, and proceeded in civilian dress to Jacksonville, Florida, and thence to various points in the United States. All were taken into custody in New York or Chicago by agents of the Federal Bureau of Investigation. All had received instructions in Germany from an officer of the German High Command to destroy war industries and war facilities in the United States, for which they or their relatives in Germany were to receive salary payments from the German Government. They also had been paid by the German Government during their course of training at the sabotage school and had received substantial sums in United States currency, which were in their possession when arrested. The currency had been handed to them by an officer of the German High Command, who had instructed them to wear their German uniforms while landing in the United States [footnote omitted].

The President, as President and Commander in Chief of the Army and Navy, by Order of July 2, 1942 [footnote omitted], appointed a Military Commission and directed it to try petitioners for offenses against the law of war and the Articles of War, and prescribed regulations for the procedure on the trial and for review of the record of the trial and of any judgment or sentence of the Commission. On the same day, by Proclamation [footnote omitted], the President declared that "all persons who are subjects, citizens or residents of any nation at war with the United States or who give obedience to or act under the direction of any such nation, and who during time of war enter or attempt to enter the United States . . . through coastal or boundary defenses, and are charged with committing or attempting or preparing to commit sabotage, espionage, hostile or warlike acts, or violations of the law of war, shall be subject to the law of war and to the jurisdiction of military tribunals."

The Proclamation also stated in terms that all such persons were denied access to the courts.

Pursuant to direction of the Attorney General, the Federal Bureau of Investigation surrendered custody of petitioners to respondent, Provost Marshal of the Military District of Washington, who was directed by the Secretary of War to receive and keep them in custody, and who thereafter held petitioners for trial before the Commission.

On July 3, 1942, the Judge Advocate General's Department of the Army prepared and lodged with the Commission the following charges against petitioners, supported by specifications:

1. Violation of the law of war.
2. Violation of Article 81 of the Articles of War, defining the offense of relieving or attempting to relieve, or corresponding with or giving intelligence to, the enemy.
3. Violation of Article 82, defining the offense of spying.
4. Conspiracy to commit the offenses alleged in charges 1, 2 and 3.

The Commission met on July 8, 1942, and proceeded with the trial, which continued in progress while the causes were pending in this Court. On July 27th, before petitioners' applications to the District Court, all the evidence for the prosecution and the defense had been taken by the Commission and the case had been closed except for arguments of counsel. It is conceded that ever since petitioners' arrest the state and federal courts in Florida, New York, and the District of Columbia, and in the states in which each of the petitioners was arrested or detained, have been open and functioning normally.

While it is the usual procedure on an application for a writ of habeas corpus in the federal courts for the court to issue the writ and on the return to hear and dispose of the case, it may without issuing the writ consider and determine whether the facts alleged by the petition, if proved, would warrant discharge of the prisoner [citations omitted]. Presentation of the petition for judicial action is the institution of a suit. Hence denial by the district court of leave to file the petitions in these causes was the judicial determination of a case or controversy, reviewable on appeal to the Court of Appeals and reviewable here by certiorari [citations omitted].

Petitioners' main contention is that the President is without any statutory or constitutional authority to order the petitioners to be tried by military tribunal for offenses with which they are charged; that in consequence they are entitled to be tried in the civil courts with the safeguards, including trial by jury, which the Fifth and Sixth Amendments guarantee to all persons charged in such courts with criminal offenses. In any case it is urged that the President's Order, in prescribing the procedure of the Commission and the method for review of its findings and sentence, and the proceedings of the Commission under the Order, conflict with Articles of War adopted by Congress—particularly Articles 38, 43, 46, 50½ and 70—and are illegal and void.

The Government challenges each of these propositions. But regardless of their merits, it also insists that petitioners must be denied access to the courts, both because they are enemy aliens or have entered our territory as enemy belligerents, and because the President's Proclamation undertakes in terms to deny such access to the class of persons defined by the Proclamation, which aptly describes the character and conduct of petitioners. It is urged that if they are enemy aliens or if the Proclamation has force, no court may afford the petitioners a hearing. But there is certainly nothing in the Proclamation to preclude access to the courts for determining its applicability to the particular case. And neither the Proclamation nor the fact that they are enemy aliens forecloses consideration by the courts of petitioners' contentions that the Constitution and laws of the United States constitutionally enacted forbid their trial by military commission. As announced in our per curiam opinion, we have resolved those questions by our conclusion that the Commission has jurisdiction to try the charge preferred against petitioners. There is therefore no occasion to decide contentions of the parties unrelated to this issue. We pass at once to the consideration of the basis of the Commission's authority.

We are not here concerned with any question of the guilt or innocence of petitioners [footnote omitted]. Constitutional safeguards for the protection of all who are charged with offenses are not to be disregarded in order to inflict merited punishment on some who are guilty [citations omitted]. But the detention and trial of petitioners—ordered by the President in the declared exercise of his powers as Commander in Chief of the Army in time of war and of grave public danger—are not to be set aside by the courts without the clear conviction that they are in conflict with the Constitution or laws of Congress constitutionally enacted.

Congress and the President, like the courts, possess no power not derived from the Constitution. But one of the objects of the Constitution, as declared by its preamble, is to "provide for the common defence." As a means to that end, the Constitution gives to Congress the power to "provide for the common Defence," Art. I, § 8, cl. 1; "To raise and support Armies," "To provide and maintain a Navy," Art. I, § 8, cl. 12, 13; and "To make Rules for the Government and Regulation of the land and naval Forces," Art. I, § 8, cl. 14. Congress is given authority "To declare War, grant Letters of Marque and Reprisal, and make Rules concerning Captures on Land and Water," Art. I, § 8, cl. 11; and "To define and punish Piracies and Felonies committed on the high Seas, and Offences against the Law of Nations," Art. I, § 8, cl. 10. And finally, the Constitution authorizes Congress "To make all Laws which shall be necessary and proper for carrying into Execution the foregoing Powers, and all other Powers vested by this Constitution in the Government of the United States, or in any Department or Officer thereof." Art. I, § 8, cl. 18.

The Constitution confers on the President the "executive Power," Art. II, § 1, cl. 1, and imposes on him the duty to "take Care that the Laws be faithfully executed." Art. II, § 3. It makes him the Commander in Chief of the Army and Navy, Art. II, § 2, cl. 1, and empowers him to appoint and commission officers of the United States. Art. II, § 3, cl. 1.

The Constitution thus invests the President, as Commander in Chief, with the power to wage war which Congress has declared, and to carry into effect all laws passed by Congress for the conduct of war and for the government and regulation of the Armed Forces, and all laws defining and punishing offenses against the law of nations, including those which pertain to the conduct of war.

By the Articles of War, 10 U. S. C. §§ 1471–1593, Congress has provided rules for the government of the Army. It has provided for the trial and punishment, by courts martial, of violations of the Articles by members of the armed forces and by specified classes of persons associated or serving with the Army. Arts. 1, 2. But the Articles also recognize the "military commission" appointed by military command as an appropriate tribunal for the trial and punishment of offenses against the law of war not ordinarily tried by court martial. See Arts. 12, 15. Articles 38 and 46 authorize the President, with certain limitations, to prescribe the procedure for military commissions. Articles 81 and 82 authorize trial, either by court martial or military commission, of those charged with relieving, harboring or corresponding with the enemy and those charged with spying. And Article 15 declares that "the provisions of these articles conferring jurisdiction upon courts martial shall not be construed as depriving military commissions . . . or other military tribunals of concurrent jurisdiction in respect of offenders or offenses that by statute or by the law of war may be triable by such military commissions . . . or other military tribunals." Article 2 includes among those persons subject to military law the personnel of our own military establishment. But this, as Article 12 provides, does not exclude from that class "any other person who by the law of war is subject to trial by military tribunals" and who under Article 12 may be tried by court martial or under Article 15 by military commission.

Similarly the Espionage Act of 1917, which authorizes trial in the district courts of certain offenses that tend to interfere with the prosecution of war, provides that nothing contained in the act "shall be deemed to limit the jurisdiction of the general courts-martial, military commissions, or naval courts-martial." 50 U. S. C. § 38.

From the very beginning of its history this Court has recognized and applied the law of war as including that part of the law of nations which prescribes, for the conduct of war, the status, rights and duties of enemy nations as well as of enemy individuals [footnote omitted]. By the Articles of War, and especially Article 15, Congress has explicitly provided, so far as it may constitutionally do so, that military tribunals shall have jurisdiction to try offenders or offenses against the law of war in appropriate cases. Congress, in addition to making rules for the government of our Armed Forces, has thus exercised its authority to define and punish offenses against the law of nations by sanctioning, within constitutional limitations, the jurisdiction of military commissions to try persons for offenses which, according to the rules and precepts of the law of nations, and more particularly the law of war, are cognizable by such tribunals. And the President, as Commander in Chief, by his Proclamation in time of war has invoked that law. By his Order creating the present Commission he has undertaken to exercise the authority conferred upon him by Congress, and also such authority as the Constitution itself gives the Commander in Chief, to direct the performance of those functions which may constitutionally be performed by the military arm of the nation in time of war.

An important incident to the conduct of war is the adoption of measures by the military command not only to repel and defeat the enemy, but to seize and subject to disciplinary measures those enemies who in their attempt to thwart or impede our military effort have violated the law of war. It is unnecessary for present purposes to determine to what extent the President as Commander in Chief has constitutional power to create military commissions without the support of Congressional legislation. For here Congress has authorized trial of offenses against the law of war before such commissions. We are concerned only with the question whether it is within the constitutional power of the National Government to place petitioners upon trial before a military commission for the offenses with which they are charged. We must therefore first inquire whether any of the acts charged is an offense against the law of war cognizable before a military tribunal, and if so whether the Constitution prohibits the trial. We may assume that there are acts regarded in other countries, or by some writers on international law, as offenses against the law of war which would not be triable by military tribunal here, either because they are not recognized by our courts as violations of the law of war or because they are of that class of offenses constitutionally triable only by a jury. It was upon such grounds that the Court denied the right to proceed by military tribunal in Ex parte

Milligan, supra. But as we shall show, these petitioners were charged with an offense against the law of war which the Constitution does not require to be tried by jury.

It is no objection that Congress in providing for the trial of such offenses has not itself undertaken to codify that branch of international law or to mark its precise boundaries, or to enumerate or define by statute all the acts which that law condemns. An Act of Congress punishing "the crime of piracy, as defined by the law of nations" is an appropriate exercise of its constitutional authority, Art. I, § 8, cl. 10, "to define and punish" the offense, since it has adopted by reference the sufficiently precise definition of international law [citations omitted] [footnote omitted].

Similarly, by the reference in the 15th Article of War to "offenders or offenses that . . . by the law of war may be triable by such military commissions," Congress has incorporated by reference, as within the jurisdiction of military commissions, all offenses which are defined as such by the law of war [citations omitted], and which may constitutionally be included within that jurisdiction. Congress had the choice of crystallizing in permanent form and in minute detail every offense against the law of war, or of adopting the system of common law applied by military tribunals so far as it should be recognized and deemed applicable by the courts. It chose the latter course.

By universal agreement and practice, the law of war draws a distinction between the armed forces and the peaceful populations of belligerent nations [footnote omitted] and also between those who are lawful and unlawful combatants. Lawful combatants are subject to capture and detention as prisoners of war by opposing military forces. Unlawful combatants are likewise subject to capture and detention, but in addition they are subject to trial and punishment by military tribunals for acts which render their belligerency unlawful [footnote omitted]. The spy who secretly and without uniform passes the military lines of a belligerent in time of war, seeking to gather military information and communicate it to the enemy, or an enemy combatant who without uniform comes secretly through the lines for the purpose of waging war by destruction of life or property, are familiar examples of belligerents who are generally deemed not to be entitled to the status of prisoners of war, but to be offenders against the law of war subject to trial and punishment by military tribunals [citations omitted].

Such was the practice of our own military authorities before the adoption of the Constitution [footnote omitted], and during the Mexican and Civil Wars [footnote omitted].

Paragraph 83 of General Order No. 100 of April 24, 1863, directed that: "Scouts or single soldiers, if disguised in the dress of the country, or in the uniform of the army hostile to their own, employed in obtaining information, if found within or lurking about the lines of the captor, are treated as spies, and suffer death." And Paragraph 84, that "Armed prowlers, by whatever names they may be called, or persons of the enemy's territory, who steal within the lines of the hostile army, for the purpose of robbing, killing, or of destroying bridges, roads, or canals, or of robbing or destroying the mail, or of cutting the telegraph wires, are not entitled to the privileges of the prisoner of war" [footnote omitted]. These and related provisions have been continued in substance by the Rules of Land Warfare promulgated by the War Department for the guidance of the Army [citations omitted]. Paragraph 357 of the 1940 Rules provides that "All war crimes are subject to the death penalty, although a lesser penalty may be imposed." Paragraph 8 (1940) divides the enemy population into "armed forces" and "peaceful population," and Paragraph 9 names as distinguishing characteristics of lawful belligerents that they "carry arms openly" and "have a fixed distinctive emblem." Paragraph 348 declares that "persons who take up arms and commit hostilities" without having the means of identification prescribed for belligerents are punishable as "war criminals." Paragraph 351 provides that "men and bodies of men, who, without being lawful belligerents . . . nevertheless commit hostile acts of any kind" are not entitled to the privileges of prisoners of war if captured and may be tried by military commission and punished by death or lesser punishment. And Paragraph 352 provides that "armed prowlers . . . or persons of the enemy territory who steal within the lines of the hostile army for the purpose of robbing, killing, or of destroying bridges, roads, or canals, of robbing or destroying the mail, or of cutting the telegraph wires, are not entitled to be treated as prisoners of war." As is evident from reading these and related Paragraphs 345–347, the specified violations are intended to be only illustrative of the applicable principles of the common law of war, and not an exclusive enumeration of the punishable acts recognized as such by that law. The definition of lawful belligerents by Paragraph 9 is that adopted by Article 1, Annex to Hague Convention No. IV of October 18, 1907, to which the United States was a signatory and which was ratified by the Senate in 1909. The preamble to the Convention declares: "Until a more complete code of the laws of war has been issued, the High Contracting Parties deem it expedient to declare that, in cases not included in the Regulations adopted by them, the inhabitants and the belligerents remain under the protection and the rule of the principles of the law of nations, as they result from the usages established among civilized peoples, from the laws of humanity, and the dictates of the public conscience."

Our Government, by thus defining lawful belligerents entitled to be treated as prisoners of war, has recognized that there is a class of unlawful belligerents not entitled to that privilege, including those who, though combatants, do not wear "fixed and distinctive emblems." And by Article 15 of the Articles of War Congress has made provision for their trial and punishment by military commission, according to "the law of war."

By a long course of practical administrative construction by its military authorities, our Government has likewise recognized that those who during time of war pass surreptitiously from enemy territory into our own, discarding their uniforms upon entry, for the commission of hostile acts involving destruction of life or property, have the status of unlawful combatants punishable as such by military commission. This precept of the law of war has been so recognized in practice both here and abroad, and has so generally been accepted as valid by authorities on international law [footnote omitted] that we think it must be regarded a rule or principle of the law of war recognized by this Government by its enactment of the Fifteenth Article of War.

Specification 1 of the first charge is sufficient to charge all the petitioners with the offense of unlawful belligerency, trial of which is within the jurisdiction of the Commission, and the admitted facts affirmatively show that the charge is not merely colorable or without foundation.

Specification 1 states that petitioners, "being enemies of the United States and acting for ... the German Reich, a belligerent enemy nation, secretly and covertly passed, in civilian dress, contrary to the law of war, through the military and naval lines and defenses of the United States ... and went behind such lines, contrary to the law of war, in civilian dress ... for the purpose of committing ... hostile acts, and, in particular, to destroy certain war industries, war utilities and war materials within the United States."

This specification so plainly alleges violation of the law of war as to require but brief discussion of petitioners' contentions. As we have seen, entry upon our territory in time of war by enemy belligerents, including those acting under the direction of the armed forces of the enemy, for the purpose of destroying property used or useful in prosecuting the war, is a hostile and warlike act. It subjects those who participate in it without uniform to the punishment prescribed by the law of war for unlawful belligerents. It is without significance that petitioners were not alleged to have borne conventional weapons or that their proposed hostile acts did not necessarily contemplate collision with the Armed Forces of the United States. Paragraphs 351 and 352 of the Rules of Land Warfare, already referred to, plainly contemplate that the hostile acts and purposes for which unlawful belligerents may be punished are not limited to assaults on the Armed Forces of the United States. Modern warfare is directed at the destruction of enemy war supplies and the implements of their production and transportation, quite as much as at the armed forces. Every consideration which makes the unlawful belligerent punishable is equally applicable whether his objective is the one or the other. The law of war cannot rightly treat those agents of enemy armies who enter our territory, armed with explosives intended for the destruction of war industries and supplies, as any the less belligerent enemies than are agents similarly entering for the purpose of destroying fortified places or our Armed Forces. By passing our boundaries for such purposes without uniform or other emblem signifying their belligerent status, or by discarding that means of identification after entry, such enemies become unlawful belligerents subject to trial and punishment.

Citizenship in the United States of an enemy belligerent does not relieve him from the consequences of a belligerency which is unlawful because in violation of the law of war. Citizens who associate themselves with the military arm of the enemy government, and with its aid, guidance and direction enter this country bent on hostile acts, are enemy belligerents within the meaning of the Hague Convention and the law of war [citation omitted]. It is as an enemy belligerent that petitioner Haupt is charged with entering the United States, and unlawful belligerency is the gravamen of the offense of which he is accused.

Nor are petitioners any the less belligerents if, as they argue, they have not actually committed or attempted to commit any act of depredation or entered the theatre or zone of active military operations. The argument leaves out of account the nature of the offense which the Government charges and which the Act of Congress, by incorporating the law of war, punishes. It is that each petitioner, in circumstances which gave him the status of an enemy belligerent, passed our military and naval lines and defenses or went behind those lines, in civilian dress and with hostile purpose. The offense was complete when with that purpose they entered—or, having so entered, they remained upon—our territory in time of war without uniform or other appropriate means of identification. For that reason, even when committed by a citizen, the offense is distinct from the crime of treason defined in Article III, § 3 of the Constitution, since the absence of uniform essential to one is irrelevant to the other [citation omitted].

But petitioners insist that, even if the offenses with which they are charged are offenses against the law of war, their trial is subject to the requirement of the Fifth Amendment that no person shall be held to answer for a capital or otherwise infamous crime unless on a presentment or indictment of a grand jury, and that such trials by Article III, § 2, and the Sixth Amendment must be by jury in a civil court. Before the Amendments, § 2 of Article III, the Judiciary Article, had provided, "The Trial of all Crimes, except in Cases of Impeachment, shall be by Jury," and had directed that "such Trial shall be held in the State where the said Crimes shall have been committed."

Presentment by a grand jury and trial by a jury of the vicinage where the crime was committed were at the time of the adoption of the Constitution familiar parts of the machinery for criminal trials in the civil courts. But they were procedures unknown to military tribunals, which are not courts in the sense of the Judiciary Article [citations omitted], and which in the natural course of events are usually called upon to function under conditions precluding resort to such procedures. As this Court has often recognized, it was not the purpose or effect of § 2 of Article III, read in the light of the common law, to enlarge the then existing right to a jury trial. The object was to preserve unimpaired trial by jury in all those cases in which it had been recognized by the common law and in all cases of a like nature as they might arise in the future [District of Columbia v. Colts, 282 U.S. 63], but not to bring within the sweep of the guaranty those cases in which it was then well understood that a jury trial could not be demanded as of right.

The Fifth and Sixth Amendments, while guaranteeing the continuance of certain incidents of trial by jury which Article III, § 2 had left unmentioned, did not enlarge the right to jury trial as it had been established by that Article [citation omitted]. Hence petty offenses triable at common law without a jury may be tried without a jury in the federal courts, notwithstanding Article III, § 2, and the Fifth and Sixth Amendments [citations omitted]. Trial by jury of criminal contempts may constitutionally be dispensed with in the federal courts in those cases in which they could be tried without a jury at common law [citations omitted]. Similarly, an action for debt to enforce a penalty inflicted by Congress is not subject to the constitutional restrictions upon criminal prosecutions [citations omitted].

All these are instances of offenses committed against the United States, for which a penalty is imposed, but they are not deemed to be within Article III, § 2, or the provisions of the Fifth and Sixth Amendments relating to "crimes" and "criminal prosecutions." In the light of this long-continued and consistent interpretation we must conclude that § 2 of Article III and the Fifth and Sixth Amendments cannot be taken to have extended the right to demand a jury to trials by military commission, or to have required that offenses against the law of war not triable by jury at common law be tried only in the civil courts.

The fact that "cases arising in the land or naval forces" are excepted from the operation of the Amendments does not militate against this conclusion. Such cases are expressly excepted from the Fifth Amendment, and are deemed excepted by implication from the Sixth [citations omitted]. It is argued that the exception, which excludes from the Amendment cases arising in the armed forces, has also by implication extended its guaranty to all other cases; that since petitioners, not being members of the Armed Forces of the United States, are not within the exception, the Amendment operates to give to them the right to a jury trial. But we think this argument misconceives both the scope of the Amendment and the purpose of the exception.

We may assume, without deciding, that a trial prosecuted before a military commission created by military authority is not one "arising in the land . . . forces," when the accused is not a member of or associated with those forces. But even so, the exception cannot be taken to affect those trials before military commissions which are neither within the exception nor within the provisions of Article III, § 2, whose guaranty the Amendments did not enlarge. No exception is necessary to exclude from the operation of these provisions cases never deemed to be within their terms. An express exception from Article III, § 2, and from the Fifth and Sixth Amendments, of trials of petty offenses and of criminal contempts has not been found necessary in order to preserve the traditional practice of trying those offenses without a jury. It is no more so in order to continue the practice of trying, before military tribunals without a jury, offenses committed by enemy belligerents against the law of war.

Section 2 of the Act of Congress of April 10, 1806, 2 Stat. 371, derived from the Resolution of the Continental Congress of August 21, 1776 [footnote omitted], imposed the death penalty on alien spies "according to the law and usage of nations, by sentence of a general court martial." This enactment must be regarded as a contemporary construction of both Article III, § 2, and the Amendments as not foreclosing trial by military tribunals, without a jury, of offenses against the law of war committed by enemies not in or associated with our Armed Forces. It is a construction of the Constitution which has been followed since the founding of our Government, and is now continued in the 82nd Article of War. Such a construction is entitled to the greatest respect [citations omitted]. It has not hitherto been challenged, and, so far as we are advised, it has never been suggested in the very extensive literature of the subject that an alien spy, in time of war, could not be tried by military tribunal without a jury [footnote omitted].

The exception from the Amendments of "cases arising in the land or naval forces" was not aimed at trials by military tribunals, without a jury, of such offenses against the law of war. Its objective was quite different—to authorize the trial by court martial of the members of our Armed Forces for all that class of crimes which under the Fifth and Sixth Amendments might otherwise have been deemed triable in the civil courts. The cases mentioned in the exception are not restricted to those involving offenses against the law of war alone, but extend to trial of all offenses, including crimes which were of the class traditionally triable by jury at common law [citations omitted].

Since the Amendments, like § 2 of Article III, do not preclude all trials of offenses against the law of war by military commission without a jury when the offenders are aliens, not members of our Armed Forces, it is plain that they present no greater obstacle to the trial in like manner of citizen enemies who have violated the law of war applicable to enemies. Under the original statute authorizing trial of alien spies by military tribunals, the offenders were outside the constitutional guaranty of trial by jury, not because they were aliens but only because they had violated the law of war by committing offenses constitutionally triable by military tribunal.

We cannot say that Congress in preparing the Fifth and Sixth Amendments intended to extend trial by jury to the cases of alien or citizen offenders against the law of war otherwise triable by military commission, while withholding it from members of our own armed forces charged with infractions of the Articles of War punishable by death. It is equally inadmissible to construe the Amendments—whose primary purpose was to continue unimpaired presentment by grand jury and trial by petit jury in all those cases in which they had been customary—as either abolishing all trials by military tribunals, save those of the personnel of our own armed forces, or, what in effect comes to the same thing, as imposing on all such tribunals the necessity of proceeding against unlawful enemy belligerents only on presentment and trial by jury. We conclude that the Fifth and Sixth Amendments did not restrict whatever authority was conferred by the Constitution to try offenses against the law of war by military commission, and that petitioners, charged with such an offense not required to be tried by jury at common law, were lawfully placed on trial by the Commission without a jury.

Petitioners, and especially petitioner Haupt, stress the pronouncement of this Court in the Milligan case, supra, p. 121, that the law of war "can never be applied to citizens in states which have upheld the authority of the government, and where the courts are open and their process unobstructed." Elsewhere in its opinion, the Court was at pains to point out that Milligan, a citizen twenty years resident in Indiana, who had never been a resident of any of the states in rebellion, was not an enemy belligerent either entitled to the status of a prisoner of war or subject to the penalties imposed upon unlawful belligerents. We construe the Court's statement as to the inapplicability of the law of war to Milligan's case as having particular reference to the facts before it. From them the Court concluded that Milligan, not being a part of or associated with the armed forces of the enemy, was a non-belligerent, not subject to the law of war save as—in circumstances found not there to be present, and not involved here—martial law might be constitutionally established.

The Court's opinion is inapplicable to the case presented by the present record. We have no occasion now to define with meticulous care the ultimate boundaries of the jurisdiction of military tribunals to try persons according to the law of war. It is enough that petitioners here, upon the conceded facts, were plainly within those boundaries, and were held in good faith for trial by military commission, charged with being enemies who, with the purpose of destroying war materials and utilities, entered, or after entry remained in, our territory without uniform—an offense against the law of war. We hold only that those particular acts constitute an offense against the law of war which the Constitution authorizes to be tried by military commission.

Since the first specification of Charge I sets forth a violation of the law of war, we have no occasion to pass on the adequacy of the second specification of Charge I, or to construe the 81st and 82nd Articles of War for the purpose of ascertaining whether the specifications under Charges II and III allege violations of those Articles or whether if so construed they are constitutional [citation omitted].

There remains the contention that the President's Order of July 2, 1942, so far as it lays down the procedure to be followed on the trial before the Commission and on the review of its findings and sentence, and the procedure in fact followed by the Commission, are in conflict with Articles of War 38, 43, 46, 50½ and 70. Petitioners argue that their trial by the Commission, for offenses against the law of war and the 81st and 82nd Articles of War, by a procedure which Congress has prohibited, would invalidate any conviction which could be obtained against them and renders their detention for trial likewise unlawful [citations omitted] that the President's Order prescribes such an unlawful procedure; and that the secrecy surrounding the trial and all proceedings before the Commission, as well as any review of its decision, will preclude a later opportunity to test the lawfulness of the detention.

Petitioners do not argue and we do not consider the question whether the President is compelled by the Articles of War to afford unlawful enemy belligerents a trial before subjecting them to disciplinary measures. Their contention is that, if Congress has authorized their trial by military commission upon the charges preferred—violations of the law of war and the 81st and 82nd Articles of War—it has by the Articles of War prescribed the procedure by which the trial is to be conducted; and that, since the President has ordered their trial for such offenses by military commission, they are entitled to claim the protection of the procedure which Congress has commanded shall be controlling.

We need not inquire whether Congress may restrict the power of the Commander in Chief to deal with enemy belligerents. For the Court is unanimous in its conclusion that the Articles in question could not at any stage of the proceedings afford any basis for issuing the writ. But a majority of the full Court are not agreed on the appropriate grounds for decision. Some members of the Court are of the opinion that Congress did not intend the Articles of War to govern a Presidential military commission convened for the determination of questions relating to admitted enemy invaders, and that the context of the Articles makes clear that they should not be construed to apply in that class of cases. Others are of the view that—even though this trial is subject to whatever provisions of the Articles of War Congress has in terms made applicable to "commissions"—the particular Articles in question, rightly construed, do not foreclose the procedure prescribed by the President or that shown to have been employed by the Commission, in a trial of offenses against the law of war and the 81st and 82nd Articles of War, by a military commission appointed by the President.

Accordingly, we conclude that Charge I, on which petitioners were detained for trial by the Military Commission, alleged an offense which the President is authorized to order tried by military commission; that his Order convening the Commission was a lawful order and that the Commission was lawfully constituted; that the petitioners were held in lawful custody and did not show cause for their discharge. It follows that the orders of the District Court should be affirmed, and that leave to file petitions for habeas corpus in this Court should be denied.

MR. JUSTICE MURPHY took no part in the consideration or decision of these cases.

German and Italian Detention and Internment in World War II

Very few presidential acts have had as much effect on a group of United States residents as the execution of Executive Order 9066 by President Franklin Roosevelt on February 19, 1942.[530] This proclamation gave American military and justice officials broad—nearly unfettered—power to "evacuate" and "exclude" any person from areas that the government declared prohibited military areas.[531] The regions that were designated as restricted were sweeping.

Attorney General Biddle described the orders he made regarding those identified as enemy aliens:

> Under regulations promulgated by me shortly after the first detentions, enemy aliens were not allowed to travel without federal authority, were barred from areas surrounding forts, camps, arsenals, airports, power plants, and dams; factories, warehouses, or storage yards for implements of war; and from canals, wharfs, piers, and docks. They could not change their residence, or travel outside the city in which they

lived, except under prescribed rules. They were forbidden to possess firearms, bombs, explosives, short-wave receiving and transmitting sets, signal devices, codes or ciphers, and photographs and maps of any military installation.[532]

The implementation of Executive Order 9066 had a devastating effect on Japanese-Americans and Japanese nationals living in the United States. The number of those on the West Coast who were taken from their homes and moved into "relocation camps" reached 120,000. An additional 40,000 people living in the United States who had been born in Japan were declared enemy aliens by the government.[533]

Although by no means to the same degree as Japanese-Americans, many German and Italians living in the United States were also swept into the enemy-alien net. By 1948, the government had arrested and detained almost 11,000 German-Americans.[534] In 1942, the FBI arrested 9,405 enemy aliens. This included 4,764 Japanese, 3,120 Germans, and 1,521 Italians.[535] Many of those arrested would be detained for the duration of the war in camps spread throughout America. The camps were located across the United States from Angel Island in San Francisco Bay to Ellis Island in New York.[536] By the end of the war, 31,275 enemy aliens had been interned by the government. This included 16,849 Japanese, 10,905 Germans, 3,278 Italians, 52 Hungarians, 25 Romanians, and 5 Bulgarians.[537]

President Roosevelt wanted all German aliens and German-Americans to be interned. In the 1940s, there were more than five million people of German ancestry living in the United States and more than 1.2 million German immigrants.[538]

Attorney General Biddle felt that there were too many Germans and Italians in the country to carry out the President's wishes. Biddle described that, after Roosevelt signed the order, they discussed the Germans and Italians.

"How many Germans are there in the country," he asked. "Oh, about 600,000," I told him. "And you're going to intern all of them," he said—by that time he was back in the chair. "Well, not quite all," I answered. "I don't care so much about the Italians," he continued.

"They are a lot of opera singers, but the Germans are different, they may be dangerous."[539]

In the end, the president would not order the mass internment of German and Italian Americans.

In addition to those who were detained, many Germans and Italians were told to leave their homes. Along the central and northern coast of California, where more than two-thirds of the California fishing fleet was owned and operated by Italians, the long-established fishing industry was such a part of the culture that they were immortalized in books like Steinbeck's *Cannery Row*. In the early part of 1942, however, approximately 10,000 Italian aliens were forced to move out of prohibited areas there.[540] Under the government regulations, they were kept from the water and their boats, and were forced to move, giving up their livelihood and their homes. The Coast Guard used many of the fishing boats to prowl the coast in search of Japanese submarines. In the meantime, the boats' owners were paid a nominal rent.[541]

Attorney General Biddle, working with the FBI, developed the process used to classify a person as an enemy alien. Once the FBI identified a person as a potential enemy alien, a warrant was obtained from the United States Attorney's Office. The individual was then arrested and brought before an enemy alien parole board. The board members were "respected citizens" selected to volunteer service on the Board. The tribunals were "informal" and, in most cases, there were no lawyers on the Board. The accused were not allowed to have a lawyer represent them at the hearing. Biddle maintained that the exclusion of lawyers for the accused "greatly expedited action, saved time, and put the procedure on a prompt and commonsense basis."[542] The United States attorney represented the government. If the board determined that the person was an enemy alien, they were detained for the duration.[543]

The internment of enemy aliens even reached beyond America's borders. Concerned for Americans being held by Axis powers, the United States negotiated with the governments of several South

UNITED STATES DEPARTMENT OF JUSTICE

★

NOTICE
TO ALIENS OF ENEMY
NATIONALITIES

★ The United States Government requires all aliens of German, Italian, or Japanese nationality to apply at post offices nearest to their place of residence for a Certificate of Identification. Applications must be filed between the period February 9 through February 28, 1942. *Go to your postmaster today for printed directions.*

EARL G. HARRISON,
Special Assistant to the Attorney General.

FRANCIS BIDDLE,
Attorney General.

AVVISO

Il Governo degli Stati Uniti ordina a tutti gli stranieri di nazionalità Tedesca, Italiana e Giapponese di fare richiesta all' Ufficio Postale più prossimo al loro luogo di residenza per ottenere un Certificato d'Identità. Le richieste devono essere fatte entro il periodo che decorre tra il 9 Febbraio e il 28 Febbraio, 1942.

Andate oggi dal vostro Capo d'Ufficio Postale (Postmaster) per ricevere le istruzioni scritte.

BEKANNTMACHUNG

Die Regierung der Vereinigten Staaten von Amerika fordert alle Auslaender deutscher, italienischer und japanischer Staatsangehoerigkeit auf, sich auf das ihrem Wohnorte naheliegende Postamt zu begeben, um einen Personalausweis zu beantragen. Das Gesuch muss zwischen dem 9. und 28. Februar 1942 eingereicht werden.

Gehen Sie noch heute zu Ihrem Postmeister und verschaffen Sie sich die gedruckten Vorschriften.

敵國外人注意

日獨伊諸國ノ國籍ヲ有スル在留外人ハ二月九日ヨリ二十八日マデノ間ニ其居所ニ一番近イ郵便局デ自分證明書ヲ申込ム可シ。

今日モ早速郵便局ヘ行キテ説明書ヲ賴ム様ニ願ヒマス。

Post This Side In All States EXCEPT
Arizona, California, Idaho, Montana, Nevada, Oregon, Utah, Washington

American countries to bring more than 2,000 enemy aliens into the United States to be used in exchange with the Axis powers for detained Americans. Many of those who were brought to the United States were arrested in Peru.[544]

The threat of arrest and internment remained with Japanese and Germans living in the United States for the duration of the war. On Columbus Day—October 12, 1942—the attorney general delivered a speech to a packed house at Carnegie Hall after being introduced by New York Mayor Fiorello La Guardia to an audience assembled at Carnegie Hall.

Biddle spoke of the rich Italian heritage and mentioned Dante, Galileo, da Vinci, Michelangelo, Tasso, and Ariosto. He then told the assembled crowd that the United States would no longer classify Italians as enemy aliens.[545]

The next day the Italian language paper, *L'Italo Americano*, ran the headline, *"Non Piu' Nemici—!"* No Longer Enemies![546]

Operation Pastorius: Fifty-Six Days in America

June 13, 1942—Dasch, Quirin, Heinck, and Burger land in Amagansett.

June 17, 1942—Kerling, Haupt, Thiel, and Neubauer land in Ponte Vedra, Florida.

June 27, 1942—J. Edgar Hoover announces the arrest of the eight Nazi terrorists.

June 28, 1942—Newspapers around the country carry the story of the FBI's arrests of the eight Germans.

July 2, 1942—President Roosevelt announces the creation of a military commission to try the eight Nazis.

July 8, 1942—The military commission trial begins in the Department of Justice, Washington, D.C.

July 13, 1942—The FBI announces the arrest of fourteen people accused of assisting the eight Nazis. The arrests include Herbert Haupt's mother and father.

July 20, 1942—The prosecution concludes its case in chief and rests.

July 27, 1942—The Supreme Court announces that it will convene in special session to hear the case of the eight accused spies. The defense rests in the military commission trial.

July 29, 1942—The case is argued before the United States Supreme Court.

July 31, 1942—The United States Supreme Court rejects the defendants' arguments and upholds the jurisdiction and authority of the military commission.

August 1, 1942—Closing arguments are completed. The commission takes the case under submission.

August 3, 1942—The commission submits its findings and the evidence to the president.

August 4, 1942—The White House announces that President Roosevelt is studying the evidence.

August 7, 1942—The White House informs the press that the president has not completed his review of the case.

August 8, 1942—Herbert Hans Haupt, Heinrich Harm Heinck, Edward John Kerling, Hermann Otto Neubauer, Richard Quirin, and Werner Thiel are executed in the electric chair. Ernst Peter Burger and George John Dasch are sentenced to prison.

Bibliography

Books:

Allen, Thomas B. and Norman Pollmar. *World War II, Encyclopedia of the War Years: 1941–1942*. New York: Random House, 1946.

Baldwin, Neil. *Henry Ford and the Jews: The Mass Production of Hate*. New York: Public Affairs Books, 2001.

Berg, A. Scott. *Lindbergh*. New York: Putnam, 1998.

Biddle, Francis. *In Brief Authority*. Garden City: Doubleday & Company, 1962.

Birkheimer, General William E. *Military Government and Martial Law*. London: Franklin Publishing, 1914.

Blackstone, Sir William. *Commentaries on the Laws of England 1723–1780* (1794).

Blum, George P. *The Rise of Fascism in Europe*. Westport, CT: Greenwood Press, 2001.

Brissaud, André. *Canaris: The Biography of Admiral Canaris, Chief of German Military Intelligence in the Second World War*. New York: Grosset & Dunlap, 1974.

Bullock, Allan. *Hitler and Stalin: Parallel Lives*. New York: Alfred A. Knopf, 1992.

Carlson, John Roy. *Undercover*. New York: E. P. Dutton, 1943.

Cicero, Marcus Tullius. *Pro Milone*. 44 B.C.

Cohen, Stan. *V for Victory: America's Home Front during World War II*. Missoula: Pictorial Histories Publishing, 1991.

Cohn, Norman. *Warrant for Genocide: The Myth of the Jewish World Conspiracy and the Protocols of the Elders of Zion*. New York: Harper & Row, 1967.

Conspiracy and Aggression. Vol. VIII. Washington: GPO, 1946.

Dasch, George J. *Eight Spies Against America*. New York: Robert M. McBride & Company, 1959.

Dear, Ian. *Sabotage and Subversion: The SOE and OSS at War*. London: Castle Military Paperbacks, 1996.

Diamond, Sander. *The Nazi Movement in the U.S., 1924–1941*. New York: Cornell University Press, 1974.

DiStasi, Lawrence. *Una storia segreta: The Secret History of Italian American Evacuation and Internment During World War II*. Berkeley: Heyday Books, 2001.

Eatwell, Roger. *Fascism: A History*. New York: Penguin Books, 1997.

Fox, Stephen. *America's Invisible Gulag: A Biography of German American Internment and Exclusion in World War II*. New York: Peter Lang Publishing, 2000.

———. *UnCivil Liberties: Italian Americans Under Siege During World War II*. Parkland, FL: Universal Publishers, 2000.

Gabler, Neal. *Walter Winchell: Gossip, Power and the Culture of Celebrity.* New York: Knopf, 1994.

Gannon, Michael. *Operation Drumbeat: The Dramatic True Story of Germany's First U-Boat Attacks Along the American Coast in World War II.* New York: Harper Perennial, 1990.

Gentry, Curt. *J. Edgar Hoover: The Man and His Secrets.* New York: W. W. Norton & Company, 1991.

Gisevius, Hans Bernd. *To the Bitter End: An Insider's Account of the Plot to Kill Hitler, 1933–1944.* London: Da Capo Press, 1998.

Gurock, Jeffrey S., ed. *Anti-Semitism in America.* Vol. 6. Parts I and II. New York: Routledge, 1998.

Harris, Whitney R. *Tyranny on Trial: The Trial of the Major German War Criminals at the End of World War II at Nuremberg, Germany, 1945–1946.* Dallas: Southern Methodist University Press, 1999.

Harvey, Robert. *A Few Bloody Noses: The Realities and Mythologies of the American Revolution.* New York: The Overlook Press, 2002.

Heide, Robert and John Gilman. *Home Front America: Popular Culture of the World War II Era.* San Francisco: Chronicle Books, 1995.

Higham, Charles. *American Swastika.* New York: Doubleday, 1985.

———. *Errol Flynn: The Untold Story.* New York: Doubleday, 1980.

———. *Trading with the Enemy.* New York: Barnes & Noble, 1983.

Hoffman, Bruce. *Inside Terrorism.* New York: Columbia University Press, 1963.

Hofstadter, Richard. *Social Darwinism in American Thought.* Boston: Beacon Press, 1944.

Hohne, Heinz. *Canaris: Hitler's Master Spy.* New York: University Press of America, 1999.

Howard, Michael. *Strategic Deception in the Second World War.* New York: W. W. Norton & Company, 1995.

Kessler, Ronald. *The Bureau: The Secret History of the FBI.* New York: St. Martin's Press, 2002.

Kramer, Arnold. *Undue Process: The Untold Story of America's German Alien Internees.* London: Rowman & Littlefield, 1997.

Laqueur, Walter, ed. *Fascism: A Reader's Guide.* Los Angeles: University of California Press, 1976.

Leckie, Robert. *George Washington's War: The Saga of the American Revolution.* New York: Harper Perennial, 1992.

Lee, Martin A. *The Beast Reawakens.* Boston: Little, Brown & Company, 1997.

Mallmann Showell, Jack P. *U-Boats at War: Landings on Hostile Shores.* Surrey: Ian Allan Publishing, 2000.

Mason, Alpheus Thomas. *Harlan Fiske Stone: A Pillar of Law.* New York: Viking, 1956.

Newfield, Michael J. *The Rocket and the Reich.* Cambridge: Harvard University Press, 1995.

Persico, Joseph E. *Nuremberg: Infamy on Trial.* New York: Penguin Books, 1994.

———. *Piercing the Reich.* New York: Barnes & Noble, 1979.

———. *Roosevelt's Secret War: FDR and World War II Espionage.* New York: Random House, 2001.

Pinza, Ezio. "Autobiography of an Italian Internee." *"Only What We Could Carry": The Japanese American Internment Experience.* Ed. Lawson Fusao Inada. Berkeley: Heyday Books, 2000.

Rachlis, Eugene. *They Came To Kill.* New York: Popular Library, 1961.

Rehnquist, William H. *All the Laws but One: Civil Liberties in Wartime.* New York: Vintage Books, 2000.

———. *The Supreme Court.* New York: Knopf, 2001.

Ribuffo, Leo P. *Protestantism on the Right: William Dudley Pelley, Gerald B. Winwood and Gerald L. K. Smith.* 2 vols. New Haven: Yale University Press, 1976.

Rossiter, Clinton. *The Supreme Court and the Commander in Chief.* Ithaca: Cornell University Press, 1976.

Salvimini, Gaetano. *Italian Fascist Activities in the U.S.* New York: Center for Migration Studies, 1977.

Seldes, George. *Facts & Fascism.* New York: In Fact Inc., 1943.

Shirer, William. *The Rise and Fall of the Third Reich: A History of Nazi Germany.* New York: Simon & Schuster, 1960.

Snyder, Dr. Lewis L. *Encyclopedia of the Third Reich.* New York: Marlowe & Company, 1976.

Spivak, John L. *Secret Armies: The New Technique of Nazi Warfare.* New York: Modern Age Books, 1939.

Starr, Kevin. *Embattled Dreams: California in War and Peace, 1940–1950.* New York: Oxford University Press, 2002.

Strong, Donald. *Organized Anti-Semitism in America: The Rise in Group Prejudice During the Decade 1930–1940.* Washington: American Council on Public Affairs, 1941.

Swanson, James L. and Daniel R. Weinberg. *Lincoln's Assassins: Their Trial and Execution.* Chicago: Arena Editions, 2001.

Takaki, Ronald, *Double Victory: A Multicultural History of America in World War II.* New York: Little, Brown & Company, 2000.

Theoharis, Ethan G., ed. *The FBI: A Comprehensive Reference Guide.* New York: Oryx Press, 1996.

Turner, William H. *Hoover's FBI.* New York: Thunder's Mouth Press, 1993.

Waller, John H. *The Unseen War in Europe.* New York: Random House, 1996.

Warren, Donald. *Radio Priest: Charles Coughlin, the Father of Hate Radio.* New York: The Free Press, 1996.

Winks, Robert W. *Cloak and Gown: Scholars in the Secret War, 1939–1961.* New Haven: Yale University Press, 1996.

Winthrop, Colonel William. *Military Law and Precedents.* Washington: GPO, 1920.

Publications:

Cahan, Richard. "A Terrorist's Tale." *Chicago Magazine,* February 2002.

Cohen, Gary. "The Keystone Kommandos." *Atlantic Monthly,* February 2002.

"D. Milton Ladd." *The Investigator.* J. J. McGuire, ed. FBI Recreation Association, U.S. Department of Justice, Washington, D.C. Vol. 11, No. 9., September 15, 1942.

Lardner, George, Jr. "Nazi Saboteurs Captured!" *Washington Post Magazine.* January 13, 2002: W12.

Lobb, David. "Fascist Apocalypse: William Pelley and Millennial Extremism." *Journal of Millennial Studies* (November 1999).

Nelinson, Jerome. "Enemies on the Beach." *The Reservist*, July 1997.

Peel, Peter H. "The Great Brown Scare: The Amerika Deutscher Bund in the Thirties and the Hounding of Fritz Julius Kuhn." *The Journal for Historical Review* VII, no. 4 (Winter 1986): 419 ff.

Pelley, William Dudley. "Seven Minutes in Eternity." *American Magazine*, March 1929.

Safire, William. "Truthout." November 26, 2001.

Silverstein, Ken. "Ford and the Fuhrer." *The Nation* 24 (January 2000): 11–16.

Interviews:

Interview with Retired FBI Agent Duane L. Traynor.
Interview with Retired FBI Agent Kenneth Crosby.
Interview with Retired FBI Agent John J. Walsh.
Interview with Retired FBI Agent Joseph O' Connor.
Interview with Retired FBI Agent Thomas Scott.

Documents from the United States National Archives, College Park, Maryland:

Record Group 38, Records of the Office of the Chief of Naval Operations. Office of Naval Intelligence, Security-Classified Administrative Correspondence, 1942–46.

RG 38, Eastern Sea Frontier War Diary.

RG 60, General Records of the Department of Justice. Nazi Saboteur Records, 1942–45.

RG 55, Records of the Federal Bureau of Investigation, FBI Headquarters Files.

RG 65, FBI Headquarters Files.

RG 87, Records of the US Secret Service, General Correspondence and Subject File, 1932–1950.

RG 107, Records of the Office of the Secretary of War, Stimson's Safe Files.

RG 153, Records of the Office of the Judge Advocate General (Army), Court-Martial Case Files.

RG 319, Records of the Army Staff.

RG 407, Records of the Adjutant General's Office, 1940–42 (formerly) Classified Central Decimal Files

Documents From the Franklin D. Roosevelt Library:

Roosevelt, Franklin D., Papers as President, File: Nazi Saboteurs: Stenographic Transcripts of Trial, 1942.

Roosevelt, Franklin D., President's Personal File, Speeches File: Statement re: Execution of Sentences of 8 Nazi Saboteurs

Roosevelt, Franklin D. Speech Files, 1419–1427, April 28, 1942–August 31, 1942. Presidential Radio Address. April 28, 1942. Presidential Message to Winston Churchill. August 14, 1942.

Other Documents:

Nuremberg Trials, Volume 3. Morning Session, December 12, 1945.

U.S. 74th Congress. *Report of the McCormack Committee*. Report No. 153. 1st Session, February 15, 1935.

U.S. 76th Congress. Special Committee on Un-American Activities. *Investigation of Un-American Propaganda Activities in the U.S.* Vol. 6. Washington: GPO, 1939.

———. Special Committee on Un-American Activities. *Investigation of Un-American Propaganda Activities in the U.S.* Vol. 4. Washington: GPO, 1940.

U.S. 78th Congress. Special Committee on Un-American Activities. *Investigation of Un-American Propaganda Activities in the U.S.* Vol. 7. Washington: GPO, 1943.

Law Review Articles:

Bittker, Boris L. "The World War II German Saboteurs' Case and Writs of Certiorari before Judgment by the Court of Appeals: A Tale of Nunc Pro Tunc Jurisdiction." 14 Const. Comment 431 (1997).

Corona, Spencer J. and Neal A. Richardson. "Justice for War Criminals of Invisible Armies: A New Legal and Military Approach to Terrorism." *Oklahoma City University Law Review* 21 (1996): 349.

Currie, David P. "The Constitution in the Supreme Court: The Second World War, 1941–1946." *Catholic University Law Review* 1 (1987): 37.

Lacey, Michael O. Major. "Military Commissions: A Historical Survey," *The Army Lawyer*. March 2002.

Mason, Alpheus Thomas. "Inter Arma Silent Leges: Chief Justice Stone's Views," *Harvard Law Review* 69 (1956): 806.

Cases:

Chandler v. United States 171 F.2d 921 (1949).
Cramer v. United States 325 U.S. 1, 65 S.Ct. 918 (1945).
Ex Parte Milligan 71 U. S. 2 (1866).
Ex Parte Quirin 317 U.S. 1, 63 S.Ct. 2 (1942).
Haupt v. United States 330 U.S. 631 (1947).
United States v. Haupt 152 F. 2d 771 (1946).
United States v. Haupt, et al. 136 F.2d 661 (1943).

Endnotes

Chapter 1: Four Lucky Porcupines

[1]Michael Gannon, *Operation Drumbeat: The Dramatic True Story of Germany's First U-Boat Attacks Along the American Coast in World War II* (New York: Harper Perennial, 1990), 455–456; citing King & Whitehill, Fleet Admiral King; indicating that the original of Marshall's memorandum is in the George C. Marshall Research Library, Lexington, VA.

[2]*Los Angeles Times*, June 29, 1942.

[3]Ibid.

[4]*New York Times*, June 19, 1942.

[5]FBI Memorandum, Special Agent D. Traynor to Special Agent Tramm, July 15, 1942, Records of the Federal Bureau of Investigation, Record Group 55, National Archives at College Park, College Park, MD (hereinafter: National Archives, RG 55); Jack P. Mallmann Showell, *U-Boats at War: Landings on Hostile Shores* (Surrey: Ian Allen Publishing, 2000), 29.

[6]FBI statement of George John Dasch, 25–26; National Archives, RG 55.

[7]Ibid., 37.

[8]Ibid.

[9]George J. Dasch, *Eight Spies Against America* (New York: Robert M. McBride & Company, 1959), 65.

[10]FBI statement of George John Dasch, 73, National Archives, RG 55.

[11]Ibid., 102.

[12]Ibid., 89.

[13]*New York Times*, July 29, 1942.

[14]Jerome Nelinson, "Enemies on the Beach," *The Reservist*, July 1997.

[15]Dasch, *Eight Spies Against America*, 99.

[16]Stenographic Transcript of Proceedings Before the Military Commission to Try Persons with Offenses Against the Law of War and the Articles of War, 104; July 8, 1942–August 1, 1942, Record Group 55, National Archives at College Park, College Park, MD (hereinafter: Reporter's Transcripts of Military Commission Proceedings).

[17]Special Agent T. J. Donegan, FBI Memorandum to the Director, July 9, 1942, National Archives, RG 55.

[18]FBI statement of George John Dasch, 44, National Archives, RG 55.

[19]Dasch, *Eight Spies Against America*, 99.

[20]Ibid., 100.

[21]Ibid., 102.

[22]Ibid.

[23]FBI Memorandum, Dictated by E. J. Connelley, Assistant Director, June 19, 1942, National Archives, RG 55.

[24]Dasch, *Eight Spies Against America*, 103.

[25]Eugene Rachlis, *They Came to Kill* (New York: Popular Library, 1961), 86.

[26]Dasch, *Eight Spies Against America*, 104.

Chapter 2: "This is What We Germans Are Supposed to Do"

[27]*New York Times*, July 2, 1942.

[28]FBI statement of George John Dasch, 29, National Archives, RG 55; Joseph E. Persico, *Roosevelt's Secret War: FDR and World War II Espionage* (New York: Random House, 2001), 199.

[29]Hans Bernd Gisevius, *To the Bitter End: An Insider's Account of the Plot to Kill Hitler, 1933–1944* (London: Da Capo Press, 1998), 471.

[30]Statement by Col. Edwin von Lahousen, former chief of Abwehr II-Sabotage Section. *Nuremberg Trials*, Volume 3. Morning Session, December 12, 1945.

[31]André Brissaud, *Canaris: The Biography of Admiral Canaris, Chief of German Military Intelligence in the Second World War* (New York: Grosset & Dunlap, 1974), 26.

[32]Ibid., 158, 318.

[33]John H. Waller, *The Unseen War in Europe* (New York: Random House, 1996), 354.

³⁴When Canaris signed the final orders for the Pastorius mission he remarked, "This will cost these poor men their lives." Persico, *Roosevelt's Secret War*, 200.

³⁵FBI Memorandum for the Director, Prepared by E. J. Connelley, July 8, 1942, National Archives, RG 55.

³⁶FBI statement of George John Dasch, 26, National Archives, RG 55.

³⁷FBI statement of Heinrich Harm Heinck, June 23, 1942, 3, National Archives, RG 55.

³⁸Ibid.

³⁹FBI statement of Richard Quirin, June 23, 1942, 3, National Archives, RG 55.

⁴⁰FBI statement of Heinrich Harm Heinck, June 23, 1942, 4, National Archives, RG 55.

⁴¹FBI statement of George John Dasch, 27–29, National Archives, RG 55.

⁴²Dasch, *Eight Spies Against America*, 73.

⁴³FBI statement of George John Dasch, 24, National Archives, RG 55.

⁴⁴Ibid., 2.

⁴⁵Ibid., 3–4.

⁴⁶Dasch, *Eight Spies Against America*, 16.

⁴⁷Ibid., 17.

⁴⁸FBI Memorandum, Re: George John Dasch, June 25, 1942, National Archives, RG 55.

⁴⁹Ibid.

⁵⁰Dasch, *Eight Spies Against America*, 17.

⁵¹FBI statement of George John Dasch, 7, National Archives, RG 55.

⁵²Dasch, *Eight Spies Against America*, 23–24.

⁵³Ibid., 27–28.

⁵⁴Rachlis, *They Came to Kill*, 30.

⁵⁵Ibid., 28.

⁵⁶Dasch, *Eight Spies Against America*, 31.

⁵⁷FBI Memorandum for Mr. Ladd, Re: George John Dasch, by Special Agent C. F. Lanman, August 2, 1942, 10, National Archives, RG 55.

⁵⁸FBI statement of George John Dasch, 57-b, National Archives, RG 55.

[59]FBI Report, on Interview of Ernst Peter Burger, by Special Agents B. D. Rice, J. G. Fellner, and C. F. Lanman, NY File 65–11065, National Archives, RG 55.

[60]FBI Report, File No. 65–11065, Re: Richard Quirin, by Special Agent B. F. Wiand, June 20, 1942, National Archives, RG 55.

[61]FBI statement of Heinrich Harm Heinck, June 21, 1942, 4, National Archives, RG 55.

[62]FBI Memorandum, Re: Heinrich Harm Heinck, June 25, 1942, National Archives, RG 55.

[63]FBI Memorandum for Special Agent Ladd, from Special Agent R. F. Cooper, June 20, 1942, National Archives, RG 55.

[64]FBI Report, Neubauer Interview by Agents W. W. Fisher and E. F. Emrich, July, 1, 1942, National Archives, RG 55.

[65]FBI statement of George John Dasch, 68, National Archives, RG 55.

[66]FBI Memorandum Re: Herbert Haupt, June 2, 1942, National Archives, RG 55.

[67]Richard Cahan, "A Terrorist's Tale," *Chicago Magazine*, February 2002.

[68]Ibid.

[69]FBI statement of George John Dasch, 70, National Archives, RG 55.

[70]Confidential FBI Memo, from Op-16-F-9, by John L. Rihaldaffer, July 7, 1942, National Archives, RG 55.

[71]FBI statement of George John Dasch, 70, National Archives, RG 55.

[72]FBI statement of Walter Froehling, 10, National Archives, RG 55.

[73]FBI statement of George John Dasch, 70, National Archives, RG 55.

[74]Rachlis, *They Came to Kill*, 60.

[75]Dasch, *Eight Spies Against America*, 30–32.

[76]FBI statement of George John Dasch, 192–196, National Archives, RG 55.

[77]Ibid., 79–82.

[78]Ibid., 98, 192.

[79]Ibid., 96.

[80]Ibid., 145, 163.

[81]Gary Cohen, "The Keystone Kommandos," *Atlantic Monthly*, February 2002.

[82]FBI statement of George John Dasch, 107–110, National Archives, RG 55.

[83]FBI statement of Heinrich Harm Heinck, June 23, 1942, 12, National Archives, RG 55.

[84]FBI statement of George John Dasch, 183, National Archives, RG 55.

[85]Ibid., 110.

[86]Ibid., 145–146; FBI statement of Heinrich Harm Heinck, June 23, 1942, 10, National Archives, RG 55.

[87]FBI statement of Heinrich Harm Heinck, June 23, 1942, 13, National Archives, RG 55.

[88]Ibid., 14.

[89]FBI statement of George John Dasch, 110, National Archives, RG 55.

[90]Dasch, *Eight Spies Against America*, 85.

[91]FBI statement of Heinrich Harm Heinck, June 23, 1942, 15, National Archives, RG 55.

[92]Dasch, *Eight Spies Against America*, 86.

[93]Dasch, *Eight Spies Against America*, 87.

[94]FBI statement of George John Dasch, 189, National Archives, RG 55.

[95]Dasch, *Eight Spies Against America*, 89.

[96]FBI statement of George John Dasch, 208, National Archives, RG 55.

[97]Rachlis, *They Came to Kill*, 72.

[98]FBI statement of George John Dasch, 39, National Archives, RG 55.

[99]*New York Times*, July 2, 1942.

[100]*New York Times*, July 5, 1942.

Chapter 3: The Friendly Sea

[101]Jeffrey S. Gurock, ed., *Anti-Semitism in America*. Vol. 6, Parts I and II (New York: Routledge, 1998), 469–470.

[102]George Seldes, *Facts & Fascism* (New York: In Fact Inc., 1943), 141.

[103]Gaetano Salvimini, *Italian Fascist Activities in the U.S.* (New York: Center for Migration Studies, 1977), 444.

[104]According to U.S. Congressman Dextrin in 1937, there were 350,000 members, quoted in Donald Strong, *Organized Anti-Semitism in America: The Rise in Group Prejudice During the Decade 1930–1940* (Washington: American Council on Public Affairs, 1941), 30. Most experts put the figure at closer to 100,000, with up to 50,000 in the Bund and 50,000 in a host of other pro-Fascist organizations such as Pelley's Silver Shirts, the Knights of the

White Camellias, and the Italian-American Black Shirts. Others list the membership at a much more conservative 10,000. Fritz Kuhn, the Bund Leader, quoted Bund membership between 8,299 and 230,000. *See also* Arnold Kramer, *Undue Process: The Untold Story of America's German Alien Internees* (London: Rowman & Littlefield, 1997), 5.

[105]House Special Committee on Un-American Activities, *Investigation of Un-American Propaganda Activities in the U.S.*, Vol. 4, 76th Congress, (Washington: GPO, 1940), 1465.

[106]John Roy Carlson, *Undercover* (New York: E. P. Dutton, 1943), 116–117.

[107]Strong, *Organized Anti-Semitism in America*, 26.

[108]Carlson, *Undercover*, 112.

[109]Strong, *Organized Anti-Semitism in America*, 27.

[110]*New York Times*, June 29, 1942.

[111]House Special Committee, *Un-American Propaganda Activities*, 76th Congress, 3786.

[112]Strong, *Organized Anti-Semitism in America*, 25.

[113]Neil Baldwin, *Henry Ford and the Jews: The Mass Production of Hate* (New York: Public Affairs Books, 2001), 284.

[114]*New York Times*, July 1942.

[115]Strong, *Organized Anti-Semitism in America*, 30.

[116]Ibid., 30.

[117]Ibid.

[118]Peter H. Peel, "The Great Brown Scare: The Amerika Deutscher Bund in the Thirties and the Hounding of Fritz Julius Kuhn," *The Journal for Historical Review* VII, no. 4 (Winter 1986), 419 ff.

[119]Strong, *Organized Anti-Semitism in America*, 29.

[120]Charles Higham, *American Swastika* (New York: Doubleday, 1985), 6.

[121]Carlson, *Undercover*, 108–110.

[122]Strong, *Organized Anti-Semitism in America*, 26.

[123]FBI Memorandum for the Director, Prepared by E. J. Connelley, July 8, 1942, 3, National Archives, RG 55.

[124]FBI Memorandum, Re: George John Dasch, with aliases, *et al*, on Walter Kappe, July 8, 1942, 8, National Archives, RG 55.

[125]*New York Times*, July 1942.

[126] House Special Committee on Un-American Activities, *Investigation of Un-American Propaganda Activities in the U.S.*, Vol. 7, 78th Congress (Washington: GPO, 1943), 1466.

[127]Peel, "The Great Brown Scare," 419 ff.

[128]Carlson, *Undercover*, 27.

[129]Ibid., 28.

[130]Peel, "The Great Brown Scare," 419 ff.

[131]Strong, *Organized Anti-Semitism in America*, 23.

[132]House Special Committee on Un-American Activities, *Investigation of Un-American Propaganda Activities in the U.S.*, Vol. 6, 76th Congress (Washington: GPO, 1939), 3768.

[133]Peel, "The Great Brown Scare," 419 ff.

[134]House Special Committee, *Un-American Propaganda Activities*, 76th Congress, 3768.

[135]Strong, *Organized Anti-Semitism in America*, 39.

[136]House Special Committee, *Un-American Propaganda Activities*, 78th Congress, 64.

[137]Ibid.

[138]Ibid.

[139]Ibid.

[140]*Los Angeles Times*, July 4, 1942.

[141]Statement by Attorney General Francis Biddle, *Los Angeles Times*, July 5, 1942.

[142]*New York Times*, July 10, 1942.

Chapter 4: Franz Daniel Pastorius

[143]Special Agent T. J. Donegan, FBI Memorandum for the Director, Re: George John Dasch, National Archives, RG 55.

[144]Rachlis, *They Came to Kill*, 87.

[145]Dasch, *Eight Spies Against America*, 104.

[146]Ibid., 105.

[147]FBI statement of George John Dasch, 136, National Archives, RG 55.

[148]Rachlis, *They Came to Kill*, 90.

[149]FBI statement of George John Dasch, 137, National Archives, RG 55.

[150]Dasch, *Eight Spies Against America*, 106.

[151]Ibid., 107–110.

[152]Ibid.

[153]Ibid.

[154]FBI statement of George John Dasch, 129, National Archives, RG 55.

[155]Ibid., 130.

[156]Dasch, *Eight Spies Against America*, 115.

[157]Ibid.

[158]FBI Memorandum for Mr. Tolson from John Edgar Hoover, Director, June 19, 1942, National Archives, RG 55.

[159]Ibid., 117.

[160]Reporter's Transcripts of Military Commission Proceedings, 2853, National Archives, RG 55.

[161]FBI Memorandum for Mr. Ladd from Agent Duane L. Traynor, June 25, 1942, 1, National Archives, RG 55.

[162]Duane Traynor, interview by Alex Abella, May 2002.

[163]Kenneth Crosby, interview by Alex Abella, May 2002.

[164]Ibid.

[165]Duane Traynor, interview by Alex Abella, May 2002.

[166]Memorandum to Mr. Ladd from Special Agent R. P. Kramer, June 19, 1942, National Archives, RG 55.

[167]FBI Memorandum, NY File 65–11065, National Archives, RG 55.

[168]FBI Memorandum for Mr. Ladd from Agent Duane L. Traynor, June 25, 1942, 4, National Archives, RG 55.

[169]Duane Traynor, interview by Alex Abella, May 2002.

[170]Ronald Kessler, *The Bureau: The Secret History of the FBI* (New York: St. Martin's Press, 2002), 26.

[171]Duane Traynor, interview by Alex Abella, May 2002.

[172]Memorandum to Mr. Ladd from Special Agent R. P. Kramer, June 19, 1942, National Archives, RG 55.

[173]Duane Traynor, interview by Alex Abella, May 2002.

[174]Reporter's Transcripts of Military Commission Proceedings, 2505, National Archives, RG 55.

[175]Duane Traynor, interview by Alex Abella, May 2002.

[176]FBI Memorandum, Activity Log, Re: George John Dasch, June 19–25, 1942, National Archives, RG 55.

[177]Duane Traynor, interview by Alex Abella, May 2002.

[178]Kessler, *The Bureau*, 14.

[179]Ibid., 31.

[180]Ibid., 64.

[181]Ibid., 182.

[182]Ibid., 95.

[183]FBI statement of George John Dasch, 79, National Archives, RG 55.

[184]FBI statement of George John Dasch, 32, National Archives, RG 55.

[185]FBI statement of George John Dasch, 64, National Archives, RG 55.

[186]FBI statement of Heinrich Harm Heinck, June 23, 1942, 25, National Archives, RG 55.

[187]FBI statement of Heinrich Harm Heinck, June 21, 1942, 8, National Archives, RG 55.

[188]Kessler, *The Bureau*, 46.

[189]Reporter's Transcripts of Military Commission Proceedings, 2865, National Archives, RG 55.

[190]FBI Report, NY File 65–11065, June 21, 1942, 7, National Archives, RG 55.

[191]Kessler, *The Bureau*, 21.

[192]FBI statement of George John Dasch, 79, National Archives, RG 55.

[193]Ibid., 110.

[194]Kessler, *The Bureau*, 43.

[195]Ibid.

[196]Ibid., 65, quoting Francis Biddle.

[197]FBI statement of George John Dasch, 29, National Archives, RG 55.

[198]Duane Traynor, interview by Alex Abella, May 2002.

[199]*New York Times*, July 18, 1942.

Chapter 5: Welcome In America

[200]FBI Memorandum from SAC Johnson to Mr. E. A. Tamm, Re: George John Davis, transcribed phone call, June 21, 1942, National Archives, RG 55.

[201]FBI report, NY File 65–11065, June 25, 1942, National Archives, RG 55.

[202]Rachlis, *They Came to Kill*, 68.

[203]FBI Memorandum, dictated by E. J. Connelley, NY File 65–11065, National Archives, RG 55.

[204]FBI Report by Special Agents B. D. Rice and Earl Hirsch, NY File 65–11065, June 20–27, 1942, National Archives, RG 55.

[205]FBI Memorandum, NY File 65–11065, 6, National Archives, RG 55.

[206]Ibid.

[207]Ibid.

[208]FBI Memorandum for the Director from Special Agent D. M. Ladd, July 23, 1942, National Archives, RG 55.

[209]Rachlis, *They Came to Kill*, 103.

[210]FBI Memorandum, NY File 65–11065, National Archives, RG 55.

[211]Rachlis, *They Came to Kill*, 104.

[212]Ibid., 106.

[213]FBI Memorandum for Mr. Ladd, Re: George John Dasch, from Duane L. Traynor, June 22, 1942, National Archives, RG 55.

[214]Ibid.

[215]FBI Memorandum for Special Agent Mr. Ladd from Special Agent Duane L. Traynor, June 25, 1942, 3, National Archives, RG 55.

[216]FBI File No. 65–2441, Title: George John Dasch with aliases et al, Statement from Hans Max Haupt, July 1–2, 1942, National Archives, RG 55.

[217]Ibid.

[218]FBI File No. 65–2441, Title: George John Dasch with aliases et al, Report of Special Agent P. V. Robe, July 23, 1942, National Archives, RG 55.

[219]Ibid.

[220]Statement by Walter Otto Froehling to FBI Agents George D. O'Connor and John F. Hennessey, July 3, 1942, National Archives, RG 55.

[221]Ibid.

[222]FBI File No. 65–2441, Title: George John Dasch with aliases et al, Statement from Hans Max Haupt, July 1–2, 1942, 3, National Archives, RG 55.

[223]Ibid., 4.

[224]Ibid.

[225]Ibid., 5.

[226]Ibid.

[227]FBI statement of Walter Froehling, 6, National Archives, RG 55

[228]Ibid.

[229]FBI File No. 65–2441, Title: George John Dasch with aliases et al, Statement from Erna Haupt, July 3, 1942, 8, National Archives, RG 55.

[230]FBI File No. 65–2441, Title: George John Dasch with aliases et al, Report of Special Agent P. V. Robe, July 23, 1942, National Archives, RG 55.

[231]FBI statement of Hans Haupt, 8, National Archives, RG 55.

[232]Ibid.

[233]Rachlis, *They Came to Kill*, 96.

[234]FBI statement of Hans Haupt, 8, National Archives, RG 55.

[235]Letter from C. Farrel, Pontiac car dealer, to Attorney General Francis Biddle, June 25, 1942, National Archives, RG 55.

[236]FBI File No. 65–2441, Title: George John Dasch with aliases et al, Report of Special Agent P. V. Robe, July 23, 1942, National Archives, RG 55.

[237]Rachlis, *They Came to Kill*, 97.

[238]FBI File No. 65–2441, Title: George John Dasch with aliases et al, Report of Special Agent P. V. Robe, July 23, 1942, 5, National Archives, RG 55.

[239]Rachlis, *They Came to Kill*, 121.

[240]FBI statement of Hans Haupt, 9, National Archives, RG 55.

[241]FBI Memorandum, Special Agent Kove, July 1942, 17, National Archives, RG 55.

[242]FBI Memorandum, NY File 65–11065, by Agents B. D. Rice and Earl Hirsh, June 27–30, 1942, National Archives, RG 55.

[243]FBI Report, Neubauer interview by agents W. W. Fisher and E. F. Emrich, July 1, 1942, National Archives, RG 55.

[244]*New York Times*, July 21, 1942.

Chapter 6: Dinner with the Yugoslav Ambassador

[245]Francis Biddle, *In Brief Authority* (Garden City: Doubleday & Company, 1962), 325–326.

[246]Ibid., 327.

[247]Persico, *Roosevelt's Secret War*.

[248] Biddle, *In Brief Authority*, 325–326.

[249] *See also* Gannon, *Operation Drumbeat* for a full discussion of Operation Drumbeat—its extent and origins.

[250]*New York Times*, June 28, 1942.

[251]Biddle, *In Brief Authority*, 328.

[252]Ibid., 330.

[253]FBI statement of George John Dasch, 76, National Archives, RG 55.

[254]Biddle, *In Brief Authority*, 330.

[255]FBI Memorandum to the Director by Edward A. Tamm, June 25, 1942—declassified June 10, 1982, National Archives, RG 55.

[256]Ibid.

[257]Section 88 of Title 18, United States Code.

[258]FBI Memorandum to the Director by Edward A. Tamm, June 25, 1942—declassified June 10, 1982, National Archives, RG 55.

[259]J. Edgar Hoover, Director of the FBI, Memorandum to Special Agents Tolson, Tamm, and Ladd, June 29, 1942, National Archives, RG 55.

[260]Ibid.

[261]Ibid.

[262]Reporter's Transcripts of Military Commission Proceedings, 2885, National Archives, RG 55.

[263]Ibid., 2885–2886.

[264]J. Edgar Hoover, Director of the FBI, Memorandum to Special Agents Tolson, Tamm, and Ladd, June 29, 1942, National Archives, RG 55.

[265]Ibid.

[266]Ibid.

[267]Ibid.

[268]Ibid.

[269]Ibid.

[270]*New York Times*, July 22, 1942.

Chapter 7: "A Wholesome and Desirable Safeguard to Civil Liberty in a Time of War"

271*Ex Parte Milligan* (1866) 71 U.S. 2, 18 L.Ed. 281.

272William H. Rehnquist, *All the Laws but One: Civil Liberties in Wartime* (New York: Vintage Press, 1998), 89.

273*Ex Parte Milligan* (1866) 71 U.S. 2, 18 L.Ed. 281.

274On September 24, 1862, President Lincoln issued the following proclamation:

> That during the existing insurrection, and as a necessary means for suppressing the same, all rebels and insurgents, their aiders and abettors, within the United States, and all persons discouraging volunteer enlistments, resisting militia drafts, or guilty of any disloyal practice, affording aid and comfort to rebels, against the authority of the United States, shall be subject to martial law, and liable to trial and punishment by courts martial or military commission.
>
> Second. That the writ of habeas corpus is suspended in respect to all persons arrested, or who now, or hereafter during the Rebellion shall be, imprisoned in any fort, camp, arsenal, military prison, or other place confinement, by any military authority, or by the sentence of any court martial or military commission. (*Ex Parte Milligan* (1866) 71 U.S. 24–25)

275Robert Leckie, *George Washington's War: The Saga of the American Revolution* (New York: Harper Perennial, 1992).

276 Major Michael O. Lacey, "Military Commissions: A Historical Survey," *The Army Lawyer*, March 2002.

277Leckie, *George Washington's War.*

278Robert Harvey, *A Few Bloody Noses: The Realities and Mythologies of the American Revolution* (New York: The Overlook Press, 2002), 346.

279Colonel William Winthrop, United States Army, *Military Law and Precedents* (Washington: GPO, 1920), 832.

280Lacey, "Military Commissions."

281Winthrop, *Military Law and Precedents*, 464.

282Ibid, 464.

283*Ex Parte Milligan* (1866) 71 U.S. 2, 51.

284General William E. Birkheimer, United States Army, *Military Government and Martial Law* (London: Franklin Publishing, 1914).

285*Ex Parte Quirin* (1942) 317 U.S. 1, 31, 63 S.Ct. 2, 13 *citing* Department of the Pacific, G.O. No. 52, June 27, 1865.

[286]James L. Swanson and Daniel R. Weinberg, *Lincoln's Assassins: Their Trial and Execution* (Chicago: Arena Editions, 2001), 18–20.

[287]Ibid, 20.

[288]Ibid, 23.

[289]*Ex Parte Quirin* (1942) 317 U.S. 1, 31, 63 S.Ct. 2, 13, *citing* Department of the East, G.O. No. 14, February 14, 1865.

[290]*Ex Parte Quirin* (1942) 317 U.S. 1, 31, 63 S.Ct. 2, 13, *citing* G.C.M.O. No. 107, April 18, 1866.

[291]Rehnquist, *All the Laws but One*, 83.

[292]*Ex Parte Milligan* (1866) 71 U.S. 2, 4.

[293]Rehnquist, *All the Laws but One*, 83.

[294]*Ex Parte Milligan* (1866) 71 U.S. 2.

[295]*Ex Parte Milligan* (1866) 71 U.S. 2, 18 L.Ed. 281.

[296]William H. Rehnquist, *The Supreme Court* (New York: Knopf, 2001), 77.

[297]Ibid., citing *Ex Parte Milligan* (1866), 4 Wallace 2, 71 U.S. 281, 295.

[298]Rehnquist, *The Supreme Court*, 76–77.

[299]*Ex Parte Milligan* (1866) 71 U.S. 2, 124–126 18 L.Ed. 281, 296–298.

[300]Ibid.

[301]Ibid.

[302]*New York Times*, July 23, 1942.

[303]Ibid.

Chapter 8: The Halls Of Justice

[304]*New York Times*, July 7, 1942.

[305]Dasch, *Eight Spies Against America*, 128.

[306]Ibid.

[307]FBI Investigative Reports, July 5, 1942; *Washington Times Herald*, July 5, 1942.

[308]Biddle, *In Brief Authority*, 332.

[309]Rachlis, *They Came to Kill*, 142.

[310]*Los Angeles Examiner*, July 6, 1942.

³¹¹Ibid.

³¹²Ibid.

³¹³*New York Times*, July 9–16, 1941; *Los Angeles Times*, July 9–16, 1942.

³¹⁴Reporter's Transcripts of Military Commission Proceedings, 4–5, National Archives, RG 55.

³¹⁵Ibid.

³¹⁶Ibid., 8.

³¹⁷Ibid., 11.

³¹⁸Ibid., 12.

³¹⁹*New York Times*, July 23, 1942.

³²⁰Reporter's Transcripts of Military Commission Proceedings, 101, National Archives, RG 55.

³²¹Ibid., 103.

³²²Ibid.

³²³Ibid., 103–112.

³²⁴Ibid., 112.

³²⁵Ibid., 112–113.

³²⁶Ibid.

³²⁷Ibid.

³²⁸Reporter's Transcripts of Military Commission Proceedings, National Archives, RG 55.

³²⁹Ibid.

³³⁰Reporter's Transcripts of Military Commission Proceedings, National Archives, RG 55.

³³¹Rachlis, *They Came to Kill*, 161.

³³²*New York Times*, July 9, 1942.

³³³Ibid.

³³⁴Rachlis, *They Came to Kill*, 134.

³³⁵*Los Angeles Times*, July 9, 1942.

³³⁶Rachlis, *They Came to Kill*, 167–178; Reporter's Transcripts of Military Commission Proceedings, National Archives, RG 55.

³³⁷Rachlis, *They Came to Kill*, 177.

³³⁸*New York Times*, July 23, 1942.

Chapter 9: The Meeting At The Farm

[339]Reporter's Transcripts of Military Commission Proceedings, National Archives, RG 55.

[340]Biddle, *In Brief Authority*, 325–326.

[341]*New York Times*, July 31, 1942.

[342]Alpheus Thomas Mason, *"Inter Arma Silent Leges:* Chief Justice Stone's Views," *Harvard Law Review* 69 (1956): 806.

[343]Biddle, *In Brief Authority*, 325–326.

[344]Ibid.

[345]*New York Times*, July 28, 1942.

[346]Cahan, "A Terrorist's Tale."

[347]*New York Times*, July 28, 1942.

[348]Mason, *Harlan Fiske Stone*, 655.

[349]*New York Times*, July 28, 1942.

[350]Ibid.

[351]Mason, *Harlan Fiske Stone*, 654.

[352]*New York Times*, July 28, 1942.

[353]Mason, *"Inter Arma Silent Leges."*

[354]*New York Times*, July 29, 1942, citing polls conducted by the American Institute of Public Opinion.

[355]Sir William Blackstone, *Commentaries on the Laws of England 1723–1780* (1794).

[356]U.S. Constitution, art. 1, sec. 9.

[357]*New York Times*, July 29, 1942.

[358]*New York Times*, July 31, 1942.

[359]*New York Times*, July 30, 1942.

[360]Ibid.

[361]Biddle, *In Brief Authority*, 337.

[362]*New York Times*, July 31, 1942.

[363]Mason, *Harlan Fiske Stone*, 654.

[364]Biddle, *In Brief Authority*, 337–338.

[365]Joseph E. Persico, *Nuremberg: Infamy on Trial* (New York: Penguin Books, 1994).

366The description of Colonel Royall as referenced in the *New York Times*, July 29, 1942; and from the Reporter's Transcripts of Military Commission Proceedings, National Archives, RG 55.

367Mason, *Harlan Fiske Stone*, 655.

368Ibid., 656.

369*New York Times*, July 30, 1942.

370Ibid.

371Ibid.

372Ibid.

373Ibid.

374Ibid.

375Ibid.

376Ibid.

377*New York Times*, August 1, 1942.

378*Ex Parte Quirin* (1942) 317 U.S. 1, 63 S.Ct. 2.

379William Safire, "Truthout," November 26, 2001.

380*New York Times*, August 1, 1942.

381*New York Times*, July 27, 1942.

382*New York Times*, July 28, 1942.

Chapter 10: Invaders or Refugees?

383Reporter's Transcripts of Military Commission Proceedings, National Archives, RG 55.

384Mason, *Harlan Fiske Stone*, 654; FBI records, National Archives, RG 55.

385Reporter's Transcripts of Military Commission Proceedings, National Archives, RG 55.

386Ibid.

387Ibid.

388Ibid.

389Ibid.

390Ibid.

391Ibid.

[392]Noted expert on terrorism Bruce Hoffman explains in *Inside Terrorism* (New York: Columbia University Press, 1998): "Terrorism, in the most widely accepted contemporary usage of the term, is fundamentally and inherently political. It is also ineluctably about power: the pursuit of power, the acquisition of power, and the use of power to achieve political change. Terrorism is thus violence—or equally important, the threat of violence—used and directed in pursuit of, and in service of, a political aim," 14–15.

[393]Carl von Clausewitz, *On War*, (London: Penguin Books, 1982), 104.

[394]Reporter's Transcripts of Military Commission Proceedings, National Archives, RG 55.

[395]Ibid.

[396]Ibid., 2885.

[397]Ibid., 2887–2889.

[398]Ibid., 2889.

[399]Ibid., 2890.

[400]Ibid., 2891.

[401]Ibid., 2895.

[402]Ibid., 2889.

[403]Ibid., 2907–2908.

[404]Ibid., 2914.

[405]Ibid., 2927.

[406]*Gideon v. Wainwright* (1963) 372 U.S. 335, 339.

[407]Reporter's Transcripts of Military Commission Proceedings, 2941–2953.

[408]Biddle, *In Brief Authority*, 468.

[409]Ibid., 476.

[410]Reporter's Transcripts of Military Commission Proceedings, 2960–2961, National Archives, RG 55.

[411]Ibid.

[412]Special Agent D. H. Ladd, Petition by defendants to the President attached to FBI Memorandum, August 3, 1942, National Archives, RG 55.

Chapter 11: The Executions: We're Here To Help!

[413]*New York Times*, August 8, 1942.

[414]*New York Times*, August 7, 1942.

[415]Biddle, *In Brief Authority*, 339.

[416]*New York Times*, August 9, 1942.

[417]Details regarding the notification of the defendants of the findings of the Commission and the President's sentences from: Memorandum from Brigadier General Albert L. Cox to the President of the United States, August 19, 1942, National Archives, RG 55.

[418]Cohen, "The Keystone Kommandos," 59.

[419]Memorandum from Special Agent McGee to Director Hoover, August 10, 1942, National Archives, RG 55.

[420]*New York Times*, August 8, 1942.

[421]Memorandum from Special Agent McGee to Director Hoover, August 10, 1942, National Archives, RG 55.

[422]Persico, *Roosevelt's Secret War*, 204–205.

[423]*New York Times*, August 9, 1942.

[424]FBI Memorandum to the Director, August 9, 1942, National Archives, RG 55.

[425]Dr. Louis L. Snyder, *The Encyclopedia of the Third Reich* (New York: Marlowe & Company, 1976), 171.

[426]*New York Times*, August 9, 1942.

[427]Ibid.

[428]*New York Times*, August 12, 1942.

[429]Brissaud, *Canaris*, 319.

[430]*New York Times*, August 13, 1942.

[431]Persico, *Roosevelt's Secret War*, 205.

[432]Duane Traynor, interview by Alex Abella, May 2002.

[433]Memorandum from Special Agent McGee to Director Hoover, August 10, 1942, National Archives, RG 55.

[434]Franklin D. Roosevelt Library, Speech Files, 1419–1427, Presidential Message to Winston Churchill, August 14, 1942.

Chapter 12: Writings From Sugar Hill

[435]*New York Times*, July 28, 1942; Robert Heide and John Gilman, *Home Front America: Popular Culture of the World War II Era* (San Francisco: Chronicle Books, 1995), 58.

[436]Rehnquist, *All the Laws but One*, 193.

[437]*Girouard v. United States* (1946) 328 U.S. 61.

[438]Mason, *Harlan Fiske Stone*, 805–806.

[439]Ibid, 658.

[440]Ibid, 745.

[441]Mason, *"Inter Arma Silent Leges,"* 819–820.

[442]Ibid.

[443]Mason, *Harlan Fiske Stone*, 659.

[444]Ibid, 824.

[445]Mason, *Harlan Fiske Stone*, 662–663.

[446]Mason, *"Inter Arma Silent Leges,"* 806, 820, 828.

[447]Marcus Tullius Cicero, *Pro Milone*, ch. 4, sct. 11, 44–43 B.C.

[448]*Ex Parte Quirin* (1942) 317 U.S. 1, 63 S.Ct.2, 6.

[449]Ibid.

[450]*Ex Parte Quirin* (1942) 317 U.S. 1, 63 S.Ct.2, 7.

[451]*Ex Parte Quirin* (1942) 317 U.S. 1, 63 S.Ct.2.

[452]U.S. Constitution, amend. 5.

[453]U.S. Constitution, amend. 6.

[454]*Ex Parte Quirin* (1942) 317 U.S. 1, 63 S.Ct.2.

[455]*Ex Parte Quirin* (1942) 317 U.S. 1, 63 S.Ct.2, 9.

[456]Mason, *Harlan Fiske Stone*, 659.

[457]Ibid.

[458]Ibid., 660.

[459]Ibid.

[460]Ibid.

[461]*Ex Parte Quirin* (1942) 317 U.S. 1, 47–48, 63 S.Ct.2, 20.

[462]*Ex Parte Quirin* (1942) 317 U.S. 1, 45, 63 S.Ct.2, 19.

[463]*Ex Parte Quirin* (1942) 317 U.S. 1, 40, 63 S.Ct.2, 17.

[464]Mason, *Harlan Fiske Stone*, 661.

[465]Ibid, 665.

[466]Ibid.

[467]Mason, *Harlan Fiske Stone*, 660, quoting Cushman, *"Ex Parte Quirin, et al, The Nazi Saboteur Case,"* *Cornell Law Quarterly* (November 1942).

[468]*New York Times*, July 31, 1942.

Chapter 13: Plaques, Condos, and Porcupines

[469]C. F. Lanman, Special Agent, Memorandum to Special Agent Ladd, August 22, 1942, National Archives, RG 55.

[470]Ibid.

[471]Ibid.

[472]Ibid.

[473]Ibid.

[474]Ibid.

[475]D. M. Ladd, Special Agent, FBI Memorandum to the Director, July 9, 1942, National Archives, RG 55.

[476]D. M. Ladd, Special Agent, FBI Memorandum for the Director, July 22, 1942; J. Edgar Hoover, Director, FBI Memorandum, July 13, 1942, National Archives, RG 55.

[477]D. M. Ladd, Special Agent, FBI Memorandum to the Director, July 9, 1942, National Archives, RG 55.

[478]*United States v. Haupt, et al.* (1943) 136 F.2D 661.

[479]Cahan, "A Terrorist's Tale."

[480]*United States v. Haupt, et al.* (1943) 136 F.2d 661.

[481]Ibid.

[482]Cahan, "A Terrorist's Tale."

[483]*United States v. Haupt, et al.* (1943) 136 F.2d 661.

[484]Ibid.

[485]Ibid.

[486]Ibid.

[487]*Miranda v. Arizona* (1966) 384 U.S. 436, 86 S.Ct. 1602.

[488]*United States v. Haupt, et al.* (1943) 136 F.2d 661, 671.

[489]Cahan, "A Terrorist's Tale."

[490]*United States v. Haupt* (1945) 152 F.2d 771, 793.

[491]Ibid.

[492]Ibid.

[493]Cahan, "A Terrorist's Tale."

[494]*Haupt v. United States* (1947) 330 U.S. 631, 645.

[495]Ibid., 648–649.

[496]Cahan, "A Terrorist's Tale."

[497]*Cramer v. United States* (1945) 325 U.S. 1, 5, 65 S.Ct. 918, 920.

[498]Ibid., 937–938.

[499]Ibid., 920.

[500]Ibid., 920.

[501]*Cramer v. United States* (1945) 325 U.S. 1, 46–57, 65 S.Ct. 918, 940, citing *Ex Parte Bollman* (1807) 8 U.S. 75, 2 L.Ed. 554.

[502]Warden Joseph W. Sanford, Letter to FBI Special Agent Loveland, July 25, 1945, National Archives, RG 55.

[503]Ibid.

[504]Colonel James R. Pierce, United States Army-Deputy Chief Public Information Division Office of the Judge Advocate General, Memorandum dated February 11, 1948, National Archives, RG 55.

[505]White House Press Release, March 20, 1948, National Archives, RG 55.

[506]Memorandum from Lt. Col. Bradlee, United States Army to the War Department, Washington, D.C., April 27, 1948, National Archives, RG 55.

[507]Dasch, *Eight Spies Against America*, 223.

[508]Ibid., 238–239.

[509]Duane Traynor, interview by Alex Abella, May 2002.

[510]Mallmann Showell, *U-Boats at War*, 29.

[511]Persico, *Roosevelt's Secret War,* 387–388.

[512]Mallmann Showell, *U-Boats at War,* 33.

[513]Persico, *Roosevelt's Secret War,* 444.

[514]Biddle, *In Brief Authority,* 342.

Appendix 1: William Dudley Pelley and His Silver Shirt Legion

[515]Strong, *Organized Anti-Semitism in America*, 46.

[516]David Lobb, "Fascist Apocalypse: William Pelley and Millennial Extremism," *Journal of Millennial Studies*, November 1999.

[517]House Special Committee, *Un-American Propaganda Activities*, 76th Congress, 7205.

[518]William Dudley Pelley, "Seven Minutes in Eternity," *American Magazine*, March 1929.

[519]House Special Committee, *Un-American Propaganda Activities*, 76th Congress, 7280.

[520]Strong, *Organized Anti-Semitism in America*, 41.

[521]Lobb, "Fascist Apocalypse."

[522]Ibid.

[523]House Special Committee, *Un-American Propaganda Activities*, 76th Congress, 7243.

[524]Strong, *Organized Anti-Semitism in America*, 49.

[525]Ibid., 52.

[526]House Special Committee, *Un-American Propaganda Activities*, 76th Congress, 7234.

[527]Strong, *Organized Anti-Semitism in America*, 50.

[528]Lobb, "Fascist Apocalypse."

[529]Ibid.

Appendix 2: German and Italian Detention And Internment In World War II

[530]Following is the full text of the order:

Executive Order 9066

AUTHORIZING THE SECRETARY OF WAR

TO PRESCRIBE MILITARY AREAS

WHEREAS the successful prosecution of the war requires every possible protection against espionage and against sabotage to national-defense material, national-defense premises, and national-defense utilities as defined in section 4, Act of April 20, 1918, 40 Stat. 533, as amended by the act of November 30, 1940, 54 Stat. 1220, and the Act of August 21, 1941, 55 Stat. 655 (U. S. C., Title 50, Sec. 104):

NOW, THEREFORE, by virtue of the authority vested in me as President of the United States, and Commander in Chief of the Army and Navy, I hereby authorize and direct the Secretary of War, and the Military Commanders whom he may from time to time designate, whenever he or any designated Commander deems such actions necessary or desirable, to prescribe military areas in such places and of such extent as he or the appropriate Military Commanders may determine, from which any or all persons may be excluded, and with such respect to which, the right of any person to enter, remain in, or leave shall be subject to whatever restrictions the Secretary of War or the appropriate Military Commander may impose in his discretion. The Secretary of War is hereby authorized to provide for residents of any such area who are excluded therefrom, such transportation, food, shelter, and other accommodations as may be necessary, in the judgment of the Secretary of War or the said Military Commander, and until other arrangements are made, to accomplish the purpose of this order. The designation of military areas in any region or locality shall supersede designations of prohibited and restricted areas by the Attorney General under the Proclamations of December 7 and 8, 1941, and shall supersede the responsibility and authority of the Attorney General under the said Proclamations in respect of such prohibited and restricted areas.

I hereby further authorize and direct the Secretary of War and the said Military Commanders to take such other steps as he or the appropriate Military Commander may deem advisable to enforce compliance with the restrictions applicable to each Military area hereinabove authorized to be designated, including the use of Federal troops and other Federal Agencies, with authority to accept assistance of state and local agencies.

I hereby further authorize and direct all Executive Departments, independent establishments and other Federal Agencies, to assist the Secretary of War or the said Military Commanders in carrying out this Executive Order, including the furnishing of medical aid, hospitalization, food, clothing, transportation, use of land, shelter, and other supplies, equipment, utilities, facilities and services.

This order shall not be construed as modifying or limiting in any way the authority heretofore granted under Executive Order No. 8972, dated December 12, 1941, nor shall it be construed as limiting or modifying the duty and responsibility of the Federal Bureau of Investigation, with respect to the investigation of alleged acts of sabotage or the duty and responsibility of the Attorney General and the Department of Justice under the Proclamations of December 7 and 8, 1941, prescribing regulations for the conduct and control of alien enemies, except as such duty and responsibility is superseded by the designation of military areas hereunder.

FRANKLIN D. ROOSEVELT

February 19, 1942

[531]Kramer, *Undue Process*, 55.

[532]Biddle, *In Brief Authority*, 208–209.

[533]Ronald Takaki, *Double Victory: A Multicultural History of America in World War II* (New York: Little, Brown & Company, 2000), 134.

[534]Stephen Fox, *America's Invisible Gulag: A Biography of German American Internment and Exclusion in World War II* (New York: Peter Lang Publishing, 2000), xvi.

[535]Kramer, *Undue Process*, 71.

[536]Facilities that held German and Italian internees included:
Angel Island, California (San Francisco Bay)
Camp Forrest Enemy Internment Camp, Tennessee
Crystal City, Texas
Detroit, Michigan
Ellis Island, New York
Fort Screven, Georgia
Fort Sill, Oklahoma
Fort Lincoln, North Dakota
Fort Meade, Maryland
Gloucester City, New Jersey
Jung Hotel, New Orleans, Louisiana
Kenedy, Texas
Lordsburg, New Mexico
Miami, Florida
Niagara Falls, New York
Pine Island, Cuba
San Juan, Puerto Rico
Seagoville, Texas
Sharp Park Alien Detention Camp, California (eight miles south of Daly City)
Spokane County Jail, Washington
Stringtown Internment Camp, Oklahoma
Tujunga, California
(*See* Fox, *America's Invisible Gulag*, 130–149; Kramer, *Undue Process*, 175–176).

[537]Kramer, *Undue Process*, 171.

[538]Takaki, *Double Victory*, 132.

[539]Biddle, *In Brief Authority*, 205.

[540]Lawrence DiStasi, *Una storia segreta: The Secret History of Italian American Evacuation and Internment During World War II* (Berkeley: Heyday Books, 2001), 19.

[541]DiStasi, *Una storia segreta*, 20.

[542]Biddle, *In Brief Authority*, 209.

[543]Ibid., 208; Ezio Pinza, "Autobiography of an Italian Internee," *"Only What We Could Carry": The Japanese American Internment Experience."* Ed. Lawson Fusao Inada (Berkeley: Heyday Books, 2000), 196.

[544]DiStasi, *Una storia segreta*, 15–16.

[545]DiStasi, *Una storia segreta*, 188.

[546]Ibid.

Index